BATTLE OF BUNKER HILL.

REVOLUTIONARY SOLDIERS

AND THEIR DESCENDANTS.

GENEALOGICAL RECORDS.

"Biography preserves the deeds of mankind when monuments will have crumbled to dust."

MISSOURI EDITION.

Southern Historical Press, Inc.
Greenville, South Carolina

This volume was reproduced
from a personal copy located in
the Publishers private library

All rights reserved. No part of this publication may be reproduced,
stored in a retrieval system, transmitted in any form, posted
on the web in any form or by any means without the
prior written permission of the publisher.

Please direct all correspondence and book orders to:
SOUTHERN HISTORICAL PRESS, Inc.
1071 Park West Blvd.
Greenville, SC 29611

Published 1906 by:
American Historical Publishing Company
ISBN #978-1-63914-620-8
Printed in the United States of America

PREFACE.

The chief object of the publishers is to produce a work which will give a faithful and complete genealogy of the descendants of the Revolution and their ancestry; to perpetuate a broader spirit of patriotism and revive the popular interest in the glorious deeds of the Revolutionary heroes, who gave us our independence, thus rendering it a valuable reference book. All Americans, and especially descendants of Revolutionary fame, should take pride in keeping constantly before the public mind the memory of the services of their ancestors, the heroic principles for which they fought and died, and not allow the splendor of their achievements to fade, be forgotten and lost in the shadows of time, as their acts command the admiration of the world deservedly, and it is but proper that the record of their labors should be spread before the gratified vision of the present and future generations.

The work, outside of containing the most vital matters of interest to Americans, will naturally be exclusive, as every American is not a descendant from Revolutionary ancestry. The names of every descendant of Revolutionary fame in Missouri of record, or that may be obtained before the publication of this work, will be printed. One aim of the publishers is to produce the portraits of the ancestors, and where this is impossible, they will be properly represented by placing the portraits of their descendants, thus beautifully portraying the value of a portrait down through the ages in honor of the immortal services of the soldiers of the Revolution.

Americans should take as much pride in preserving the genealogy and history of their families, as the nobility, aristocracy and landed gentry of Europe.

The work will be handsomely illustrated, and its value largely enhanced by life-like portraits of soldiers of the American Revolution and their descendants, a fitting tribute to hand down to posterity, more valuable than monuments of bronze, gold or marble; and will be a standard reference book of its kind. The data now in the hands of the editors has necessitated large expenditure of money, labor and considerable time. This work, from the nature of things, cannot be bulky, the plan being to confine it exclusively to the Revolutionary descendants of Missouri, necessarily limiting it to a few. This, of course, greatly enhances the value of the volume to its fortunate possessor.

THE PUBLISHERS.

INDEX TO PORTRAITS.

Alban, George	face p.	38
Barret, Richard Aylett	"	54
Backus, Rev. Clarence Walworth, D. D.	"	89
Backus Coat of Arms	"	89
Burnham, Rev. Michael	"	58
Cadle, Henry	"	63
Catlin, Daniel	"	74
Clark, Gen. William	"	49
Comstock, Thomas Griswold, M. D.	"	51
Comstock Coat of Arms	"	52
Crane, Charles Samuel	"	61
Edgar, Timothy Bloomfield	"	42
Edgar Coat of Arms	"	44
Fogg, Josiah	"	64
Funkhouser, Robert Monroe	"	33
Gadsden, Gen. Christopher	"	14
Glasgow, Wm. Henry	"	24
Gentry, Richard	"	91
Greenwood, Moses	"	46
Greenwood Coat of Arms	"	46
Gross, George Peery	"	88
Haddaway, Walter Scott	"	35
Holmes, John Beriah	"	67
Hopkins, Lieutenant-Colonel Samuel	"	39
Hopkins, Innis	"	40
Huse, William Lee	"	52
Huse Coat of Arms	"	53
Husted, Edward Chapin	"	25
Hughes, Charles Hamilton	"	65
Hughes Coat of Arms	"	66
Humphrey, Frank W.	"	76
Humphrey Coat of Arms	"	77
Irwin, James Harvey	"	34
Jewell, Erwin S.	"	82
Leighton, George Eliot	"	16
Lemoine, Edwin S., M. D.	"	72
Lincoln, William Shattuck	"	17
Lucas, John Baptiste Charles	"	27
Mason, Isaac Mason	"	29

INDEX TO PORTRAITS.

Mayfield, W. H., M. D.	face p.	36
Mayfield, Stephen	"	36
Mayfield, Eli Burton, M. D.	"	37
Mansur, Alvah	"	68
Morrill, Henry Leighton	"	22
McLure, Charles Derickson	"	69
McLure, Margaret A. E.	"	83
McCulloch, Robert	"	84
Napton, Charles McClurg	"	50
O'Fallon, Anna M. Harris	"	48
Robbins, Alexander	"	30
Robertson, George	"	86
Sands, James Thomas	"	19
Sands Coat of Arms	"	19
Shields, George Howell	"	10
Shapleigh, Augustus Frederick	"	12
Shapleigh, A. L. and J. B.	"	13
Shapleigh Coat of Arms	"	70
Spencer, Horatio Nelson, M. D.	"	20
Spencer Coat of Arms	"	20
Slavens, Luther Clay	"	80
Slavens, James W. L.	"	79
Tuttle, Rt. Rev. Daniel S.	"	9
Twiss, Stephen Prince	"	81
Wyman, Henry Purkett	"	18
Wyman Gravestone	"	18

INDEX TO BIOGRAPHIES.

Alban, George ....page	38
Backus, Rev. Clarence Walworth ...."	89
Baker, George Arnold ...."	98
Barret, Richard Aylett ...."	53
Block, George Montgomery ...."	98
Burnham, Rev. Michael ...."	58
Brier, Robert Emmet ...."	22
Brinsmade, Hobart ...."	37
Brown, James Newton ...."	39
Clark, Gen. William ...."	49
Comstock, Thomas Griswold, M. D ...."	51
Crane, Charles Samuel ...."	61
Cadle, Henry ...."	62
Catlin, Daniel ...."	74
Crum, Rev. John Horace, S. T. D ...."	93
Derivaux, Armand ...."	32
Doddridge, William Brown ...."	98
Edgar, Timothy Bloomfield ...."	41
Fogg, Josiah ...."	64
Funkhouser, Robert Monroe, M. D ...."	33
Gage, John Cutter ...."	86
Gadsden, Gen. Christopher ...."	13
Glasgow, William Henry ...."	24
Gentry, Richard ...."	91
Grant, Lee Wiley ...."	97
Greenwood, Moses ...."	46
Gross, George Peery ...."	88
Gregg, Norris B ...."	40
Gregg, William Henry ...."	73
Husted, Edward Chapin ...."	25
Haddaway, Walter Scott ...."	35
Hopkins, Lieut.-Col. Samuel ...."	39
Hopkins, Innis ...."	39
Huse, William Lee ...."	52
Hughes, Charles Hamilton ...."	66
Holman, John B ...."	67
Humphrey, Frank W ...."	76
Hutchings, Charles F ...."	93
Irwin, James H ...."	34

INDEX TO BIOGRAPHIES.

Jewett, Erwin S	page	82
Leighton, George Eliot	"	15
Lincoln, William S	"	16
Lucas, J. B. C	"	26
Lemoine, Edwin S., M. D	"	71
Lathrop, William, A. H	"	25
Lathrop, Joseph	"	25
Morrill, Henry Leighton	"	21
Mason, Isaac M	"	28
Mayfield, W. H., M. D	"	36
Mayfield, George W	"	36
Mayfield, Eli Burton, M. D	"	37
Mansur, Alvah	"	68
McLure, Charles D	"	69
McLure, Margaret A. E	"	83
McCulloch, Robert	"	84
Napton, Charles McClurg	"	50
O'Fallon, Anna M. H	"	47
Prince, Lawrence L	"	98
Robbins, Alexander Henry	"	72
Robbins, Alexander	"	30
Robertson, George	"	85
Randall, Jno. F	"	23
Robinson, Paul Gervais, M. D	"	31
Sands, James T	"	19
Shields, George H	"	9
Shapleigh, Agustus F	"	11
Shapleigh, Alfred Lee	"	70
Shapleigh, John Blasdel, M. D	"	12
Spencer, Horatio Nelson, M. D	"	20
Spencer, Hon. Selden Palmer	"	98
Slavens, James W. L	"	79
Slavens, Luther Clay	"	79
Swasey, William Albert	"	98
Swentzel, William E	"	97
Stanard, Edwin O	"	14
Shelley, George Madison	"	86
Siegrist, Vera Lawrence	"	98
Tuttle, Rt. Rev. Daniel S	"	9
Twiss, Stephen Prince	"	80
Williams, Walter	"	84
Wyman, Henry Purkett	"	18
Yost, Charles C	"	95

Sandys Portraits and Scrooby Manor.— This interesting group of pictures easily connects the busy rush and hurry of to-day with the calm, staid and almost classic days of Queen Elizabeth and James I. Then, as now, Spain was the antagonist of the Anglo-Saxon. Then, as now, there was an Armada. Then 'twas Spain's disaster, while now it is the Anglo-Saxon's success, and Saxon of the Saxons was the family of Sands, Sandis, Sandes, Sandys. Ulnod, a Saxon, dwelt at a place called Sande, on the Isle of Wight, and in the time of Edward the Confessor took the name of Sande; from this man was descended Edwin Sandys, Archbishop of York in the time of Elizabeth. Edwin was Chancellor of Cambridge about the time of the death of Edward Sixth, and a relative of Lady Jane Grey. He preached a sermon at Cambridge proclaiming Lady Jane Queen; but Mary coming into power soon afterwards he was thrown into the Tower, from which, after some months, he was liberated and fled to Strasburg, Germany, where he remained until the accession of Elizabeth, when he returned to England and became successively Bishop of Worcester, London, and Archbishop of York. He was liberal in his views; so much so that some writers have called him the first Puritan.

At the time of the accession of Elizabeth, nine-tenths of all the real and personal property of England was under the control of the Church; the title was vested in the Bishops. It was the habit of good Queen Bess to repay her courtiers for compliments they might make her, by commanding a Bishop to make a lease at a nominal rental; and should the Bishop hesitate she would threaten to unfrock him. Archbishop Sandes was no exception. He resisted for many years but at last, realizing the inevitable distribution of much of the Church property, entered into a sort of a compromise with the Queen, giving her and each of his five sons in preference to outsiders a number of leases, thus raising up a powerful family, and his second son, Sir Edwin,* became one of the foremost workers in a cause which has resulted in establishing this great Republic of North America.

Sir Edwin was born December 9, 1561, graduated at Oxford, traveled extensively, and wrote books of his travels; he became the first statesman of England. He was the author of all the Charters of the London Virginia Company. He wrote the Code for the establishment of the House of Burgesses in Virginia, and the Charter for the Mayflower Company. He loaned the Pilgrims one thousand pounds for five years without interest. In 1620 he was the Governor of the London Virginia Company and foremost in advancing its affairs.

Spain viewed the effort to colonize Virginia with disfavor, and the Spanish Ambassador watched every movement of the Company, reporting constantly to the King of Spain, and little by little influencing King James until he became the implacable enemy of Sir Edwin Sandys, emphasizing his enmity by sending word to the Electors of the London Virginia Company in 1621 to "choose the Devil if you will, but not Sir Edwin Sandys." In consequence of which a compromise was effected and the Earl of Southampton — the patron of Shakespeare — was elected Governor or Treasurer as the office was called. Sir Edwin however remained in its councils, the moving spirit, until the Charter was canceled and the government resumed by the Crown.

---

*The picture of Sir Edwin Sandys, in this group, is presented through the kindness of Mr. Alexander Brown, author of The First Republic in America — Houghton, Mifflin and Co., Publishers, Boston, 1898.

Mr. Alexander Brown, author of the Genesis of the United States, in his recent excellent work "The First Republic in America," on page 632, says: —

"In brief, although the King put a stop to their proceedings even before many of their plans were fully developed, and the Privy Council succeeded in obscuring many of the objects, ideas, and accomplishments of the company by licensing incorrect histories and by concealing or destroying most of their records, sufficient evidence has now been found to show that the planting of the first Republic in America under the popular charters, drafted by Sir Edwin Sandys, was in every way a most interesting — and to us the most important — event in our annals. When the Colony was resumed by the Crown, 'the present estate of Virginia was but small,' yet it was sufficient for its destined purpose. The managers of the company in England and America had planted colonies in North and South Virginia, and in so doing under the authority derived by them from their charters, had laid the true foundation of the new nation in the new world, upon which it has grown to be the greatest nation in the whole world."

George Sandys, youngest son of the Archbishop, was born March 2d, 1577, and educated at Oxford. In 1621 Sir Thomas Wyatt was appointed by the London Company, Governor of the Colony of Virginia; he sailed with his wife, a daughter of Sir Samuel Sandys, eldest son of the Archbishop, and George Sandys, who became the resident Treasurer of Virginia. George was a gentleman of fine parts and well esteemed as a poet, and here, in the wilds of Virginia, he made his translation of "Ovid's Metamorphosis." He was a valuable member of the Colony — established iron works and aided in defenses against the Indians. In 1624 he returned to England but was more or less interested in Virginia matters until his death in 1643.

On the 24th of April, 1626, King Charles issued a concession, in which he relates that "our trusty and well-beloved George Sandys, Esquier, hath with great care and industry translated into English verse the fifteen books of Ovid's Metamorphoses, which he hath to his great charge caused to be imprinted and made ready to be published in print, rather for the delight and profit of our living subjects, than for the hope of any great benefit to be by him reaped thereby, and hath humbly besought us to vouchsafe him a privilege for the sole printing of the said work for such term of years as we should think fit and convenient, the better to encourage him and others to employ their labors and studies in good literature," and then grants him the privilege to print and sell the same for twenty-one years.

John Brown, in his interesting book, "The Pilgrim Fathers of New England," says: "The manor of Scrooby as far back as Domesday Book belonged to the Archbishop of York and was one of the palaces occupied by them when they moved from one part of their diocese to another, administering various civic as well as ecclesiastical functions, dispensing hospitality, and taking with them a numerous and splendid retinue. Being also near to one of the post stations on the great north road, it was frequently a hospice for distinguished travelers on their way south or north. It is recorded that Margaret, Queen of Scotland, daughter of King Henry VII., slept here on the 12th of June, 1603, on her way to Scotland.

"For the space of several weeks also, toward the close of his strangely chequered career, Cardinal Wolsey made the old manor house his abiding place, planting the mulberry tree in the garden which till recent days was associated with his name. It was in 1530 that Wolsey visited Scrooby and by reason of his kindness of heart and many good works endeared himself to the people; but an aching heart must have followed him everywhere, for it was during these Scrooby days Wolsey learnt that all his most cherished plans had come to nothing, that the king had dissolved his

college at Ipswich, seizing all its lands and possessions, and that at Oxford the name of Christ Church had obliterated that of Cardinal College. 'I am put away from my sleep and meat,' he wrote, 'for such advertisements as I have had of the dissolution of my college.'

"After three months spent at Scrooby, towards the end of September, the fallen minister set out for York, and two months later he had taken that long journey from which there is no return. As the end drew near he sent a message to the king requesting ' His grace in God's name that he have a vigilant eye to depress this new pernicious sect of Lutherans, that it do not increase within his dominions through his negligence.' As if either King or Cardinal could keep back the oncoming tide! Little did Wolsey dream that from that same manor house at Scrooby he had so lately left there would in process of time go forth a little band of earnest men, who would carry across to the new world beyond the Atlantic the principles of freedom and self-government, born of that very Reformation he was trying to crush with his dying hand. He could not foresee this, nor could he anticipate that even when, eleven years later, in 1541, the king himself slept a night at Scrooby on his way to the north, the mighty change would have come, and that ' this new pernicious sect of Lutherans ' would be supreme in the State. Yet so it was. In that brief space the king had become a Lutheran himself, the Act of Supremacy had become a law, the monasteries were dissolved, the nation had passed over to the Protestant faith, and England was severed from the See of Rome.

"The stateliness of Scrooby manor with its thirty-nine chambers and apartments suffered a decline after the Reformation. In 1576 Archbishop Sandys appointed William Brewster, the father of Elder Brewster of later days, his receiver of Scrooby and all its liberties in Nottinghamshire, and also bailiff of the manor house, to hold both offices for life.

"Subsequently, when the Archbishop's son, Sir Samuel Sandys, became the owner of Scrooby, Elder Brewster became the tenant and Scrooby manor became a regular Post House on the great North Road ; and here the first Separatist Church was formed by William Brewster, William Bradford, John Robinson and the people living near by, and regular meetings were held within the old Manor walls until forced by circumstances, the Church removed to Leyden, Holland.

After a few years the desire to be on English soil became a factor in the councils of the Separatist Church, and it was but natural that they should look to the Sandys family for advice and assistance.

The following letter written by Sir Edwin Sandys, to John Robinson and William Brewster, in reply to one from them, is found in the record of the London Virginia Company :

"After my hartie salutations. The agents of your congregation, Robert Cushman and John Carver have been in communication with diverse selecte gentlemen of his Majesties Counsell for Virginia ; and by ye writing of 7 Articles subscribed with your names, have given them yet good degree of satisfaction, which hath caried them on with a resolution to sett forward your desire in ye best sorte y may be for your owne and the publick good. Divers perticulers whereof we leave to their faithfull reports ; having carried themselves heere with that good discretion as is both to their owne and their credite from whence they came. And wheras being to treate for a multitude of people, they have requested further time to conferr with them that are to be interested in this action, about ye severall particularities which in ye prosecution thereof will fall out considerable, it hath been very willingly assented too. And so they doe now returne unto you. If therefore it may please God so to directe your desires as that in your parts there shall fall out no just impediments, I trust by ye same direction it shall likewise appear, that on our parte, all forwardnes to set you forward shall be found in ye best note which with reason may be expected. And so I betake you with this designe (which I hope verily is ye worke of God), to the gracious protection and blessing of ye Highest.

"London, November 12,   Your very loving friend,
   "Anno: 1617.   EDWIN SANDYS.

To this letter an answer was sent, dated December 15, 1617, and on the 27th of the following January another letter was forwarded to Sir John Wolstenholme.

"Right Worship: with due acknowledgements of our thankfullness for your singular care and pains in the bussines of Virginia, for our & we hope the commone good, we doe remember our humble dutys unto you, and have sent inclosed, as is required a further explanation of our judgments in the 3 points specified by some of his majesties Honourable Privie Counsell; and though it be greevious unto us that such unjust insinuations are made against us yet we are most glad of ye occasion of making our just purgation unto so honourable personages. The declarations we have sent inclosed, the one more breefe and generall which we think ye fitter to be presented; the other something more large and in which we express some small accidental differences which if it seeme good unto you and other of our worship friends you may send instead of ye former. Our prayers unto God is, yet your Worship may see the frute of your worthy endeauors, which on our part we shall not faile to furder by all good meanes in us. And so praing yet you would please with ye convenientest speed yet may be, to give us knowledge of ye success of ye bussiness with his Majesties Privy Counsell, and accordingly what your further pleasure is, either for our direction or futherance in ye same, so we rest.

"Leyden Jan. 27,   Your Worship in all duty,
"Anno 1617, old stile.   JOHN ROBINSON.
                                                             "WILLIAM BRUSTER."

All the members of the Sandys family, and many of their connections were members of the London Virginia Company. Sir Samuel, eldest son of the Archbishop, residing in Worcestershire, was prominent in Parliament; he owned Scrooby Park and Manor and his son, Martin, resided at Scrooby. Martin's mother was Mercy Cullpeper of the same family as the Cullpepers of Virginia. Sir Myles Sandys, third son of the Archbishop, was a gentleman of polite parts and learning, residing in the Isle of Ely. He also served in Parliament.

Thomas, the fourth son, resided in London; his son, Robert, was married to Alice Washington, daughter of Lawrence Washington, of Sulgrave; she was aunt of Col. John Washington, the emigrant ancestor of George Washington, the father of his country.

Robert's cousin, Samuel Sandys, was married to the widow of the celebrated Colonel Henry Washington.

Henry, fifth son of the Archbishop, was born September 30th, 1572, educated at Oxford, was in holy orders, residing much of his time at Edwin's Hall, Essex; often preached at Boxford, and Grotton Suffolk; was a great friend of John Winthrop, first Governor of Massachusetts; his second wife was a daughter of Thomas Goffe, a London merchant, and Deputy Governor of the Massachusetts Bay Company, 1628. Rev. Henry died 1626 and was buried at Groton Suffolk, the seat of Adam and John Winthrop. His two small boys, Henry and James, were raised by their mother, who resided much of her time at Graces, Essex, the seat of Sir Henry Mildmay.

In 1638 they came with their uncle, Edward Goffe, to Boston, and from this

James, is descended James T. Sands whose portrait appears in another part of this book. The name was spelled differently by various branches of the family who settled in different parts of England; but their identity was preserved by their all bearing the same coat of arms, as well as by their names being spelled in official records, warrants and commissions indiscriminately Sandys, Sandis, Sandes and Sands when addressed to one and the same person.

It is interesting to look back and follow the daily life of many who were interested in the London Virginia Company and the Massachusetts Bay Company. The one follows the other as easily as the son follows the father; the spirit of civil and religious liberty in America, made possible by the London Virginia Company, seems to have been taken up by the Massachusetts Bay Company, and the people who constitute what is called the Winthrop Emigration, from 1630 to 1650; and though the Church at first wielded a strong influence in secular affairs, yet it was not destined for long, and in 1860 it was estimated that the descendants of the 30,000 who came in the Winthrop Emigration amounted to 17,000,000 people, unanimous in their love for civil and religious liberty. The number at this day (1898) must be something like 40,000,000 people, whose mode of thought controls the destinies of these United States.

Near the center of Essex, England, in the 16th and 17th centuries, there existed a Park called Woodham-Ferrers. Within this Park were a number of manor houses and a church. One of these manors was called Edwin's Hall, built by Edwin Sandes, Archbishop of York. The manor and 260 acres of land was owned by the Archbishop's eldest son, Sir Samuel Sandys, but was occupied by Sir Samuel's widowed mother, and her son, Rev. Henry Sandes.

Shoreham, belonging to the family of the Lady Jane Grey, was five miles from Edwin's Hall. It was here Lord Cavendish was arrested to prevent the duel between him and the Earl of Warwick. Cavendish had sided with Sir Edwin Sandys in a dispute about Somer's Island matters and Warwick had given him the lie.

Graces was four miles from Edwin's Hall, and here resided Sir Henry Mildmay, son of Sir Thomas Mildmay and Alice Winthrop his wife, sister of Adam Winthrop, father of John Winthrop, first Governor of Massachusetts, who resided at Groton Hall, Suffolk, a day's ride from Woodham-Ferrers. Sir Henry's wife was a daughter of Mr. Gurdon of Assington, the next parish to Groton. The widow of Rev. Henry Sandys resided much of her time at Graces with her two young sons, Henry and James, who came to Boston in 1638. James subsequently, with sixteen others, purchased Block Island and through his influence it was incorporated under the name of Shoreham. James also gave the name of Graces to a cove and point on Block Island.

John Winthrop, Governor of Massachusetts, in writing to his son in England often asks to be remembered to Mrs. Sandes at Graces. The Rev. Henry Sandes was a rural preacher with a large circuit and at times the dean of Shoreham. He was a devoted friend of both Adam and John Winthrop and often preached at Groton and other parishes, peculiars of Canterbury and in the deanry of Shoreham.

At Rettenden, three miles south from Edwin's Hall, resided Richard Humphrey, whose wife was Mary, daughter of Sir Samuel Sandys.

Purleigh, three miles north from Edwin's Hall, is memorable as the parish where from 1633 to 1643 resided, as rector, Rev. Lawrence Washington, the father of John, the emigrant ancestor of George Washington.

At Springfield, ten miles from Edwin's Hall, resided Sir Thomas Mildmay, whose wife was Alice, sister of Adam Winthrop.

At Stambridge, fifteen miles from Edwin's Hall, resided John Forth, Esq., father of Mary Forth, John Winthrop's first wife.

At Edwardstone Suffolk resided Henry Brown, father of Ann, second wife of Adam Winthrop.

At Brettenham Suffolk Rev. Henry Sandys married his second wife, a daughter of Thomas Goff, Esq., a member of the London Virginia Company, 1620, and Deputy Governor of the Massachusetts Bay Company, 1628.

The following letter, written about 1620, by Rev. Henry Sandys to John Winthrop, shows the confidential relations of Sandys and Winthrop in religious matters: —

"To my Worshipll-well-approved good friend Mr. John Winthrop at Honton Hall these.

Sir: I do understand that Stoke Vicarage is not yet given. It is a great parish. I do fro my hart persuade my selfe that at Naylond would be a good church of God if they had a good minister. Theare is one or two. There is one Mr. Watson felow of Trinitie Colledge. I take the next yere to be his yere of Bachelor of Divinitie. A Gentleman borne, hath of his owne some xx or xxx a yere. A m̄a of gret lerning for his tyme & verie quiet. Theare is another, one Mr. Gilgate, sonne unto Mr. Gilgate that dwelt at Langham, one whome I thinke Mr. Manocke knew & a verie quiet honest m̄a. A sufficient scholar. A bachelor & so I thinke it may be he will contynue, for he is of some good reasonable yeres. Let me intreat you end r in the affection that I know you beare to the Churche of God to look into it and help. If extremitie of buisnes had not hinderd I would haue bene with you afore this tyme & I purpose afore weekes be ended to come to you. In the meane tyme the thing is prsently to be done. Let me intreat importunitie to the uttermost you can. I pitie the Churche. The Lord stirre up all or harts to love it and labor for the good of it. I take my leave thus hastely this hand being wearie. Comending my selfe to yor owne selfe and Mris. Winthrop, not forgetting Mris. Hanna.

Yor Worships exceedingly behoulding to you

HEN. SANDS.

Forty miles south from Woodham Ferrers was London, the great center of English civilization. Here was the headquarters for all projects of adventure, and chiefly so the colonization of America. Here resided many interested in American affairs and here was transacted all its important business. Some ten or fifteen miles south of London is Rochester, the dean of which was Walter Balcanqual, whose wife was Elizabeth, daughter of Anthony Aucher, Esq., whose wife was Margaret, sister of Sir Samuel Sandys. Continuing on south we come to Shoreham in Kent. It is within the ecclesiastical jurisdiction of the diocese of Rochester, and being a peculiar is within its own deanry of Shoreham. The several parishes having been part of the ancient possessions of the See of Canterbury are exempt from the jurisdiction of the bishop of the diocese in which they lie, and as such are peculiar to the jurisdiction of the Archbishop only, whence they have acquired the name of the Archbishop's peculiars, all such being within the deanry of Shoreham and subject only to his prerogative.

Near Shoreham resided Anthony Aucher, Esq., and within five miles was Boxley Abbey, the home of Sir Francis Wyatt, Governor of Virginia in 1621 ; and here George Sandys made his home while in England and here died and was buried.

A day's ride from Shoreham was Northborne Court, the home of Sir Edwin Sandys.

The following memoranda from the diary of Adam Winthrop, father of Governor John Winthrop, is interesting as showing the comings and goings of different people connected with this sketch, and the distances they traveled.

"1595. The XXIIth of Sept. my brother Mildmay came to my house.
The 8th day of October my wyfe rydde to her father at Prithnell in Essex and returned the XXth.
The IXth of January Mr. Sands was taken sicke grauiter.
The Xth of ffeb I was at my ffather's and the XV at my brother Mildmay's.
1597. The XVIth day of April Mr. Gawn Harvey highe shreve of Essex came to my house and the XIXth day he and my nephew Henry Mildmay depted toward Springfield in Essex.
1601. The first day of August my cosen Adam Winthrop and my cosen Sara Frost his sister came from London to Groton.
The Vth of Decemb I ridde to Cambridge and beganne the Auditt.
22nd Jan. I did ridde to Springfield and from there to London.
1606. The thirde of Sept. we did ridde with Mr. Sands to Stambridge and the XIth my sonne took an estate.
The XIIIIth of Sept. Mr. Sands prch'd at Groton and dyned with me.
1608. The Xth of October my sonne and his wyfe departed from Groton to dwell at Stambridge in Essex.
The 2nd of Marche Mr. Sands pchd at Bexford after his return from London.
The XIth Sir Henry Mildmay my nephew came to G. * * *

Sufficient entries are here quoted to give one an idea of the activity of the rural people of those places and times.

Archbishop Sandys was born at Hawkshead, Lancashire, and here he established a grammar school. His family Bible which is kept here contains among others the following entries, which are also interesting in this connection.

Penelope Sandes was borne ye 9th April 1629 beinge Thursday about 7 at night.	God Father Sir John Washington. God Mothers Ye Lady Penelope Spencer Mrs. Margaret Washington
Thomas Sandes was borne ye 14th Mch. 1629 beinge Sunday about 5 in ye morning.	God Fathers Thomas Sandes Esquire Francis Meuce Esquire God Mother Ye Ladye Washington
Richard Sandes was borne ye 29th April 1631 beinge Friday about noone	God Fathers Richard Spencer Esquire Francis Meuce Esquire God Mother Mrs. Elizabeth Spencer
Francis Sandes was borne ye 20th day of Aprile 1636 beinge Friday about Eleven at night.	God Father Francis Meuce Esquire God Mothers Mrs. Margaret Washington Mrs. Elizabeth Washington deputy for the Ladye Washington.
Elizabeth Sandes was borne ye 23 of July 1633 beinge Tuesday about 6 in the morning	God Father Arthur Samuel Esquire God Mothers Mrs. Elizabeth Spencer Mrs. Elizabeth Meuce
Susannah Sandes was borne ye 14th of August beinge Thursday about midnight (the date of the year is not given)	God Father Simon Adams Clarke God Mothers Mrs. Margaret Washington Mrs. Ann Doheres? Deputy for Mrs. Susan Wem?

Robert Sandes was borne ye 24th day of May 1636 beinge Wednesday about 6 at night.	God Fathers Robt. Spencer Esquire Robt. Paraster ?Esquire God Mother Mrs. Margaret Anderson

Edwin Sandes May 6th between 4 & 5 at night
    Gemelli borne 1637
Myles Sandes May ye 7th between 8 & 9 at night
	God Fathers John Bulins deputy for
	    Sir Myles Sandes
	Richard Seymer Esquire
	God Mother Mrs. Elizabeth Meuce.

The majority of these entries probably relate to the children of Robert Sandys and his wife Alice Washington. Robert was the son of Thomas Sandys, Esq., of London. Robert resided in London also and both he and his father were frequently guests at Edwin's Hall.

The family of Sandys, though large at one time, in England became very much decimated during the Civil War, some siding with the King and some with Parliament. The present directory of London contains but half a dozen Sandys, and the name is known no more about Essex, Suffolk and Kent. The noble family of Lord Sandys still have their seat at Ombersly Court Worcestershire, but those of the Vine and other places are extinct.

In striking contrast is the family in America. Of the two emigrants, Henry and James, Henry's line became extinct with the death of his son John, but from James there are now in the United States 1500 bearing the name Sands or Sandys. One branch of the family were Tories and removed to Nova Scotia after the Revolution, but most of them were loyal to the American cause. Comfort and Joshua Sands, of New York, wealthy merchants, were prominent during the Revolution, and many of the name served their country at various times in both the Army and Navy; two, Benjamin F. and Joshua, attaining the rank of Rear Admiral.

It is a singular fact that while one of the most important objections raised by the Spanish Ambassador against the British colonizing in America (as revealed by the records of the London Virginia Company) and repeatedly presented to the view of the King of Spain, was the fear that a New England would rise up to fight the New Spain, it has resulted in the New England rising up to fight the old Spain for the purpose of liberating the the new Spain, and while this fact has resulted by reason of the Revolution, still the New England efforts receive the hearty approval of the old England, and the Anglo-Saxon alliance is so firm in spirit that it needs no formal declaration of a written character to impress the world at large.

JAMES T. SANDS.

St. Louis, July 28th, 1898.

    AUTHORITIES: Collins' Peerage, Hunter's Founders of New Plymouth, Brown, The First Republic in America, Sandys' Poetical Works, Life and Letters of John Winthrop, Visitation of London, Works of Captain John Smith, Norden's Essex, Livermore's History of Block Island, Thompson's Long Island, Sands Genealogy, Letters and MSS. in the British Museum, Austin's Gen. Record, Savage's Gen. Dictionary, Domesday Book, Brown's Genesis of U. S., Beginnings of N. E. Fiske, The Pilgrim Fathers of New England, John Brown, Ireland's History of Kent. Neill's Virginia Co. of London. Neill's Virginia Carolorum.

Non-Puritan Sects of Colonial Times.— Of the invaluable service to the cause of liberty rendered by the religious sects of the non-Puritan colonies, public mention is but seldom made. The orators, poets and historians of New England, with a just and commendable pride, and without stint of praise, have celebrated the deeds and kept green the memory of their Puritan ancestors.

"Bunker Hill, Old South Church, the old State house and Faneuil Hall, have long and wisely been made to serve as constant reminders of Puritan valor and patriotism. It is to be regretted that more of that filial spirit has not been shown by the descendants of the early settlers and Revolutionary sires of the non-Puritan colonies. For as the years go by, the less familiar facts are overlooked or ignored by the public, and ancestral honor is modified by the popular application of the rule, that to him that hath shall be given, but to him that hath not shall be taken away even that which he hath.

"In sermons on Thanksgiving day and various anniversary occasions it is the custom to glorify only the Puritan branch of our colonial ancestors, not only for their patriotism, but also because of the moral and religious influences which they so largely set to work in the New World. We do well to remember that they were patriotic Christian men; but let us not forget that so also were the Huguenots, who first settled in the Carolinas, the Church of England emigrants, who settled in Eastern Virginia, the Quakers, who settled Eastern Pennsylvania, the Catholics, who settled Maryland, the Swedish Lutherans, who settled New Jersey; the adherents of the Dutch Reformed church, who settled New York, the Scotch-Irish Presbyterians, who settled the central and western parts of Pennsylvania, Virginia and North Carolina, and the Baptists, who settled Rhode Island, under Roger Williams.

"It may have been providential, but certain it is, the fact that these religious settlements were thus distributed in the various non-Puritan colonies, was of the utmost importance to the cause of liberty. Some of these sects were religious refugees, but it must not be inferred that those who were not, were less zealous in the cause of liberty. Dr. Benjamin Rush of Philadelphia truly said, 'A Christian can hardly fail of being a republican, for every precept of the gospel inculcates those degrees of humility, self-denial and brotherly kindness, which are distinctly opposed to the pride of monarchy and the pageants of a court.' And yet there are those in our day, who *assume* that the 'Established' Church of England in Virginia, must have been unfriendly to American Independence. They might with equal propriety infer, that because Virginia was a British colony, her sincerity in supporting the Revolution should be discredited. The church to which Washington belonged was true to the cause he so nobly represented. There was less opposition to the Revolution in Virginia than in any other State. In 'Sabine's Loyalists of the American Revolution,' the author (who was a New Englander,) gives a list of 856 Massachusetts' Tories, 500 of whom were prominent enough to merit biographical sketches, while he gives sketches of only 59 Virginia Tories, referring in a footnote to 56 more, and expressly states that Virginia had fewer Tories than any other State, though she had the largest population.

"Without exception, the various religious sects of the non-Puritan colonies were liberty loving people. Upon them, the leaders of the Revolution largely depended for both moral and national support. Situated as they were in different colonies, or in localities then remote from each other, their aggregate influence in behalf of liberty has not been generally appreciated. But for them, we might not have secured religious liberty.

"The Baptists who settled Rhode Island were pioneers in the securement of religious liberty by legislative enactment. Referring to them Judge Story says: 'In the code of laws established by them in Rhode Island we read for the first time since Christianity ascended the throne of the Caesars, that conscience should be free, and that men should not be punished for worshiping God in the way they were persuaded He required.' This code was established in 1647. Moreover, that clause of the first amendment to the Constitution of the United States, which provides that Congress 'shall make no laws respecting an establishment of religion, nor prohibiting the free exercise thereof,' was secured by the united efforts of the Baptists. They had suffered persecution in the past, and were keenly alive to the need of constitutional safeguards for the future.

"But the Catholics who settled Maryland were really the first promoters of religious liberty in this country. As proprietary of the colony, Lord Baltimore always required the governor and the councilors to take an official oath, whereby they were expressly pledged to in no way interfere with the free exercise of religion in the colony. This executive policy was, in 1649, put into the more permanent form of a statute, known as the famous Act of Toleration. This act first recited that 'Whereas, the enforcing of conscience in matters of religion hath frequently fallen out to be of dangerous consequence,' and it then provided that no person of any Christian sect should be 'in any ways troubled, molested or discountenanced in respect of his or her religion, nor in the free exercise thereof.' All the authorities agree that this was but the putting into the form of a statute what had been the executive policy of Lord Baltimore from the beginning. It is true this act of toleration was passed by the assembly of Maryland two years after that which was adopted in Rhode Island; but the fact remains that through the effect of the oath of office thus previously required by Baltimore of both the governor and the councilors, religious liberty was by lawful authority established in Maryland before Rhode Island was settled at all. Let honor be given to whom honor is due.

"Our Scotch-Irish Presbyterian ancestors are also deserving of highest praise. They were the first religious body in this country to declare in favor of open resistance to King George. This they did at their synod in Philadelphia in 1775. In the same year, at Mecklenburg, N. C., they prepared the first Declaration of Independence, embracing many of the important features of that penned by the immortal Jefferson. Realizing how essential to liberty is education, they were enthusiasts in the founding of schools of learning in frontier settlements. These were often referred to as log colleges. Yet who can estimate the far-reaching beneficence of those early beginnings of culture?

"It was a Methodist minister, who, at the centennial commencement of Dickinson college, had the candor and the manliness to say: 'The debt which this country owes to the Scotch-Irish Presbyterians has not been understood, much less acknowledged. * * * Their history has not yet been but imperfectly told; but the time will come when the Scotch-Irish Presbyterian of Pennsylvania will take his place alongside of the New England Puritan, as one of the founders of learning and liberty in the new world. The race which has given to this country John Witherspoon, Alexander Hamilton, James Wilson, Andrew Jackson, Robert Fulton, Horace Greeley and others of equal or lesser fame is one whose memory men cannot willingly let die.

"It is our duty to honor the memory of the founders of our free institutions. As the hero of Santiago said of our last great naval victory, so let it be said of the great achievements of our colonial sires: 'There is glory enough to go round to all.'"

LUTHER CLAY SLAVENS.

Dan'l S. Tuttle
Bishop of Missouri.

GENEALOGICAL RECORD.

TUTTLE, Rt. Rev. Daniel Sylvester, President of the Society of the Sons of the Revolution in the State of Missouri, is descended from distinguished Revolutionary ancestry. His great-great-grandfather, Daniel Tuttle, born November 11, 1680, was a captain of the Southeast Military Company of Wallingford, Conn. The Bishop's great-grandfather was Jehiel Tuttle, a lieutenant, who distinguished himself in the French War in the expeditions against Ticonderoga and Crown Point, and was wounded and died in either camp or hospital in 1759. He had six children; the fifth of whom was Bishop Tuttle's grandfather, Charles Tuttle, born January 26, 1753, in Wallingford, Conn. He served five years in the Revolutionary War. He was married twice. His first wife was Anna Finch, and his second wife Sarah Bliss. He died in Prattsville, New York, April 5, 1818. Daniel B. Tuttle, father of Bishop Tuttle, was born July, 1797, in Windham, Green County, N. Y.; he was a farmer and prominent member of the M. E. Church. In 1821 he married Abigail C. Stimpson; the result of this union was four children, of whom Bishop Tuttle was the third. Daniel B. Tuttle died September 6, 1877. Daniel S. Tuttle was born in Windham, N. Y., January 26, 1837. His early tuition was under Rev. T. S. Judd, an Episcopalian clergyman. Later he attended the Delaware Academy at Delhi, N. Y.; there he prepared for college and during the last year of his course taught in the academy. He afterwards taught in a day boarding school at Scarsdale, West Chester County, N. Y., for one year. In the fall of 1854 he entered the Sophomore class of Columbia College in New York City, and graduated from that institution in 1857. For two years he was a tutor in New York and acquired sufficient funds to pay the debt of his college education. He then entered the general Theological Seminary of the Episcopal Church in New York City and graduated therefrom in the summer of 1862. Immediately after he went to Otsego County, N. Y., as assistant rector to the Rev. G. L. Foote, of Zion Church, Morris. Upon Mr. Foote's death in 1863, he became rector of that church. In September, 1865, he was married to Harriett M., daughter of Mr. Foote. In October, 1866, he was nominated for Bishop, for the Territories of Montana, Idaho and Utah, by Bishop Horatio Potter of New York, and was elected; he was but twenty-nine years of age at the time but this fact was not known. The ancient Church law requires a person to be thirty years of age to be eligible as Bishop, so the young rector returned to his post and remained until after his thirtieth birthday. On May 1, 1867, he was consecrated Bishop in Trinity Chapel, New York City. He left his family in Morris, N. Y., and reached Salt Lake City, July 2d, 1867; he then visited Idaho and Montana, and spent the balance of the year 1867 in Virginia City, Montana. In September, 1868, he returned East, and in November, 1868, with his wife and child and Mrs. Foote went to Helena, Montana, where they lived for one year. In the autumn of 1869 they removed to Salt Lake City, where they lived until September, 1886. While in Virginia City, Montana, he was elected Bishop of Missouri, but declined same, feeling that his duty laid in the mountains. Eighteen years later, in May, 1886, he was elected a second time Bishop of Missouri, and accepted, succeeding Bishop Robertson, a wise and prudent churchman. Bishop Tuttle soon recognized the fact that one Bishop could not do justice to Missouri, so in 1890 the diocese was divided, the western half being under Bishop Atwill of Kansas City. Bishop Tuttle resides in St. Louis and is beloved and respected by all who know him.

SHIELDS, George Howell, the president of the Missouri Society of the Sons of the American Revolution, was born June 19, 1842, at Bardstown, Kentucky. His

(9)

parents were George W. Shields and Martha A. Howell, daughter of Daniel S. Howell and Sarah Garnett Shipp. Daniel S. Howell was the son of Caleb Howell and Rebecca Stiles; Caleb Howell was a light horseman or dispatch bearer during the Revolution, the son of Ebenezer Howell, who was a Major in the New Jersey line during the Revolutionary War. Daniel S. Howell was one of the early settlers of Kentucky coming from New Jersey and was a member of the County Court of Nelson County, and also for many years a Magistrate. Sarah Garnett Shipp was the daughter of Edmund Shipp and Sarah Garnett, who were both of old Virginia stock; her brother Edmund Shipp was a Lieutenant in the War of 1812 and was with Col. Croghan in his defense of Fort Sandusky or Fort Stephenson against the British and the Indians, where with a little band of Western men they defied a force of over 500 men, mostly Indians, but under a British officer. In 1835 Congress voted a sword to Croghan and Shipp for bravery, although Lieutenant Shipp had died in 1817, quite young and before marriage. George W. Shields was born in Pennsylvania and was the oldest son of David Shields and Nancy McChord. Among the early records of Pennsylvania it is shown that David Shields, the father of the David Shields above mentioned, was sent in command of a company of men to Standing Rock, now Huntington, Pa., to defend the western portion of Pennsylvania from the Indians and he became noted as an Indian fighter. The family emigrated into Ohio and settled in Athens County, and from there moved near Cincinnati. George W. Shields left school and home at the age of 17 and became a civil engineer. He built quite a number of the turnpike roads in Kentucky, and surveyed the first railroad in Mississippi. He married Martha A. Howell, July 20, 1841, and moved to Missouri in 1844, settling in Hannibal. He there engaged in business, became quite wealthy but lost his property during the war. He was six times Mayor of Hannibal, and three times City Engineer. He was appointed Postmaster of Hannibal by President Johnson and lived there till his death in 1880, respected by all his townsmen. Both Mr. and Mrs. Geo. W. Shields were of Scotch-Irish descent. George H. Shields obtained the usual grammar school education in Missouri before the war, and in 1859 went to Westminster College, Fulton, Mo. He continued there till early in 1861 when the Civil War caused his return home. He then began the study of law with Hon. Wm. P. Harrison. The war rendered consecutive study impossible, so Mr. Shields became an active member of the 53d Regiment of the Enrolled Missouri Militia in Co. E, which took part in the war, and were engaged in several skirmishes, notably the fight at Palmyra, Mo. Mr. Shields was afterwards commissioned by Governor Gamble as Capt. and A. Q. M. of the 53d Regiment E. M. M. In February, 1866, he married Mary Harrison, eldest daughter of Rev. John Leighton, D. D. Mrs. Shields is also of Revolutionary stock, being a descendant of Col. Joseph Cabell of Virginia, Benjamin Harrison of Surrey, and of William Randolph and "King" Carter of Virginia, and John Crowly Richardson, all of whom took part in the Revolution. She is President of the Colonial Dames of Missouri and State Regent of the Daughters of the American Revolution, and was for two years the Secretary-General of the National Society of the Daughters of the American Revolution, of which Mrs. Benjamin Harrison was President. In 1870 Mr. Shields advocated the adoption of the amendments to the constitution of 1865 conferring the right of suffrage on the returned Confederates and otherwise modifying the restrictive clauses of the constitution, and was sent as a delegate to the State Republican Convention in 1870, in which the famous bolt of the Liberal Republican wing of his party occurred; he refused to bolt and remained with the regular organization and voted for and supported Governor McClurg at the polls. He was nominated for the Legislature for the Hannibal District and was elected, being the only Republican elected in Marion County at that election. In the Legislature of 1871 and 1872, he was a member of the Judiciary Committee and Chairman of the Committee on Constitutional Amendments. Although the Legislature was largely Democratic, Mr. Shields was considered so good a lawyer that he was elected one of the House Managers of the impeachment of Judge Philander Lucas. He was chosen Chairman of the Missouri Republican Convention in 1872 at Jefferson City, which sent delegates to the National Rebublican Convention which renominated General Grant. In the St. Louis Republican Convention of that year he was nominated for judge of the Supreme Court of Missouri, and although defeated he received quite a complimentary vote. In 1878 Mr. Shields removed to St. Louis, Mo., and formed a partnership with Hon. John B. Henderson, which continued for ten years. This firm was associated in

(10)

many celebrated cases. In 1876 Mr. Shields was an advocate of Hon. James G. Blaine for President. He was elected chairman of the Republican State Committee in that year and continued its chairman till 1880. In 1875 he was elected a member of the Constitutional Convention of Missouri. After its adoption by the convention he was largely instrumental in preventing the vote on it becoming a political one; he voted against some of its provisions, but voted for the instrument as a whole and advocated its adoption before the people. In 1876 he was elected as one of the Board of Freeholders to frame a scheme for the division of the city from the county of St. Louis, and to frame a charter for the city. Although a majority of the Board were Democrats, Mr. Shields was complimented with the chairmanship and greatly aided in its conclusions. The scheme and charter was adopted by the people. From 1877 to 1889 Mr. Shields devoted his time to his profession, but after 1880 he stumped Missouri and other States in behalf of the Republican party. He was appointed by Judge Samuel Treat, master in chancery of the United States courts, and special master in the receivership of the Cotton Belt Railroad. He discharged his duties in this behalf so well that he was never reversed, and complimented from the bench by Judges Treat and Brewer. He was also special master in chancery in the celebrated Express cases. In 1889 he was appointed by President Harrison, on the recommendation of General Noble, then Secretary of the Interior, as Assistant Attorney-General in charge of the legal business of the Interior Department of the United States, and while serving in this capacity ably handled the many complicated cases constantly arising. While serving as Assistant Attorney-General, Westminster College conferred on him the degree of LL.D. President Harrison appointed Mr. Shields as agent and counsel of the United States before the United States and Chilean Claims Commission. For a year and a half this commission sat, and all the claims of our citizens against Chili for seventy-five years were prosecuted, and all the claims of Chilean citizens against our government, were defended by Mr. Shields. Returning to St. Louis in December, 1894, Mr. Shields resumed the practice of the law. In September, 1895, Gen. Noble offered him a partnership, and the firm of Noble & Shields was formed and still continues. This firm stands among the first in the State. Mr. Shields is a Presbyterian, like his ancestors before him, and was an elder in the Lafayette Park Presbyterian church of St. Louis, the Church of the Covenant in Washington, D. C., and now of the Second Presbyterian church in St. Louis. He is greatly interested in Sunday-school work, believing in the efficacy of religious instruction of the young. He is an ardent patriot and believes that the future of the country will be brilliant and lasting. He is a member of the Frank Blair Post of the Grand Army of the Republic, and was vice-president of the District of Columbia Society of the Sons of the American Revolution for two years. Mr. and Mrs. Shields have three living children, George H. Shields, Jr., Mrs. Sara Bainbridge Leighton Warren, and Marion Leighton Shields, all of whom are members of the Societies of the American Revolution.

SHAPLEIGH, Augustus Frederick, numbers among his Revolutionary ancestors, men of distinction who served their country well. The Shapleighs date their American ancestry from Alexander Shapleigh, who was born in Devonshire, England, in 1585, and came to this country before 1635, as agent for Sir Ferdinand Gorges in the ship Benediction owned by himself with Sir Francis Champernoon. He settled at Kittery, Maine, and built the first house there. From him to the date of the Revolution, the descent was as follows: Alexander Shapleigh, born Devonshire, England, 1606, died 1642; Major Nicholas Shapleigh, born 1610, accidentally killed 1682; he occupied some of the highest offices in the Colony of Maine, being a member of Governor Vine's and Governor Godfrey's council — commander of the troops — associate judge, and was commissioner who signed the treaty with Squando, chief of the Sagamores, in 1678; Captain John Shapleigh, born 1642, killed by the Indians in 1706 — representative to the General Court; Major Nicholas Shapleigh, born 1680; representative to General Court of Massachusetts Colony, Major of York County troops, died 1756; Nicholas Shapleigh, born 1720, died 1786, was a soldier in Sir Wm. Pepperell's "Blue troupe of horse;" Captain Elisha Shapleigh, Revolutionary hero, born 1749, died 1823, married Elizabeth Waldron of Dover in 1770; he commanded the first Kittery company of Colonel Joseph Storer's Second York County (Maine) Regiment; Captain Shapleigh organized and equipped this company at his own expense, participated in the battle of Germantown and other engagements of the Revolutionary War; Captain Richard Shapleigh, born 1776 died 1813, was captain and owner of ship

(11)

"Granville" and was lost in the wreck of his ship in 1813; he married in 1799, Dorothy Blaisdell, who was the daughter of Abner Blaisdell, who served in the Revolution as Sergeant in Captain Titus Salters Company of artillery, Fort Washington, 1775, and also served in Colonel John Langdon's Company of Light Horse Volunteers in 1778. Other prominent ancestors of Mr. Shapleigh are: Lieutenant Roger Plaisted, killed by Indians 1675, in King Philip's War, was Deputy to the General Court; Captain John Pickering, Deputy to General Court, 1680, Member of Assembly; Colonel John Wheelwright, a very prominent officer in Queen's Anne's War, 1712, Judge of the Court, 1708; Samuel Wheelwright; Deputy to General Court 1671–77, judge of the Court 1694–1700. Anthony Stangan, Deputy to General Court 1654–80; Jeremy Houchin, Deputy to General Court, 1651–67; Tobias Langdon, grandfather of Governor John Langdon; John Plaisted, speaker of the New Hampshire House of Representatives; Ambrose Gibbons, Assistant Governor of Maine, 1640.

Shapleigh, Augustus Frederick, born at Portsmouth, N. H., Jan. 9, 1810. His father was Richard Waldron Shapleigh, a ship-owner, who was lost in the wreck of his ship *Granville*, off Rye Beach, N. H., in 1824. His family are of English ancestry, Alexander Shapleigh, of Dover, having immigrated to America in 1635. He settled at Kittery Point, Me., then in the Massachusetts colony. Alexander and his son, Maj. Nicholas Shapleigh, held important trusts under the British Crown, and they and their descendants were prominent in the local history of the colony. Portions of his property in Kittery are now (1896) held by his descendants. In 1824, at the death of his father, Augustus, though but fourteen years of age, was obliged to aid in the support of his family and secured a position in a hardware store in Portsmouth, at a salary of $50 per annum. After one year he gave up his position and went to sea, serving for three years on board a sailing vessel. At the earnest solicitation of his mother and sisters, he then gave up the sea and re-entered the hardware business in his native city. A few years later he accepted a position with Rogers Bros. & Co., hardware merchants of Philadelphia, with whom he remained until 1843, having then become a junior partner in the firm. In the same year the house established a Western branch, and Mr. Shapleigh removed to St. Louis to take charge of the new enterprise under the name of Rogers, Shapleigh & Co. On the death of Mr. Rogers the firm became Shapleigh, Day & Co., and in 1863, when Mr. Day retired, A. F. Shapleigh & Co. In July, 1880, the business was incorporated as the A. F. Shapleigh & Cantwell Hardware Co., and in 1888 this was changed to the A. F. Shapleigh Hardware Co., which is the present name of the corporation. In 1886 their entire stock was destroyed by fire; notwithstanding this and other minor disasters the house has enjoyed uninterrupted prosperity for over fifty years, operating extensively from the Middle States to the Pacific Coast. Since 1859 Mr. Shapleigh has been a trustee and director of the State Bank of St. Louis. He was for twenty-eight years a director of the Merchants' National Bank, and, in 1890, resigned this position in favor of his son, Alfred. He was for many years president of the Phœnix Fire Insurance Company and vice-president of the Covenant Mutual Life Insurance Company, which office he still retains (1896). Mr. Shapleigh was married, in 1838, in Philadelphia, to Miss Elizabeth Ann Umstead. Of the eight children born to them, six survive — five sons and a daughter: Frank, vice-president of the hardware company; Richard W., second vice-president; Alfred L., secretary and treasurer; Augustus F., Jr., and John B., a physician. Although Mr. Shapleigh has given over the control of the hardware company to his sons, he still maintains an active interest in the many commercial enterprises with which he is, or has been, connected.

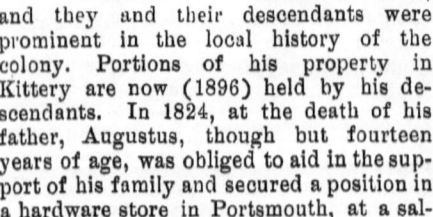

SHAPLEIGH, John Blasdel, a descendant of the Revolutionary soldiers, is a well-known and prominent physician of St. Louis, Mo., and in him the Revolutionary patriots are ably represented. Elisha Shapleigh, great-grandfather of our subject, was Captain of the 1st Company, 2nd York County Regiment, Massachusetts troops,

J. B. Shapleigh

A. F. Shapleigh

during 1776-77; he was also Captain of a Company in Colonel Joseph Storer's Regiment and took a prominent part in the battle of Germantown. Our subject is also the great-grandson of Abner Blaisdell, who was a Sergeant in Captain Titus Salter's Company of Artillery at Fort Washington, in 1775; he was also a private in Colonel John Langdon's Company of Light Horse Volunteers, New Hampshire troops, in 1778. The father of our subject, Augustus F. Shapleigh, is an honored and wealthy citizen of St. Louis, and the head of the A. F. Shapleigh Hardware Co., one of the oldest and most prosperous business houses in the West. His mother was, before her marriage, a Miss Umstead. Dr. Shapleigh was born Oct. 31, 1857. He received his academic and collegiate education at the Washington University, St. Louis, Mo., and graduated from that institution in 1878 with degree of A. B. Then took a course of medicine at the St. Louis Medical College, and graduated from there in 1881, as M. D. He then served for one year at the City Hospital and one year at the Female Hospital, in St. Louis. He then went to Europe, took a course of study on diseases of the ear in Vienna, Austria, returning to St. Louis in the spring of 1885, and began the practice of his profession, which he has continued with marked success. Dr. Shapleigh is Professor of Otology and Secretary of the Faculty of the St. Louis Medical College, and has occupied that Chair since 1895, and is the present occupant of that important post. He was formerly consulting Aurist of the City Hospital of St. Louis, Mo.; he is a member of the staff of St. Luke's Hospital, St. Louis Protestant Hospital, and is connected with the Evangelical Deaconess Hospital; is also a member of the staff of the Missouri Baptist Sanitarium, a member of the St. Louis Medical Society, a member of the City Hospital Medical Society, a member of the American Otological Society, and of the American Academy of Medicine. Socially, is a member of the University Club of St. Louis. Dr. Shapleigh was married Sept. 27, 1886, to Miss Anna T. Merritt, of St. Louis, daughter of Jacob Merritt. Dr. Shapleigh, although a young man, is recognized as a leader in the special branch of medicine he has chosen, diseases of the ear. He is dignified and reserved in manner, but is popular, not only with the members of his profession, but with all with whom he comes in contact.

GADSDEN, Gen. Christopher, great-great-grandfather of Paul Trapier Gadsden, was one of the first of all Americans to advocate independence. He was a member of the first Congress of the Colonies, the "Ovum Republicæ" which met in Boston in 1765 to protest against the "Stamp Act," and it was through his efforts, that the Colonies south of the Potomac were represented in that Congress. He took 1,000 pounds to Boston, collected from the citizens of Charleston and Georgetown, South Carolina, for relief of those who were blockaded on account of the "Tea Party" episode; and vehemently protested against payment to the British of any indemnity for loss of the tea. From 1760 to 1775, he served as Captain of Charleston Artillery. During this time he held "Liberty" meetings under a palmetto tree on the Gadsden estate on subject of Independence. The tree was called "Liberty Tree" afterwards, and a copy of the Declaration of Independence was read from under its branches. The tree was afterwards burned by the British, and from its stump a desk was made and presented to Thomas Jefferson at his request. From 1762 to 1776, Gen. Gadsden was a member of the South Carolina Assembly. When the Continental Congress proposed to retaliate on Great Britain by prohibiting exports to England, five of the South Carolina delegates requested that rice should be excepted, as it was the main source of revenue of that State. Although the exception was yielded, Gen. Gadsden alone of the South Carolina delegation opposed the concession and voted against it, although his entire fortune was invested in rice, and wharves and vessels for its export. During 1774–75–76, he was a member of the Continental Congress. In 1775 he became Colonel of the First South Carolina Regiment. From 1776 to 1777 he was Brigadier-General of the Continental Army. In February, 1776, he was ordered to take command of the troops in South Carolina, and he presented to the Provincial Congress the flag that was afterwards used by the Commander-in-Chief of the United States Navy. His absence in South Carolina prevented his signing the Declaration of Independence. In 1780 he became Lieutenant-Governor of South Carolina. When Charleston capitulated he was requested to give his parole not to further molest the British; he refused and was placed in solitary confinement in St. Augustine, Fla., for some time. In

(13)

1782 he was elected Governor of South Carolina, but declined the honor on account of advanced age. The Provincial Congress of South Carolina gave him a vote of thanks in 1776 for his distinguished services. Gen. Christopher Gadsden had three children, two sons and one daughter. Philip, his second son, was a shipowner in Philadelphia and Charleston; he had sixteen children; his second son was Gen. James Gadsden of South Carolina, Minister to Mexico, who negotiated the treaty by which the U. S. acquired what is known as the "Gadsden Purchase." His third son was a lawyer of prominence and Speaker of the South Carolina House of Representatives; his oldest son was Rt. Rev. C. E. Gadsden, fourth Bishop of South Carolina, and grandfather of Paul T. Gadsden. Rev. Thomas F. Gadsden, father of Paul T. Gadsden, was for nearly thirty years a clergyman in the missionary parishes of South Carolina. Paul Trapier Gadsden is the only living male representative of the oldest branch of the family, was born near Charleston, S. C., June 11, 1870. He attended the Porter and Anderson Military Academies of South Carolina, and graduated from the University of the South at Suwanee, Tenn., in 1891, with degrees of B. Lt. B. A. and M. A. In autumn of 1891 he entered the Columbian University Law School, Washington, D. C., and studied law under Justices Harlan and Brewer of the Supreme Court of the U. S. In 1893-94 he took the degrees of LL.B. and LL.M. at this institution. While at Suwanee, he represented the University at the intercollegiate oratorical contest in Nashville, Tenn., in 1890, and the Interstate oratorical contest in Charlottesville, Va., in 1891. He was elected president of the Columbian Law School Debating Society, and represented it three successive years in the intercollegiate debate; was admitted to the bar in St. Louis, Mo., February, 1895, where he is now practicing his profession.

STANARD, Edwin O., takes his stand in the front rank of Missourians, who, as a descendant of the Revolutionary heroes, proudly and honorably represents the noble men who secured Americans their independence. His great-grandfather, father's side, William Stanard, Sr., was a member of the Committee of Safety of Newport, N. H., a private in Captain Uriah Wilcox's company, Colonel Benjamin Bellows' New Hampshire regiment. His great-grandfather on mother's side was Samuel Webster, Lieutenant in Captain Joseph Dearborn's New Hampshire company, in the Continental service, who marched against Canada in 1776 with General Montgomery. Edwin O. Stanard, subject of this sketch, was born in Newport, N. H., January 5th, 1832. His father was one of the early New England settlers, and his mother was Miss Elizabeth Webster of the early colonial settlers. Mr. and Mrs. Stanard went West, locating in Van Buren County, Iowa, and young Edwin here received the first rudiments of education, graduating from the Keosoqua (Iowa) High School. For several years he taught school, and in 1856 secured a position as bookkeeper in Alton, Ill. He soon afterwards went to St. Louis and established a commission house. Mr. Stanard, with untiring energy and perseverance, soon built up a large business, and although but twenty-five years of age, had secured a hold in the commercial world. In 1861 he established a branch of his business in Chicago, during the blockade of the Mississippi river; afterwards opened a second branch in New Orleans. He continued to do a prosperous business until 1868, when he disposed of his interests and embarked in the milling business, which he at present conducts. The E. O. Stanard Milling Company is widely and favorably known throughout the United States. In 1866 Mr. Stanard was made President of the Merchants' Exchange of St. Louis, and made one of the ablest presidents that body has ever had.

He was afterwards elected Vice-President of the National Board of Trade. Mr. Stanard has been foremost in all matters pertaining to St. Louis interests, and was particularly conspicuous in his work of securing deep water between St. Louis and the Gulf, and in securing equitable railroad rates.

During 1893 he was President of the Board of Directors of the St. Louis Exposition, and was among the first to assist in the Autumnal Festivities Association, now known as the "Business Men's League." He is a director of the St. Louis Trust Company, and for many years President of the Citizens' Fire Insurance Company, and is a director of the Boatman's Bank.

Politically Mr. Stanard is a Republican, and in 1868 was elected Lieutenant-Governor of Missouri, and soon afterwards elected to the Forty-third Congress.

Mr. Stanard served Missouri well, during his Congressional career, securing appro-

(14)

priations for the river and harbor jetty system. On retiring from Congress he did not again take active part in politics and declined most honored nominations tendered him. Mr. Stanard is a most charitable man, and has given largely to all charities and to the M. E. Church, of which he is a member. In 1881 he was elected a delegate to London by the Missouri Conference to represent that body at the great Ecumenical Conference. Mr. Stanard married Miss Esther Kauffman of Iowa in 1856. Four children have blessed their marriage. W. K. Stanard, the eldest son, is a representative business man of St. Louis, and is a prominent member of the Merchants' Exchange.

Gov. Stanard, although he is usually a very busy man, is a genial and agreeable gentleman, and readily approachable when disengaged from business cares.

LEIGHTON, George Eliot, was born in Cambridge, Massachusetts, March 7, 1835. He is a lineal descendant of Captain John Leighton, who came to America in 1650, and settled near the mouth of the Piscataqua in what was then Kittery, now Eliot, Maine. During the early New England history the family was well and honorably known, and bore its full share in the troubles incident to the establishment of the colony. Its members served in the several wars of the times with the Indians, King Philip's War, King William's War, Queen Anne's War, the old French War, and, finally, in the war with England in the struggle for Independence. William Leighton (born 1723, died 1795), the great-grandfather of the subject of our sketch, was from 1770 to 1776 one of the select men of the town and foremost in arousing the patriotic spirit of the people. He was a member of the Committee of Correspondence of the town, appointed December 21, 1773, to whom was referred the letter relative to the tea shipped by the East India Company, and made the report upon which it was: "*Voted*, That the thanks of the town be returned to the Inhabitants of the town of Boston for their early intimation to us of a Quantity of Tea lately arrived there subject to a duty; also for the said Inhabitants' conduct in not suffering said Tea to be landed in their Town, and the Inhabitants of said town of Boston may be assured that the inhabitants of this Town will at all times be ready to assist their brethren of Boston, and every other town in the province at the risque of their lives and Fortune, in the defense of all our just rights and privileges." He was a delegate to the Congress of the Towns of York County, held at Wells, November 11, 1774, in which he protested against English taxation and recommended "the withdrawal of all commerce and dealings with those who have assisted to the enslaving of a free people." He was active in assisting in raising and equipping the 112 men, who at the call of Warren marched from Kittery under command of his cousin (Capt. Samuel Leighton) to join the army at Cambridge in April, 1775, and served at Bunker Hill and the siege of Boston. After peace came the Leightons were prominent in the merchandise and shipping and ship-building interests of Maine and New Hampshire, with extensive business connections in the larger eastern towns. Mr. Eliot Leighton, born at Eliot, Maine, in 1802, the father of the subject of this sketch, took up his residence in the city of Cincinnati as a merchant when his son George was about ten years of age. In that city the lad received his education, and at the age of eighteen graduated with honors from Woodward. His ambition was the law, and in the year 1856, after three years' study, he was admitted to the practice in the State and United States courts. Two years later (1858) he came to St. Louis. He had scarcely become established in his profession when the civil war broke out, and being an ardent Unionist, he gave his time and influence to the encouragement of the loyal sentiment of his adopted city, and in April, 1861, entered the Federal service as Lieutenant of the Third Missouri Infantry R. C. During the summer of 1861 he was engaged in active duty in the field. Later he received the appointment of Major of the Fifth Missouri S. M. Cavalry, and was subsequently transferred to the Twelfth Regiment of Cavalry. In the fall of 1861 he was assigned to duty as Provost Marshal of the St. Louis division, under General Halleck, and was in charge of the city during the trying and critical period of the winter of 1861 and 1862. His services under Generals Halleck, Curtis, Schofield, Hamilton and Davidson, during the years 1862 and 1863, won from his commanding officers the most generous expressions of approval, and resulted in his promotion to the Colonelcy of the Seventh Regiment Missouri E. M. M. Colonel Leighton's war record was an honorable one throughout, and when peace came, in the year 1865, he resumed the practice of

(15)

the law, which he soon found to be lucrative and promising. In addition to his ordinary legal business he accepted the position of General Counsel to the Missouri Pacific Railroad, and continued to occupy that position until the year 1874. His railroad and manufacturing interests in those years increased so rapidly and demanded so much of his time, that he was compelled to relinquish the practice of law. In 1875 he became president of the Bridge & Beach Manufacturing Company. This company is the oldest and one of the largest iron manufacturing establishments in the West. Colonel Leighton's other interests are diversified, and his experience and ripened judgment have made him a valuable member of the boards of directors of many important corporations. He is at present one of the trustees of Bellefontaine Cemetery, director in the Union Pacific Railroad Company, in the Union Trust Company of St. Louis, and in the Boatmen's Bank of this city. For twenty-two years he has been a member of the Board of Trustees of the Washington University, and has given much attention to its important affairs. In 1887, upon the death of Dr. William G. Eliot, he was elected president of the board, and in that capacity served the institution with a zeal and wisdom which has worked the most important results to the educational interests of St. Louis. For more than thirty years he has been a Trustee of the Church of the Messiah (Unitarian). Colonel Leighton's means are abundant, his sympathies are broad, his tastes catholic, his pride in the city of St. Louis is great, and he has been a generous contributor of time and money to the promotion of many laudable schemes for the building up of home institutions. For ten years he was president of the Missouri Historical Society, which owes its success largely to his gifts and personal efforts, and is corresponding member of several other State societies; has been president, and is now a leading member of the New England Society; he was for four years president of the Commercial Club, and took a prominent part in originating and directing the agitation which resulted in the substitution of granite streets in the down town districts of St. Louis. It is impossible to exaggerate the importance of that reform. To improved streets may be largely attributed the extraordinary growth of St. Louis in the last ten years. Colonel Leighton is a member of the St. Louis Academy of Science, of the American Economic Association, of the American Academy of Political and Social Science; is a member of the Board of Control of the St. Louis School of Fine Arts, and of the St. Louis Medical College. He is a member of the Bar Association, of the Missouri Commandery of the Loyal Legion, and also of the Missouri Society of the Sons of the American Revolution, of which he has been president. He believes in the advantages and good-fellowship of club life, and is a member of the St. Louis and University Clubs of St. Louis, as also of the Union and Union League Clubs of New York City. He is not a politician in the ordinary sense of that term, and though a Republican from principle, is independent, and not active within party lines except when the issues involved are of exceptional importance to the country, the State or the city. He has taken a prominent part in the cause of Sound Money, and is president of the national organization known as the National Sound Money League. In the year 1862 Colonel Leighton married Miss Isabella, daughter of Hon. Hudson E. Bridge, of St. Louis. She died in the year 1888. He has one son, George Bridge Leighton, born July 19th, 1864, married to Miss Charlotte Kayser of this city. Colonel Leighton's home-life is quiet, refined and dignified. The paintings and library of his residence are characteristic of the cultivated tastes of the owner. The library, the largest private library in the city, especially reflects the refined appreciations and the research of the student and lover of literature. It has a particular value in the department of discovery and exploration and settlement of the Mississippi Valley. Colonel Leighton is yet in vigorous life, with a clear intellect, active sympathies, and enjoys in a high degree the honor and respect of the community in the midst of which he has passed so many pleasant and profitable years. His summer home is at Monadnock, N. H.

LINCOLN, William Shattuck. Whether in the savage state, or throughout the changing epochs of civilized life, the true qualities of manhood, courage and duty constitute the base upon which the edifice of human respect is built. These essential characteristics of the soldier, since the earliest records of time, have been held up for the admiration of passing generations. The descendants of the soldiers and statesmen of the Revolution in organizing societies in the several States of the country to keep alive

William S Lincoln

and perpetuate the glorious memories of their distinguished ancestors, not only honor themselves and the lineage from which they spring, but they accentuate the old adage that "Pride is more priceless than gold." Pride of birth is not empty vanity; the fact that a man is the bearer of a great name is almost invariably the foundation upon which honor and truth are built. The Missouri Society of Sons of the American Revolution is particulary rich in distinguished Revolutionary ancestry. Several are descendants of signers of the Declaration of Independence. Such great names as Washington, Benjamin Lincoln, Israel Putnam, Nathaniel Greene and Patrick Henry, all are represented. W. S. Lincoln is entitled to the honor of membership in the Missouri Society S. A. R. by right of lineal descent in the following line: Major-General Benjamin Lincoln of the Continental Army, who was born in Hingham, Massachusetts, January 24, 1732, and died in Boston, May 9, 1810. Gen. Lincoln bore a conspicuous part in most of the battles of the Revolution from Lexington to Yorktown. He was not only distinguished as a military leader, but he also filled, most honorably and creditably to himself, several high offices in civil life. He was at one time Collector of the Port of Boston, was Secretary of War, and negotiated important Indian treaties in Ohio, and Buffalo Creek. In admiration of his abilities and moral worth, Washington on two occasions bestowed upon him swords of honor. These weapons, silver-hilted and appropriately engraved, are in the possession of a brother of Wm. S. Lincoln at the family seat in Dennysville, Maine. The subject of this sketch, Wm. Shattuck Lincoln, was born in Dennysville, Washington County, Maine, May 19, 1837; he was a son of Theodore and Elizabeth Cushing Lincoln; a grandson of Theodore and Anna Mayhew Lincoln, and a great-grandson of Maj.-Gen. Benjamin Lincoln and Mary Cushing, his wife. Wm. Lincoln received his primary education in the district schools of his native town, and, in 1852, entered the Lawrence Scientific School at Cambridge, Massachusetts, but was for a time compelled by ill health to relinquish his studies. He returned to Cambridge and completed his studies, leaving there in 1856, when he removed to Logansport, Indiana, securing employment on Cincinnati & Chicago R. R. Nov. 12, 1856, he was made division engineer and continued in this duty until May, 1857, when he was made chief engineer of the road. Caleb B. Smith, afterwards President Lincoln's Secretary of the Interior, was at this time its president. On August 1st, 1857, Mr. Lincoln commenced the location of an extension of the C. & C. Road to Valparaiso, Indiana, which was completed Feb. 2d, 1861; while in charge of this work as chief engineer, he still had charge of the maintenance of the Cincinnati & Chicago Road. After completing the Valparaiso extension, he was placed in charge of maintenance of the whole line, continuing in this position until Jan. 1st, 1865; in the meantime he was consulting engineer of the Chicago extension. Mr. Lincoln entered the service of the Wabash system July 25th, 1865, in charge of the rebuilding and maintenance on the Illinois division, with headquarters at Springfield. March 1st, 1868, he was appointed chief engineer of the Decatur & East St. Louis R. R.; he completed this work July 25th, 1870; in the meantime he was consulting engineer of the Pekin, Lincoln & Decatur R. R. Oct. 1st, 1870, he was transferred to the eastern division of the Wabash, with headquarters at Toledo, Ohio, in charge of maintenance of way, also in charge of building docks and elevators at Toledo. In June, 1871, in addition to his other duties he was appointed consulting engineer of the Lafayette, Bloomington & Mississippi R. R. which was completed in June, 1872. June 1st, 1877, the duties of purchasing agent were assigned to him. He left Toledo Jan. 3, 1880, for Springfield, Ill., when he was appointed chief engineer of the Wabash, St. Louis & Pacific lines, east of the Mississippi river, in the meantime being consulting engineer of the Detroit, Butler & St. Louis R. R., and in charge of the terminal facilities of same road at Detroit, which he completed July 1, 1881. Sept. 1, 1881, he was made chief engineer of the entire Wabash system, establishing his headquarters in St. Louis. The foregoing outline of Wm. Lincoln's work and experience in railroad construction, coupled with the fact that he continued in the management of the engineering department of one of the greatest railway systems in America, is the highest proof that he is one of the ablest and most distinguished members of his profession in the country. Mr. Lincoln is an indefatigable worker, and by the necessities of his official position, always a busy man. Notwithstanding this, he is an approachable and companionable gentleman, exceptionally well informed and greatly interested in the Society of Sons of the American Revolution. Wm. Lincoln most creditably, but modestly, represents the historic name he bears. On Dec. 12, 1872, he married Miss Eliza J. Higgins, of Logansport, Indiana, who died May 4, 1894.

WYMAN, Henry Purkitt, was born in Hillsboro, Montgomery County, Illinois, October 25th, 1841. Son of Edward Wyman and Elizabeth Frances Hadley, the former a native of Charlestown, Mass., the latter of Boston, Mass., was brought to St. Louis by his parents in 1848, where he has resided continuously since. His father, Edward Wyman, was a life-long and conspicuously successful educator of boys and young men, establishing and maintaining in St. Louis for nearly forty years "Wyman's English and Classical High School," an institution, the fame and usefulness of which eclipsed that of all other similar schools in the then "Great West." It numbered continuously a membership ranging between five and six hundred, and in the aggregate, educated thousands of young men whose training and tutelage have made their mark upon the progress and enlightenment of the Mississippi Valley. The subject of this sketch completed a High School course at sixteen years of age, and immediately entered upon a business career as a clerk in a leading wholesale grocery and commission house, remaining so employed until the opening of the Civil War in 1861, when he entered the service of the government, acting as Chief Clerk in the Transportation Quartermaster's Department throughout the war, and showing marked ability in transportation matters. In 1867 Mr. Wyman was appointed Special Deputy Collector of Customs under Collector Sam'l M. Breckinridge, and his efficiency and faithfulness in that responsible position caused his retention in it during the successive terms of collectors S. M. Breckinridge, Felix Coste, E. W. Fox, John F. Long, and Gustavus St. Gem, an aggregate period of fourteen years, during which his management of the St. Louis Custom House made it a recognized model for efficiency and accuracy. Mr. Wyman's special efforts were directed to the inauguration of the "Direct Importation Laws" and the establishment of regulations under which importers of St. Louis and interior cities might be freed from the agency and exactions of other importers resident at the seaboard, and the reward of his long and persistent efforts (co-laboring with Members of Congress, officers of the Treasury Department and the local press) was finally won, when Congress passed the Act of 1870, and importers of the interior became subject to no greater restrictions than are common to those at tide-water. In 1880 Mr. Wyman was elected Secretary and Treasurer of the St. Louis & New Orleans Transportation Co.,—a strong corporation formed for carrying bulk grain from St. Louis to Europe via the river and New Orleans. The directory of the company was composed of leading merchants of St. Louis, together with several New York City representatives—amongst them Messrs. Jay Gould and Russell Sage. From the start the company was phenomenally successful, and rapidly increased the number of its steamers, barges and other facilities until at the close of 1881, the company merged its business with that of the Mississippi Valley Transportation Co.—the new organization taking the name of the St. Louis & Mississippi Valley Transportation Co.—and having a paid up cash capital of two millions of dollars. This company, of which Mr. Wyman has always been the energetic and efficient secretary, has been the chief factor in making St. Louis an export grain market, wields a powerful influence in transportation circles, and contributes largely to the welfare and renown of the city. Mr. Wyman takes special interest in the patriotic and historical societies of the day and is an enthusiastic member of the Society of Colonial Wars and of the Sons of the Revolution; he is a charter member and the treasurer of the local organizations of both societies, and active in promoting their growth, influence and usefulness: his eligibility to membership is clear by right of the services of quite a number of his paternal and maternal ancestors—which are duly recorded in the Massachusetts archives of the New England Colonial wars and the War of the Revolution. Mr. Wyman traces his ancestry to Saxon origin as remote as the ninth century (the name, in common with names in earlier times, having been spelled in different ways, as Wiman, Wymant, Wymond, Wimond, and otherwise)—the family being native to Leicestershire, and later to

WYMAN GRAVESTONE.

Sands.

James T. Sands

County Herts, England. The first of the family of record in America were Francis and John Wyman, brothers, whose names are found signed to the "town orders" of Woburn, Mass., in 1640. The older brother, Francis, was the progenitor of the subject of this sketch; he was a prosperous tanner and had a town house in Woburn with a country home a few miles distant: the latter building was erected about 1646 and is *still standing in good preservation — more than two hundred and fifty years old;* his gravestone too is remarkably well preserved, and stands in the old Woburn graveyard with inscriptions clear cut and legible now as when first erected in 1699. Mr. Wyman caused it to be photographed in the winter of 1894, and a reprint of same is here inserted. The Latin inscriptions on either side are "Memento Mori" and "Fugit Hora" while the record reads as follows: "Here lyes ye body of Francis Wyman, aged about 82 years, died Nov. 28th, 1699. 'The memory of ye just is blessed.'" Following is the line of descent from Francis Wyman:

1. Francis Wyman, born England, 1617; married Abigail Read; died Woburn, Mass., 1699.
2. William Wyman, born Woburn, 1656; married Prudence Putnam; died Woburn, 1714.
3. William Wyman, born Woburn, 1685; married Abigail Stearns; died 1749.
4. Nehemiah Wyman, born Woburn, 1722; married Elizabeth Winn; died Woburn, 1775.
5. Nehemiah Wyman, born Woburn, 1762; married Susanne Stearns; died Woburn, 1820.
6. Nehemiah Wyman, born Medford, Mass., 1786; married Susan Frances Cutter; died Hillsboro, Ill., 1869.
7. Edward Wyman, born Charlestown, Mass., 1815; married Elizabeth Frances Hadley; died Upper Alton, Ill., 1888.
8. Henry Purkitt Wyman, born Hillsboro, Ill., 1841; married Annie E. Leigh, 1863.

SANDS, James Thomas. Among those who enjoy the satisfaction of having preserved the records of more than one member of his family who participated in the battles of the Revolutionary Wars, is James Thomas Sands, the subject of this sketch. On his father's side, his Revolutionary ancestors were his great-grandfather, Samuel Sands, an ensign in Col. Robert Curry's Battalion of Philadelphia County Associators in 1777, and his great-great-grandfather, John Sands, who served in the Pennsylvania Line until January 1st, 1781. These ancestors of Mr. Sands were descendants of Captain James Sands or Sandys as the name appears to have been originally spelled in England, came to Boston in 1638 and settled on Block Island, in 1665; his father was Rev. Henry Sandes, of Edwin's Hall, the fifth son of Edwin Sandes, Archbishop of York in Queen Elizabeth's reign. The oldest son of the Archbishop, Sir Samuel Sandys, was the owner of a splendid estate, Scrooby Manor; it was leased to Brewster, and here the first Separatist Church was founded. A daughter of Sir Samuel Sandys was the wife of Sir Francis Wyatt, Governor of Virginia, 1621, and resided in Virginia with her husband for a while; her cousin, Robert Sandys, was married to Alice Washington, aunt of the emigrant John and grandfather of George Washington. Another son, Sir Edwin, was Governor of the London Virginia Co., in 1620, and through him the "Mayflower" Company obtained its charter. All the sons (six in number) of Archbishop Sandes were members of the London Virginia Co., and the youngest, George, the Poet, was resident treasurer in Virginia. Edward Eggleston in his book "The Beginners of a Nation," says, "That group of liberal English statesmen who were charged with keeping a school of sedition in the courts of the Virginia Co. founded the two centers of liberal institutions in America, the Earl of Southampton, the Ferrars, Sir John Danvers, and, above all, and more than all, Sir Edwin Sandys, were the founders of representative government in New England, by the charter of February 2, 1620, as they had been of representative government in Virginia by the charter of November 13, 1618." The father of James Thomas Sands was Samuel Gilbert Sands, a native of Montgomery County, Pennsylvania; he removed to St. Louis in 1837, where he married Miss Ann Maria Wright; he went to California in 1849, where he died in 1870. Miss Wright was a daughter of Thomas Wright and Comfort Hancock, his wife, of Maryland. Thomas Wright was a grandson of Captain Job Wright of Lieut.-Col. Willett's regiment of New York troops 1781–2, a descendant of Deacon Samuel Wright, of Springfield, Massachusetts (1639), who was a son of Nathaniel Wright, one of the Assistant Governors of the Massachusetts Bay Colony, 1628–30. Comfort Hancock was a daughter of Isaac Hancock, a cousin of Governor John Hancock of Massachusetts, a signer

(19)

of the Declaration of Independence. Mr. James T. Sands was born in St. Louis; he is well-known in business, financial and social circles, and is especially interested in hereditary patriotic societies, being a member of the Society of Colonial Wars in the State of Missouri, by right of Captain James Sandys of Block Island, Sons of the Revolution in Missouri, the Society of the War of 1812 in Philadelphia, by right of Lieutenant James Sands Thirteenth Company, Third Regiment, Pennsylvania V. R., 1814–15, the New York Society Order of Founders and Patriots of America, and the New York Commandery of Military Order of Foreign Wars. Mr. Sands enjoys the distinction of being the representative of a long line of aristocratic and patriotic ancestors, on both the paternal and maternal sides. The history of this family is an exceptionally interesting one to every student of American biography, who, at the present day, and in the years to come, may have the good fortune to acquire from this book a knowledge of the nobility of American manhood, the soldiers of the Revolution and their descendants.

SPENCER, Horatio Nelson, M. D., is descended on both sides from a line of honored Revolutionary ancestry. Dr. Spencer is eighth in descent from Rev. John Wilson, seventh in descent from Rev. Thomas Hooker, seventh in descent from Sergeant Richard Church, seventh in descent from John Clark, sixth in descent from Lieut. William Pratt, sixth in descent from Lieut. Alexander Marsh, sixth in descent from Ensign Jared Spencer, fifth in descent from Capt. William Pratt, fourth in descent from Isaac Spencer, third in descent from Capt. Israel Spencer, second in descent from Israel Selden Spencer, and third in descent from Capt. William Brockway. Rev. John Wilson was a chaplain in the Pequot War, and the first pastor of the first church in Boston, Mass. Rev. Thomas Hooker founded the Connecticut Colony in 1636, and on January 14, 1639, drew up the constitution of the Government of the Colony; "it was the first written constitution known to history which created a government, and marked the beginning of American Democracy of which Thomas Hooker deserves more than any other man to be called the father."— (*Fiske*.) Dr. John Wilson, son of Rev. John Wilson, graduated in the first class that was graduated from Harvard University in 1642. The Pratt family have records back to the eleventh century, and William Pratt, an ancestor, was distinguished for his valor in preventing the capture of King Richard of England in one of the holy wars of 1191. He pretended to be the king, was captured by the Turks, and a ransom of ten emirs was paid for his release by the king, who also knighted him for his loyalty and courage. Capt. William Pratt was appointed Lieutenant of Connecticut troops in 1709, and Captain of the first company of Saybrook, Connecticut, in 1717. Lieut. William Pratt commanded the forces that fought under Mason in the Pequot War, and was deputy to the General Court during 1666–67. John Clark was a royal patentee under charter from Charles II., and was also a soldier in the Pequot War. Israel Selden Spencer was a private at the age of fifteen, in the company of Capt. John Gates, in 1777, was also a private in the company of Capt. Worthington, and a private in the company of Capt. Hungerford. Israel Spencer was a Captain in Col. Charles Burrall's regiment, Connecticut troops, and served at Quebec and Ticonderoga in 1776. Dr. Spencer's father, Horatio Nelson Spencer, was born in Lyme, Conn., November 22, 1798, and graduated from Yale College in 1821 with high honors; was admitted to the Bar, removed to Georgia and thence to Mississippi in 1828, where he practiced his profession and became one of the conspicuous men of his time and section; he acquired large wealth and finally devoted himself exclusively to planting. He married Sarah Marshall, who came of a line of distinguished ancestors. They had ten children, the subject of our sketch being the seventh. Dr. Horatio Nelson Spencer was born in Port Gibson, Mississippi, and received his preparatory education from tutors graduated at Yale. At age of sixteen years, he entered Oakland College, Mississippi, and was graduated valedictorian of his class in 1862. When the Civil War began he espoused the Southern Cause, enlisting as a private in Cowan's Battery, Loring's Division of the Confederate Army of Tennessee, and served without intermission until the close of the war. In 1865 he began the study of medicine in New York City, and was graduated in 1868. After spending one year in Germany, he settled in St. Louis, Mo., in 1870. Dr. Spencer is Professor of Diseases of the Ear in the Missouri Medical College; he also holds the degree of LL.D., which was conferred upon him by Westminster College, Missouri, in 1897. In 1868 he married Miss Anna Kirtland, of Memphis, Tenn., by which union they had five children. His wife died in 1885, and in 1887 he married

SPENCER.

again, his second wife being Miss Elizabeth Porcher Dwight, of South Carolina.

MORRILL, Henry Leighton, Major in the First Iowa Cavalry, whose distinguished services during the late Civil War have stamped him as a worthy representative of the ancestor who bore a prominent part among the heroes who assisted at the birth of this great nation, is the great-grandson of Colonel Henry Morrill, who commanded the 2d Essex Regiment in the War of the Revolution. The Morrill family first became identified with this continent when, in 1632, Abraham Morrill landed in Boston with his brother Isaac, who had accompanied him from London, England, in the ship "Lion." Early records show that they at once took a foremost place in the land of their adoption. Isaac Morrill became a freeman of Roxbury, Mass., in 1633, and died in 1661, the possessor of extensive real estate, leaving no issue. Abraham Morrill in 1635 was a citizen of Newtown, now Cambridge, and in 1639 became one of the founders of Salisbury, Mass., whither he removed in 1640, and where he died in 1662. His son Jacob was the second of a family of nine children by his wife, Sarah Clement, and was born in Salisbury, June 26, 1648. He married in 1674, Susanna Whittier, of the same stock as the poet Whittier, and died in 1814, leaving a family of eight children, of whom Aaron married Johanna Dow, a descendant of Henry Dow, one of the first settlers of Hampton, N. H., and ancestor of General Neal Dow. Their son, Henry Morrill, to whose name attaches the distinction of having been one of the founders of our liberty, was born at Salisbury, on June 27, 1731. At the commencement of the struggle for independence, he held a commission as captain of militia, and was the first in his community to respond to the call for troops. It is recorded of him that on the ordering of the draft, he mustered his men on parade and addressed them in patriotic terms, calling upon them to volunteer, at the same time ordering the drum and fife to pass down the line to head those who should volunteer; none responding, so Captain Morrill seized a musket himself and followed the music. His example so inspired his men that all "fell in" at once. At the siege of Boston he commanded a company in Col. Isaac Little's Regiment, and early in 1776 was appointed Lt.-Col. of the 2d Essex Regiment under Col. Jonathan Titcomb. On March 13, 1778, he was appointed Colonel of the same regiment and while in active command died of camp fever Oct. 20, 1778. He married Eleanor Currier Oct. 5, 1756, of Amesbury, Mass., by whom he had seven children; of these Levi, the next link in the chain of Major Morrill's descent, was the fourth son, born at Salisbury, October 15, 1765, and who married Mary Bagley, April 15, 1792; resided at Salisbury, N. H., where he died Feb. 19, 1858, leaving a family of eleven children, of whom Benjamin Franklin Morrill, our subject's father, was the ninth son, born at Salisbury, N. H., August 12, 1810. He married Sarah A. Leighton, a member of the historic family of that name. In 1837 he migrated to Illinois. In 1841 he moved to Iowa, where he settled on a farm in Van Buren County, and closed a long and honored life on Oct. 23, 1884. Of his family of eight children, his eldest son, Henry Leighton Morrill, was born in Guilford, Me., April 4, 1836. He received his education at the Academy of Van Buren County, Iowa, and graduated in 1856. He began life's career as a school teacher. Between this profession and mercantile life he was engaged until 1861, and on June 13 of that year, he enlisted at Keokuk, Iowa, in Company A, 1st Iowa Cavalry. He served with honor through the various grades of non-commissioned rank, and on Dec. 1, 1864, was commissioned First Lieutenant and Adjutant in the same regiment. March 13, 1865, was honored by President Lincoln with the brevet of Captain and Major for "gallant and meritorious services in the field." During his active service, Major Morrill participated in many memorable actions. He was at Blackwater in the battle of Dec. 18, 1861; at Silver Creek, Mo., on January 6, 1862, in the fight with Poindexter's command, at the battle of Pleasant Hill, Mo., and of Lone Jack, Mo. In October, 1862, his regiment was attached to the Army of the Frontier and fought in the battle of Prairie Grove, Ark. In June, 1863, he marched to Pilot Knob, Mo., and in July the regiment was attached to the Army of Arkansas, proceeded to Little Rock and participated in its capture. He was also engaged in the battle of Bayou Meto, Ark. In the fall of 1864 the regiment returned to Little Rock, and in February, 1865, was ordered to Memphis and remained attached to the Army of Tennessee until June, 1865, when it was ordered to Texas and attached to the Army of the Gulf under command of General Custer, marching from Alexandria, La., to Austin, Texas, where it was stationed until February, 1866. On March

16, 1866, Major Morrill was mustered out and discharged, after a continuous service of four years and nine months. Major Morrill returned in 1867 to Keokuk, Iowa, whence he had marched in the ranks six years before, and remained there until July, 1870, filling the position of Deputy Collector and Collector of Internal Revenue. In that year he first became connected with railroad interests, taking charge of the construction and operation of the St. Louis and Southeastern Railway, and of the Cairo and Vincennes Railway. In 1877 he severed his connection with these lines, having been appointed by the U. S. Circuit Court Receiver and Manager of the Iowa Central Railway. In December, 1879, he took charge of the construction of the Peoria, Decatur and Evansville Railway, and on the completion of this enterprise in March, 1881, he commenced the construction of the New York, Chicago and St. Louis Railway from Buffalo to Chicago, completing this gigantic work in eighteen months. From October, 1882, to April, 1886, he filled the position of general manager of the Boston, Hoosac Tunnel and Western Railway; and on June, 1886, was appointed general manager of the St. Louis and San Francisco Railway Company, of which corporation he was elected 2d vice-president in 1887. In July, 1896, he severed his connection with this company and has since enjoyed the leisure earned by the labors of an active and useful career. Major Morrill was married on Feb. 10, 1869, to Miss Clara White, of Des Moines, Iowa. He is a member of the St. Louis and Commercial Clubs, is Past Commander of the U. S. Loyal Legion of Missouri; a member of the Society of the Army of the Tennessee and of the Missouri Society of the Sons of the American Revolution. Among the cherished heirlooms of the family is the sword of Col. Morrill of Revolutionary fame, and no less cherished will be the war escutcheon of Major Morrill which hangs by its side in the family home in St. Louis.

BRIER, Robert Emmet, great-grandson of Benjamin Lodge, of Revolutionary Army fame, was born at Covington, Indiana, May 13, 1847. He is the son of Judge David Brier, who married Caroline A. Breckinridge, a member of the distinguished Kentucky family of that name. Judge Brier was born in Westmoreland County, Pa., August 25, 1808, and was a graduate of Wabash College, Indiana. He adopted the profession of law and commenced practice at Covington, later removing to Bloomington, Ill. While in Covington he was elected judge and in his office, the late Senator Voorhees first read law, afterwards becoming Judge Brier's partner. Judge Brier was a man of high literary culture, domestic in his tastes and retiring in his disposition. He was repeatedly a nominee for Congress, though defeated as a Whig by the overwhelming Democratic element in his district, and was one of the electors of Henry Clay at the Baltimore Convention. He passed his declining years at Topeka, Kan., where he finally closed an honorable career in April, 1883. His widow still survives in the enjoyment of a hale old age, at Denver, Col. Robert Emmet, so named in honor of the Irish patriot and orator, began his education at the High School at Bloomington, Ill., from which he was graduated in 1861, when he entered the Wesleyan University. He was not destined, however, to pursue his academic course beyond his freshman year, for on the call of his country in 1862, he, though little more than a child, not yet 15 years of age, felt the spirit of his patriotic ancestors pointing out to him the path of duty. With the encouragement of his father, prevented by physical disability from leading in the path he pointed out to his son, and the heroic consent of his mother, the young lad enlisted as a private in the 68th Illinois Infantry, for a term of three months, on the expiration of which he re-enlisted for the same period, which, completed, he again enlisted for three years in the 3rd Illinois Cavalry. He was in the second battle of Bull Run and many other engagements during his period of active service, and in 1864, his health seriously impaired by the exposure and hardships of army life, he, apparently in a dying condition was sent home, but under the loving care of his parents he partly recovered his health. He then left the service to accept the position of Treasury Aid at Memphis, by appointment of Secretary Fessenden. Here he remained until 1865. He then entered commercial life as a clerk, was again taken sick, and went north to Bloomington, where, on regaining his health, he entered a commercial college, from which he was graduated in the winter of 1865. In the spring of 1866 he was appointed clerk in the Treasury at Washington, and while there entered upon the study of law at the Columbian Law School. He faithfully performed his official duties until 1869, when he was graduated from the law school, and his health having again succumbed, to

(22)

the strain his ambition had subjected it to, he went to Santa Fe, New Mexico, where he was appointed cashier in the United States Depository, and clerk in the Paymaster's office for the United States Army. After three years' sojourn in New Mexico, Mr. Brier came to St. Louis as purchasing agent for United States Q. M. Dept., under Major E. B. Grimes. In June, 1872, he entered the house of George D. Hall, in capacity of porter. Progress marked his career, and with experience gained as salesman and traveler, he engaged with Messrs. Beck and Corbitt as salesman in 1875, and in 1878 the business having been incorporated as a joint-stock company he was appointed secretary and treasurer, and on the death of Mr. Corbitt was elected president. In addition to the presidency of the Beck & Corbitt Iron Co., he is also president of the Shelter Top Co., the St. Louis Cycle Co. and the Forrest Hardwood Mfg. Co., the latter plant located at Little Rock, Arkansas, being the largest in the South. On October 24, 1877, Mr. Brier married Miss Hannah B. Clark, daughter of Mr. Daniel B. Clark, of St. Louis. Mr. Brier is a member of Ransom Post, G. A. R., and of the Missouri Society of the Sons of the American Revolution. During his travels in Europe, which he visits every year, he makes it a point to study the sociological questions which are still awaiting solution. Mr. Brier is one of St. Louis' most prominent and progressive citizens, and it is with pride we present his name among those who so honorably represent the glorious deeds of their Revolutionary ancestors.

RANDALL, John F. The distinguished honor of membership in the Missouri Society of Sons of the Revolution comes to this gentleman from the mother's side, through one of the most widely known families of New England, the Averys, of Groton, Connecticut. Mr. Randall was born at Mystic, in that State, April 13, 1839. His father, Isaac Randall, married Adelia H. Miner, the daughter of John Owen Miner and Elizabeth Avery, who was a daughter of Lieutenant Ebenezer Avery and Phoebe Denison. Ebenezer Avery, a Revolutionary officer, whose title to fame was earned at the cost of his life, was killed September 6, 1781, in the massacre of the garrison at Fort Griswold. The gallant defense of this fort by a force of only one hundred and sixty-seven men, under Colonel Ledyard and Captain Latham, against fifteen hundred British regulars, supported by a powerful fleet of armed ships, was one of the most brilliant achievements in the War of Independence. Those who escaped death or wounds were mostly put to the bayonet, only some twenty or thirty men being made prisoners. Sixteen members of the Avery family participated in the battle of Fort Griswold, of whom nine were killed, three wounded and four captured. The scenes in that drama of actual war were at Groton, opposite New London, Conn. Rufus Avery, a Sergeant in Captain William Latham's company, has handed down to posterity a graphic and somewhat quaint account of the event, in which he was an active and fearless participant. In this battle the attacking force of the enemy was under the immediate direction of the traitor, Benedict Arnold. Every member of that little band of patriot soldiers may indeed be justly remembered as a hero of the Revolution. Captain James Avery was the founder of the family called the Groton Averys. He was born in England in 1620, coming to America with his father in his boyhood, settling first at Gloucester, Mass. He was a very prominent man, distinguishing himself while occupying many high positions, both civil and military. As a reward for his public services, the General Court of New London granted him, in 1668, a hundred acres of land for a farm, and in 1675 a similar grant was made to him by the Colony. From Captain James Avery descended Lieutenant Ebenezer Avery, the hero of Fort Griswold, and the ancestor of John F. Randall. Mr. Randall received his elementary education in the district school of Mystic, his native town, and in 1857-58 attended school at the Connecticut Literary Institute at Suffield. He afterwards studied for one year at the Pierce Academy, Middleboro, Mass., entering Yale in 1860. The sophomore year was scarcely finished when he put aside the quiet life of the student to take up the sterner and more exciting duties of the soldier. August 3rd, 1862, he enlisted in Company C, Twenty-first Connecticut Regiment, being shortly afterwards appointed Second Lieutenant of the same company. On September 15, 1862, he was promoted to the grade of First Lieutenant, and took part in many noted battles in the campaigns in Virginia. August 8, 1863, he resigned his commission, returning to his home at Mystic, where he engaged in business for a year. He went to St. Louis in November, 1864, and was in the employ of Appleton, Noyes & Co.,

(23)

until March, 1865, when he went to Vicksburg, Miss., with a stock of goods. In May of the same year he opened a store, with an assorted stock of merchandise, at Jackson, Miss., which business he conducted until the fall of 1866; during this period he engaged in cotton planting. He returned to St. Louis in 1866, and shortly thereafter engaged in the fire and marine insurance business, to which he has devoted thirty-one years of his life, being a partner in the well-known insurance firm of Martin Collins, Son & Co. Mr. Randall was married in March, 1870, to Miss Elizabeth F. Stark of Mystic, Conn., a relative of General Stark, of Revolutionary fame. Their family consists of two daughters. Mr. Randall is a Republican in politics, and cast his first vote in 1860, for Abraham Lincoln. In religion he is a Baptist. In addition to his membership in the Sons of the Revolution, Mr. Randall is a member of the Grand Army of the Republic, the Loyal Legion, the Society of Colonial Wars, and is one of the "Mayflower" descendants.

GLASGOW, William Henry. In presenting the name of William Henry Glasgow before the world in the Missouri edition of "Revolutionary Soldiers and their Descendants," we present that of an honored and prominent resident of St. Louis, whose career both as soldier and citizen has reflected so much credit on his distinguished ancestry. He is the grandson of Edward Mitchell, who was Captain and Quartermaster of Col. William Campbell's Rifle Regiment, of Virginia Line. Captain Mitchell did valiant service in the cause of Independence and was among the first of the patriots to take up arms in that grand cause. William Henry Glasgow, the subject of our sketch, was born in Belleville, Ill., Feb. 19, 1822. His early education was received in the private schools of St. Louis, completing his studies at St. Charles, Mo. He began life's labors at the age of 17 years, as clerk in a grocery store, and in 1841 went to Mexico; from there on horseback to the Gulf of California, thence across the mountains to Chihuahua, Mexico, thence to Santa Fe, N. M., thence to Independence, Mo., and from there to St. Louis; here he met an old steamboat friend of his father's, who gave him a position as clerk on the steamboat "Oceana," and after holding same three months, occupied a similar position on the steamboat "Lexington," plying between St. Louis and St. Joseph, Mo., in the summer, and St. Louis and Cincinnati in the winter; he soon afterwards bought this boat, and ran it up the Missouri river for one year; he then purchased the steamboat "Congress," and ran her until the winter of '44 in connection with the New Orleans trade; during same year and in the winter of '46, he bought a stock of goods in Philadelphia, shipped by water to Independence, Mo., and from there in wagons to Santa Fe, N. M. On reaching the Arkansas river, Mr. Glasgow and his party were stopped by a company of U. S. Dragoons, sent out for the purpose by Gen. Stephen Kearney, who was on his way to capture New Mexico, who informed them that war had been declared and was in progress between the U. S. and Mexico. They then proceeded by slow and cautious marches into Mexico, and reached the mouth of the Jornada del Muerte, and remained there until February, 1847, when he and his party followed Gen. Donovan to El Paso, where they all volunteered, and were mustered into the U. S. Army. They began their march to Chihuahua, but before reaching that city, encountered Gov. Trias, at the head of 4,000 men, who were entrenched at Sacramento Mt. and had fought the battle of Sacramento, where the Mexicans were defeated and driven off the ground; the following day Mr. Glasgow and his company marched into the city of Chihuahua. During this time Mr. Glasgow was Lieutenant in Co. A., Col. Samuel Owens' Battalion, of which his brother, Edward J. Glasgow, was Captain. They remained in Chihuahua about one month, when Col. Donovan, fearing the return of the Mexicans with reinforcements from Durango, quietly bought from the traders all their horses and teams for use of his army, and left Mr. Glasgow and his four companions to their fate in an enemy's country. He was in a fearfully trying and dangerous situation, but proved himself equal to the occasion. He made arrangements with the Alcalde of the city of Chihuahua, who proceeded to Parral, to which place the capital had been removed, where he made a treaty with the Mexicans, by which Mr. Glasgow and his companions were allowed to remain in Chihuahua and sell their goods. In the spring of 1848, Gen. Sterling Price with his army proceeded from Santa Fe by forced marches to retake Chihuahua, and engaged the Mexicans at Santa Cruz, where the Mexicans were defeated in a battle lasting all day. Shortly after the battle an armistice was concluded be-

E.C. Husted.

tween Gen. Scott and Gen. Santa Anna, and forthwith Gen. Price detailed Capt. Greer with fifty men, under a flag of truce, to communicate with the U. S. Army in possession of Monterey, Mex., and Mr. Glasgow accompanied the party. On reaching Monterey he at once set out for Matamoras, and upon arrival there, took steamer and went to New Orleans, and soon after returned to St. Louis, where he engaged in the wholesale grocery business until 1886, at which time he was elected president of the St. Charles Car Co., a large corporation engaged in the manufacture of all kinds of railroad equipments, both freight and passenger, to which business he gives his exclusive attention. Mr. Glasgow's father, Wm. Glasgow, was born in Christine, Delaware; he went to Spain and France as assistant to the U. S. Consul in both countries. In 1814 he went to St. Louis, Mo., where he became a prominent merchant, and died there in his eighty-ninth year.

LATHROP, William Addison Howe, is the great-great-grandson of General Seth Pomeroy, who served as a delegate to the Provincial Congress of Massachusetts in 1774–1775, by which he was elected a General Officer in October, 1774, and a Brigadier-General in February, 1775.

He served as a volunteer at the battle of Bunker Hill, and his presence as an old veteran of the Colonial War gave inspiration to the troops.

LATHROP, Joseph, is the great-great-grandson of General Seth Pomeroy, who served as a delegate to the Provincial Congress of Massachusetts in 1774–1775, by which he was elected a General Officer in October, 1774, and a Brigadier-General in February, 1775.

He served as a volunteer at the battle of Bunker Hill, and his presence as an old veteran of the Colonial War gave inspiration to the troops.

HUSTED, Edward Chapin, is a worthy representative of a long line of distinguished ancestors from whom he has by heredity derived those qualities which have placed him in the front ranks in the community. Through his mother he is the great-grandson of William Harvey, one of those heroes of Revolutionary times who assisted at the birth of this great republic and to whom we are indebted for the liberty we enjoy; and through his father he is the eighth in line of direct descent from Louis DuBois, a nobleman of France who came to America in 1660. William Harvey was born at East Haddam, Conn., October 26, 1754, and was one of the first to answer to the trumpet call of freedom, though barely of man's estate, enlisting in Captain Abraham Filer's Company of the Eighth Connecticut Regiment, commanded by Col. Huntington. At the battle of Monmouth he was captured by the enemy and for eighteen months was immured in a British prison ship. He lived to a good age, dying at Lyndon, Vt., August 26, 1826. His widow, Jane Harvey, who was born October 15, 1757, survived him until July 21, 1840. Their daughter Lucretia married, in 1805, Daniel Stoddard, born in Vermont, January 29, 1787, and who afterwards removed to Ohio, being one of the earliest settlers of the Western Reserve, and the founder of the town of Woodstock. Their daughter, Cassandra Louisa, the mother of our subject, was born January 6, 1823, at Stowe, Vt.; died May 21, 1892. She was endowed by nature with sterling characteristics. She married John Arthur Husted in Springboro, Ohio, December 21, 1848. He was a native of Indiana, born March 10, 1823, of a family originally from New Jersey and directly descended from Louis DuBois, a nobleman of fame and a victim of the Huguenot persecution, who was first driven from his native country to Holland and thence to this country in the early part of the Seventeenth Century. J. A. Husted settled in Muncie, Indiana, of which town he became a highly respected citizen. Ably seconded by his wife, a woman of great force of character and a typical descendant of the early New England Puritans, he was always deeply interested in building up the town where their memories are still loved. He was one of the principal organizers of the present school system, was the first school trustee elected, serving as treasurer of the School Board for fifteen consecutive years, and his death in 1882 was widely mourned. His eldest son, Edward Chapin Husted, whose name heads this article, was born in Indiana. His primary education was received at the public schools of Muncie and Terre Haute, supplemented by a course under private tutors, and a commercial course at a business college in Terre Haute. Thus well equipped for the battle of life, he, after about a year's business experience in his native place, as reporter for the Muncie *Daily News*, sought a wider field and traveled south to Texas, where he remained for some years as financial manager for a firm of railroad contractors. In 1883 he went to Leadville, Col., where he became largely interested in min-

(25)

ing and also was associate proprietor of the Clarendon Hotel, then the leading hostelry of that part of the country, and himself the youngest hotel proprietor in the United States. His geniality, tact and business acumen brought success in his new venture but in 1885 he was forced by failing health to retire from business and he traveled for one year in California. In 1886 he went to Chicago, where he engaged in insurance business until 1890, when he accepted a position with the Wabash Railway Co., eventually being transferred to St. Louis. In 1892 he became connected with the St. Joseph Lead Co. at their mines at Bonne Terre, where he remained a few months, and was then placed in charge of its affairs, as general agent at St. Louis, controlling all territory west of the Alleghany mountains. By his unaided efforts Mr. Husted has gained thus early a position in the community of which his friends are proud, and his success as a business man and the unlimited confidence he commands, are due to his unswerving adherence to the high standard of life and conduct he had maintained and which has been handed down to him by his Puritan Scotch and Irish maternal ancestry, and the French and Dutch Huguenot blood on the paternal side. The example set by his purity of life is one to be emulated. A keen student of human nature, his judgment of men is unerring and the conferring of his friendship is recognized as a valuable indorsement of character.

LUCAS, John Baptiste Charles, is the present most prominent living descendant of that honored name in Missouri and the seventh in line of descent from the Lucas side and the fourth in descent of his Revolutionary ancestor. Our subject's life reflects the magnitude and grandeur of a great family and has himself beautifully illustrated the heritage of a great name, is one of St. Louis most prominent citizens. He is a great-grandson of Andrew Vanoy, who was Captain of a company of militia in North Carolina, commanded by Colonel Abraham Shepard. He enlisted in 1777 and served his country with great credit until the close of the war. His company was prominent in the Revolutionary War and was actively engaged in battles of note. No name is more prominent in the history of Missouri than that of Lucas. The earliest date of record from grandfather's side of the Lucas family is that of Nicholas Lucas, who was born in 1572 and died in 1650, aged 78 years. Second in descent was Robert Lucas. Third in descent was James Lucas. Fourth in descent was Robert Lucas, 2nd. Fifth in descent was Robert Joseph Lucas. Sixth in descent was Robert Joseph Edward Lucas; records show he was born in 1725 and died in 1783. From 1760 onwards he was the Procureur du Roi (King's prosecuting attorney) of Port Audemur, Normandy, France. He married La Mademoiselle de L'Arche. From this union there were seven children, John Baptiste Charles Lucas being their third child and second son, and the grandfather of our subject. John Baptiste Charles Lucas was married in France to Mademoiselle Sebin; he was educated in law with a view to becoming Procureur du Roi at the University of Caen (Cadomum) which was founded by Henry the Sixth, King of England. Its charter was taken out in 1793. The rules of this institution governing the fitness and worthiness of candidates were very rigorous and were prescribed by his Majesty the King. John Baptiste Charles Lucas and his wife left Ostend, Belgium, April 17, 1784, came to America, arriving in Philadelphia, Pa., and purchased a tract of land called Montpelier, situated at Coal Hill, on the Monongahela River near Fort Pitt, now Pittsburg, where they lived until 1805. He brought to this country with him a letter of introduction from Benjamin Franklin, then Minister to France, recommending him to President Jefferson as an able jurist whose counsels would be valuable in framing the laws of the new-born Republic. He became prominently identified with the history of Pennsylvania. He first occupied the bench with Judge Addison, then was elected to the State Legislature in 1795, and was elected to Congress in 1803. About 1801 he was sent by President Jefferson to ascertain the temper of the French and Spanish residents of Louisiana respecting the Louisiana purchase. He traveled incognito to St. Louis, Mo., from there to St. Genevieve and thence to New Orleans, assuming the name of Des Peintreaux. So well and ably did he execute his commission that in 1803, the President appointed him Judge of the Territorial Court and Commissioner of Land Claims of Upper Louisiana. After serving his country well and to the entire satisfaction of the President, he resigned the honored and responsible positions which he so ably filled and returned to St. Louis in 1805. He immediately invested his money in real estate, realizing enormous returns. He had a great love for his family and the sad loss of his five sons caused him to retire from public life and assume only the management of his estate. His law

James H. Lucas

practice was very large and the care of that and other matters fully occupied his time. He was a staunch friend to his debtors and although he was the creditor of thousands, foreclosure was never made unless it was the pleasure of his debtor. The historic speech made by him in St. Louis County, April 20, 1820, wherein he defined his views in consenting to allow his name to be used as a candidate for delegate to the Constitutional Convention of Missouri, created a great sensation at that time. He strongly opposed the introduction of slavery in the State of Missouri, and his speech caused him to incur the enmity of the wealthy slave-owners. That portion of his speech which caused it is as follows: "I could not see our inhabitants and other persons who have no slaves, pillaged, harassed and robbed by such slaves who are poor and miserable in proportion as their masters are wealthy. I would not like to see our citizens obliged to purchase peace and repose in selling their land at any price and going to seek better fortunes far from the rich. I would not like to see our white free population exchanged for the black slave, neither the humble and industrious inhabitants for the proud and effeminate nabobs." The grand words he used in giving his reasons for opposing slavery were as follows: " The whole world is agreed that slavery is a deviation from the rules of morality and justice; that it is in itself an evil that brings in its train a long succession of evils; in consequence it seems to me to be the duty of a public servant to do all in his power to arrest the increase, providing that can be done without affecting the rights of the people of our State. I am then of the opinion that it would be advantageous to a majority of the present population, and much more to future generations, to prevent by the Constitution the introduction of slaves into the State of Missouri, from no matter what State or Territory they may come." From the foregoing sketch can be adjudged the character of the man who during his reclining years reaped the fruits of a well-spent life. Such was the glorious record he handed down to posterity. James H. Lucas, father of our subject, was born November 12, 1800. He was educated at the College of St. Thomas, in Nelson County, Kentucky. In 1817 he left Kentucky and went to New Hampshire, from there to Hudson or Poughkeepsie, New York, to study law. He returned to St. Louis in 1819 and started to South America by boat, going as far as Montgomery Point on the White River, when changing his mind he took a pirogue up the river, by means of a cut-off, and landed at Arkansas Post, thence to Little Rock. He read law during his stay at both places and supported himself by setting type on the Arkansas *Gazette* and running the ferry. His superior ability was soon manifested and he was appointed County Clerk but resigned after being admitted to the bar. He then began to practice his profession, riding the Circuit, as was the custom in those days. He was appointed Major of Militia by Gov. James Miller in 1825, and was later made Judge of the Probate Court. May 10, 1832, he was married to Miss Emilie Desruisseaux; from this union there were thirteen children. At the urgent request of his father, J. B. C. Lucas, who was aged and very feeble, he returned to St. Louis October, 1837. August 17, 1842, his father died, and to his two children, James H. Lucas and Annie L. Hunt, he left his entire estate. James H. Lucas then assumed charge of his father's estate and was very prominent in the history of St. Louis, being its chief benefactor. He was State Senator from 1844 to 1847, and took an active part in the affairs of the State. To his generosity is largely due the building up of St. Louis; he subscribed $100,000 to build the Missouri Pacific R. R. and was twice elected president of that system. He was instrumental in organizing the St. Louis Gas Co., was elected president of same, and was a director in the Boatman's Savings Institution. After 1851 he established a banking house in St. Louis with a branch at San Francisco, Cal. In 1853 a change was made and the institution was reorganized. Among the names of the corporation appear others prominent in history outside of the Lucas family: that of Wm. T. Sherman, Henry S. Turner, John Simonds and Henry L. Patterson. Thus can be judged the class of men whom Mr. Lucas selected as his business associates. The original agreement bearing these signatures given at San Francisco, October 21, 1853, is at present the valued property of J. B. C. Lucas and is an heirloom worthy of preservation. During the panicky times following, both the St. Louis and San Francisco houses failed, but Mr. Lucas assumed and paid their entire liabilities with interest at 10 per cent at a clear loss to himself of half a million dollars and no loss to any of his partners. He was a large contributor to the city of St. Louis and it is indebted to him for a quit-claim deed to the site of the old jail lot. He built Lucas market, gave the Historical Society real estate valued at $10,000 and gave $10,

000 towards the erection of the Southern Hotel; also contributed largely to charitable institutions. His wife died December 24, 1878, after forty-seven years of wedded life. James H. Lucas after a residence of thirty-six years in St. Louis, died November 11, 1873, leaving an estate of 225 stores and dwellings to be divided among his eight surviving children, six sons and two daughters. Our subject, John Baptiste Charles Lucas, was born December 30, 1847, and was educated at Washington University, St. Louis, Mo., and Seaton Hall College, South Orange, N. J. After completing his collegiate course he returned to St. Louis and entered his father's office as a clerk, where he remained two years, when he assumed entire charge of his father's business. At the death of his father, he was appointed one of his executors and settled his estate. In 1890 our subject was elected President of the Citizens' Bank, which position of honor and trust he still holds (1897). He is one of the seven originators and owners of the Planters Hotel and was one of the chief promoters of that enterprise. Mr. Lucas has five children: Mrs. Francis K. Sawyer, Francene, Mary, Charles and James Morton Lucas. Our subject was first married in 1876 to Miss Mollie C. Morton of Little Rock, Ark.; they had two children who died in Colorado. His second marriage was to Isabel Lee Morton; three children from this union. His wife is a descendant from the Nortredes, a very prominent French family, the oldest in the State of Arkansas. Mr. Lucas is vice-president and acting president of Calvary Cemetery and has held this honorable trust ten years. In politics he is conservative, affiliating with such party as in his opinion would best serve the interests of the country.

MASON, Isaac Mason, who has been prominently identified with the city of St. Louis for nearly half a century, is a worthy descendant of one of those patriots who wrested liberty from the hands of tyranny in the War of the Revolution, and bequeathed us our glorious heritage of freedom. His great-grandfather, John Stevenson, who was a native of Baltimore and a member of one of the foremost families of that State, enlisted August 13, 1776, as a private in Captain James Watson's Company, of Colonel Thomas Porter's Battalion, of Lancaster County, Penn., and marched to New Jersey. On the expiration of his term of enlistment he re-enlisted in April, 1780, in Colonel Robert Elder's Battalion, of Lancaster County, under Captain James Murray. After the war he settled down on his farm where he died at the age of 83 years. His second son, Asa Stevenson, by his marriage with Hester Bond, cousin of Shadrach Bond, the first Governor of Illinois, was born in Baltimore in 1780, prior to the removal of the family to Pennsylvania, which took place in 1790, and which was effected by means of a six-horse team, traveling through what was then a wilderness, at the risk of massacre by the Indians. At the farm, on the Monongahela river, the family settled down, and in due time Asa Stephenson married Priscilla, daughter of Richard Gregg, one of the pioneer settlers of the county. After his marriage he gave up farming and went to the town of Jefferson, where he embarked in trade, teaming to Baltimore, while his wife conducted a hotel. He was drafted for service in the War of 1812, and was stationed at Baltimore, which was garrisoned to repel the threatened attack of the British. His descendants numbered four sons and six daughters, all of whom have filled honored places in the community. His daughter, Parmelia Stevenson, married Morgan Mason, father of our subject, who was born July 28th, 1808, in Washington County, Penn. He was the son of Robert Mason, miller, formerly of Virginia, who settled in Pennsylvania in 1800. The founder of the American branch of the Mason family was Robert Mason, a school teacher, who came from England and settled in Virginia in the beginning of the 17th century. His grandson, Robert, above referred to, was born in 1778, and died in Brownsville, Penn., in 1854. His son, Morgan Mason, who on the 29th of July, 1897, entered upon his ninetieth year, is a splendid specimen of American manhood; still in the enjoyment of all his faculties, his mind teeming with the memories of a long and active life, he delights in imparting his recollections of the early days of the century in the Monongahela and Ohio Valley. Starting in life with the advantages of a good education he at first assisted his father in the milling business, afterwards worked for John Walton, miller and distiller. In 1827 he made a trip to Washington with a drove of horses, the journey over the roads in those days being no small undertaking, and after selling his stock and spending some time in viewing the sights of the city, he, being frugally minded, made the return journey (330 miles) on foot. In 1829, after a short term of school teaching, he made a trip to New

(28)

Orleans on a flatboat to Louisville, where they had to land cargo, run the falls, and then reship and thence by steamer "Cavalier." Mr. Mason relates with gusto his experiences on this trip and how, in the keen competition for a market, the captain of the steamer "Porter" swore that he would reach New Orleans ahead of the "Cavalier" or blow up; the excitement of the race culminating in the blowing up of the "Porter." On his return from this trip he rented a flour and saw mill in Fayette County, where he remained six months, and on April 11, 1830, he married, as above stated, Parmelia Stevenson, and removed to Brownsville, where he commenced business as general merchant. A man of boundless energy and activity, he did not, however, long confine himself to the narrow limits of a country store. The years up to 1844 found him steamboating, farming, milling and trading, but always advancing. In 1844, having sold out his mill, he embarked on the steamer "Consul" as clerk, and remained on the river until 1854, during which time he commanded the steamers "Atlantic" and the "Jefferson." In 1854 he gave up river life and bought a large farm in Clark County, Mo., where he went extensively into stock raising, and remained there until 1877, when he opened a store at Alexandria, which he conducted until his final retirement in 1894. During his long life Mr. Mason has held many important public offices. While in Alexandria he was twice elected Justice of the Peace, and was Township Commissioner and Clerk of Council at different times. His children, numbering six, of whom three are still living, were: Isaac M., Presley S., Sarah, Priscilla, William, and Morgan. The old gentleman is now residing with his son, Capt. Isaac M. Mason, in St. Louis, is in full enjoyment of all his faculties, bidding fair to become a centenarian, and states with pride that in all his life he has never used tobacco or intoxicants in any form. His eldest son, Isaac M. Mason, was born at Brownsville, Pa., March 4, 1831. He was educated at the public schools and academy of his native place, and at the age of 15 years commenced his business life as clerk in a store. Soon after he took to steamboating and at 16 years of age was second clerk on a steamboat; one year later was promoted to first clerk, and at a little over 19, was Captain commanding steamer "Summit," plying between Pittsburg and Cincinnati. Until 1863 Capt. Mason spent his life on the river, and during the war was in command of boats carrying supplies for Gen. McClernand's Division, during which time he had many exciting experiences. In 1865 he was appointed general freight agent for the Northern line of steamers, with headquarters at St. Louis. His strong individuality soon brought him to the front in public affairs, and in 1876 he was elected Marshal of St. Louis County. The following spring, on the separation of the county from the city, he was elected Marshal of the city of St. Louis, and on the expiration of his term, in 1880, was elected Sheriff, and re-elected in 1882 for the following term. In 1884 he was appointed general superintendent of the Anchor Line, and in 1887 was chosen as its president. He administered the affairs of this corporation until 1895 when he sold out his interest and in 1897 was elected City Auditor. Captain Mason was for several terms on the directorate of the Merchants' Exchange and in 1892 was elected president of the same. In 1894 he was elected president of the Mercantile Trust Co. and has been for the past ten years president of the Phillips Mining Co. of Colorado. His wide experience of affairs has led to his being selected for many important public missions. He has been several times a delegate to the National Board of Trade at Washington, D. C., has represented St. Louis at the Trans-Mississippi Congress at Omaha, was St. Louis delegate at the launching of the "St. Louis" at Philadelphia, and was actively concerned in the committee to further Capt. Eads bill for the building of jetties at the mouth of the Mississippi and the dredging of the channel at low water between St. Louis and Vicksburg. In the winter of 1895-6 he with Mr. Webb Samuel was instrumental in again bringing this important scheme before Congress to dredge a channel in Mississippi river during low water but failed to secure the contract. Captain Mason was married Nov. 16, 1852, to Miss Mary Tiernan, of Brownsville, Pa., of whom he was bereaved in 1895, and by whom he had six children, of whom five are living, his first son, Morgan, dying in infancy. Charles, born in 1857, holds a position in his father's office; William, born in 1859, is in mercantile life and was deputy sheriff for four years; George, born 1862, contracting agent for Erie-Despatch Ry. Co., and Frank, born 1868, secretary and treasurer of the St. Louis Tarpaulin Co. His only daughter is married to Charles W. Scudder, son of John A. Scudder, capital-

(29)

ist, of St. Louis. In the social life of St. Louis, Captain Mason holds a prominent position. He is a member of the St. Louis Club, Merchants League Club, Washington Lodge, I. O. O. F. No. 24, and Encampment, Legion of Honor, Knights of Honor and the A. O. of U. W. In Freemasonry he is a charter member of Anchor Lodge No. 443, Oriental Chapter No. 78, St. Louis Council, Ascalon Commandery of Knights Templar No. 16, and holds Supreme rank in the Consistory of Scottish Rite Masons having been appointed to the rank of 33° at Washington in 1894. He is also one of the Board of Managers of the Missouri Society of the Sons of the American Revolution, and is a member of the Episcopal Church of the Redeemer, of which he is senior church warden.

ROBBINS, Alexander. Few are those now living who can boast of having listened to the stories of the heroic struggle of Revolutionary days falling from the lips of one of those who took an active part in the erection of this great republic. Captain Alexander Robbins, when a child, sat at his grandsire's knee and eagerly imbibed the lessons of heroism and self-sacrifice conveyed in the tales of the struggles of the patriots of those times. His grandfather, Abner Robbins, at the early age of 18 enlisted in Captain Harwood's Company of Colonel Larned's Massachusetts Regiment, and served with honor from December, 1775, until the triumphant close of the war. The founder of the Robbins family, Richard Robbins, came from England in 1639, landing in Charleston, and finally settled in Cambridge, Mass. Many of his descendants, as also those of Gurdon Robbins, one of the early settlers of Hartford, Conn., have been prominent in their day in the spheres of law, literature and divinity. Abner Robbins was born at Brewster, Mass., in 1757, and after having performed his duty to his country in the War of Independence, returned to his native place and married Judith Jenkins, also a native of Brewster, and there passed the remainder of his long life, during which he was for many years deacon of the Baptist Church, foremost in every good work, dying in 1848 at the ripe age of over 90 years. His son, Alexander Robbins, father of the gentleman whose name heads this article, was born at Brewster, and took to a seafaring life as master and owner of coasting and fishing vessels. He also was imbued with the same spirit of patriotism as his father and took up arms for his country in the war of 1812. Through his marriage with Eunice Sears, his descendants can boast of another honorable line of descent, the Sears family having contributed many heroes to the cause of liberty. Prominent among these was Captain Isaac Sears, who was a prominent member of the Sons of Liberty in New York, was a member of the New York Assembly and of the Provincial Congress of 1783. He bore an active part in the war and commanded the troop of horse which captured the Rivington printing house in New York, obnoxious on account of the unpatriotic stand taken by the N. Y. Gazetteer, destroying the presses and converting the type into bullets. The Sears family was founded in America by Richard Sears or Sayer, who was a great-grandson of John Sayer, alderman of Colchester, England, early in the 16th century. Richard Sears, whose father had been driven from England on account of his Puritan principles, and had taken refuge in Holland, in which country he had distinguished connections in the Van Egmond family, first settled in Yarmouth, in which place and at Chatham are many family monuments. The family is also identified with Norwich, Conn., of which they were among the founders. Captain Alexander Robbins, the eldest son of this marriage, who unites in his veins the blood of the Sears and Robbins families, was born at Brewster, Mass., January 19, 1818, and has, therefore, at the date of this writing, nearly reached his four-score years, though still in full vigor and with unimpaired faculties. He received a good education in his native place and on leaving school followed his father to sea, and in the course of years became owner and commander of his own vessels. Early in the 30's he gave up seafaring and went to Pawtucket, R. I., where, having a natural capacity for mechanics, he mastered the machine business in a short time, becoming so expert as to receive skilled journeyman's wages. In 1839 he was induced to return to the sea, and in 1840 commanded the "Harmony" schooner. In 1844 he went to Boston and after some time spent in the machine business, became connected with a varnish manufactory as salesman. In 1847 he emigrated to St. Louis where he laid the foundations of the present extensive varnish manufacturing now carried on by a joint-stock corporation known as the A. Robbins Varnish Co., of of which he is president. Captain Robbins has been, with the exception of a short period, for 50 years an active citizen of

Alexander Robbins

St. Louis but though always taking a keen interest in public affairs, has never sought civic honors. He is a charter member of Alpha Council Legion of Honor, and of the Missouri Society of the Sons of the American Revolution. In 1845 he married Eliza A. Chapman, daughter of Rev. Nathan Chapman of Massachusetts, by whom he has five sons living: Alexander Robbins, born 1846, secretary-treasurer of the A. Robbins Varnish Co.; Nelson C. Robbins, born 1851, vice-president of the same; Charles C. Robbins, born 1854, now of Las Vegas, N. M.; Lurin C. Robbins, born 1859, garden farmer in St. Louis County, and Cyrus G. Robbins, born 1863, now with the Waters-Pierce Oil Co. of St. Louis. Captain Robbins, though still president of the company, has retired from active participation in its affairs and enjoys the rest earned by the labors of his long life. A keen angler, he spends every summer in the gentle sport either in the scenes of his early life on the sea coast or at inland lakes and is able notwithstanding his great age to endure fatigue which many younger men would not care to face.

ROBINSON, Paul Gervais, M. D., is a descendant from one of the oldest and most distinguished French Protestant Huguenot families. His great-grandfather on maternal side was Jean Louis Gervais, who was born in France in 1741, died in Charleston, S. C., Aug. 8, 1789. He was a member of the "Committee of Safety" with Governor John Rutledge of South Carolina; was also a member of the Continental Congress in 1781-1782. Jean Louis Gervais was one of the colony of Charleston whom the English besieged in that city in 1780; Gov. Rutledge left the city with him and two other members of the council, feeling that the civil authority would be more advantageously employed in the interest of the colonies, than in the capital, invested as it was on every side. Jean Louis Gervais assisted Gov. Rutledge with energy in efforts to rally the dispersed militia, and persuaded them to march to the relief of Charleston; not being successful in that design, they established themselves to the north of the Santee, in order to be in communication with North Carolina, but the reduction of that city and defeat of the garrison who defended it having inspired the soldiers with terror, they retreated farther north, and after having procured succor from North Carolina and Virginia, resolutely returned to South Carolina, where they endeavored to instill more vigor and unanimity into the efforts of the inhabitants against the British. Arriving too late to save Charleston they at least opposed a formidable obstacle to the progress of the British forces, who were elated at their victory. When the province, with the exception of the capital, had been purged of the presence of the enemy, public gratitude eagerly elevated him to the dignity of President of the Senate of South Carolina, which had provisionally assembled at the village of Jacksonborro. Jean Louis Gervais was of French Huguenot descent, and before his emigration to America was a subject of the King of England and a Colonel in the Hanoverian service of the King. He went to Charleston, S. C., in 1764, with letters of introduction to Mr. Oswald (afterwards one of the commissioners of the treaty of peace between Great Britain and the United States), and Henry Lawrence, who was subsequently president of Congress, and Minister to Holland, but was captured by the English at sea and confined in the "Tower of London." Col. Gervais became a merchant and planter on Cooper river, where rice was first cultivated on its introduction in South Carolina. During the Revolutionary War he was one of the counsel of John Rutledge, the Governor, or, as was styled, the President of the State of South Carolina. He was also a member of the convention which met at Philadelphia and adopted the Articles of Confederation. In 1782, he was President of the State Senate of South Carolina. Col. Gervais married Mary Sinclair, daughter of Col. David Sinclair, of South Carolina — authority for above — Weiss' History of the French Protestant Refugees — Appleton's Cyclopædia of American Biography, Ramsey's History of the American Revolution, first edition. Stephen (Etienne) Thomas is the great-grandfather of Dr. Paul Gervais Robinson, on father's side. Stephen was born in the village of Eymet, La Dordoyne, France, August 19, 1750, and died in Charleston, S. C., June 17, 1839. He served with distinction in the Revolutionary War at the battle of Fort Moultrie, and afterwards under General Marion until the war ended. He was captured by the British fleet in Chesapeake Bay and was a prisoner for some time. He was an ardent Christian of the Huguenot faith, and one of the founders of the French Huguenot church of Charleston, S. C. He married Marie Frezil, daughter of Jean Frezil, pilot on board the ship "Friendship," which conveyed the emigrants from Plymouth, England, to Charleston, in January, 1764. Dr. Paul Gervais Robinson was born in Charleston, S. C., August 22, 1834. He received his academic education at Charleston College, from which he graduated in 1854. He studied medicine, entered the South Carolina Medical College, and graduated therefrom in 1856; went to Paris (France), and spent two years at Ecole de Medicine. In January, 1858, he married Elizabeth R. Dickson, daughter of Prof. Samuel Henry Dickson. He was a surgeon in the Confederate army and did noble service in that valiant cause, serving until the surrender. In 1867 he went to St. Louis, Mo., and continued the practice of medicine. From 1868 he has been Professor of Practice of Medicine in the Missouri Medical College and Dean of Faculty of same college to date (1897). In June, 1869, Dr. Robinson married Lina Pratte, daughter of Gen. Bernard Pratte, of St. Louis. Dr. Robinson's line of descent is as follows: Great-grandson of John Robinson and of Stephen (Etienne) Thomas, on paternal side. Great-grandson of John Lewis (Jean Louis) Gervais and General Micah Jenkins, on maternal side. Grandson of John Robinson and Susan Frazil, on paternal side. Grandson of Paul Trapier Gervais and Martha Perry Jenkins, on maternal side. Dr. Robinson's father was Stephen Thomas Robinson, and his mother, Mary Margaret Gervais. He is a member of Empire State Society Sons of the American Revolution, No. 543, also a member of the National Society, No. 5343.

DERIVAUX, Armand. This well-known physician of St. Louis, a native of France, is entitled to honor in our Missouri edition of "Revolutionary Soldiers and Their Descendants" as the grandson of Mathieu Derivaux, a French gentleman who accompanied the expedition under Count Rochambeau in 1781, which lent its aid to the colonists in the War of Independence. He was direct descendant of Chevalier Jean de Rivaux, a nobleman of France, who was an officer of cavalry in the French army in the reign of Louis XIV. holding the rank of "Cornette," an equivalent to the modern rank of "Chef d' Escadron" or Major, U. S. A.; and who served in the Thirty Years' war with the allied armies of France and Sweden. He was severely wounded in his last campaign and retiring from the army was rewarded for gallant service with the appointment of Superintendent of Forests in the "Province de la Basse Alsace" on the annexation of Alsace to France in 1648. The estate accompanying the appointment is still in possession of the family which inhabits the old manor-house of Holtzbad, built in the seventeenth century and still standing in good preservation. The father of Mathieu, also Jean de Rivaux, at the time of the French Revolution changed the name to Derivaux, in order to obliterate the distinguishing sign of nobility, in deference to the prevailing hatred of aristocracy during that period; and having devoted fourteen out of his twenty-one sons to service in the armies of the Convention, received his certificate of "civisme" from that body. One of these twenty-one sons was Mathieu Derivaux, grandfather of the gentleman whose name heads this sketch, who came to America with Count Rochambeau in 1781 as regimental surgeon, though only twenty-one years of age. He served through the War of Independence until the surrender at Yorktown, when he decided to remain in the country which he had assisted to take its place among the nations, and settled in Eastern Pennsylvania, where he remained in the practice of his profession until 1791, when the troubles of his mother country re-awakened his French patriotism and he again turned his face towards his native land, and on landing at Brest joined the army of General Hoche as surgeon. After the quelling of the Chouan rebellion he accompanied General Hoche on his promotion to the command of the army of the Lower Rhine and served through all the campaigns until 1805 when he was pensioned with the rank of Surgeon Major and took up his residence at Erstein in Alsace near his native place. He married Miss Rapp, cousin of General Rapp, whose name is well known in history as one of the generals of Napoleon the Great. Of the seven children of this union, Jean Baptiste Derivaux, father of our subject, was born at Erstein in 1812. He, also, took up the medical profession and settled at St. Amarin in the department of the Upper Rhine, where he married Theodorine Scheibel Girardey, and where he passed the remainder of his life, dying in 1883. His widow, who still resides at the family home in Alsace, is a member of a family whose name has become identified with American history in the persons of Dr. Girardey, uncle of Mdme. Derivaux, who served in the U. S. Army during the Texan war, where he is supposed to have been slain, never since having been heard of, and of two generals and a colonel of the same name who served with distinction in the armies

Rob't M. Funkhouser

of the Confederacy. Dr. Armand Derivaux, who represents the family in the State of Missouri, was born at St. Amarin, Alsace, Sept. 19, 1849, and received his primary education at the College of Jesuits at Metz. He then entered the University of Strasbourg, where he studied medicine until the outbreak of the Franco-Prussian war, when he joined the Third Regiment of Turcos as assistant surgeon. After the battle of Woerth he was separated from his regiment, and the refusal of the Prussians to treat for peace under any less terms than those finally exacted, having aroused the feeling of the nation and made the war national, rather than as before regarded, one of dynasty, he, like many others, enlisted in the ranks and joined the army of The Vosges in which he served until the close of hostilities, when he entered the naval service as assistant surgeon for the port of Brest. Here he remained until December, 1872, when he left the service and resumed his medical studies at the Faculty of Paris, where he received his diploma in 1876. He then determined upon taking up citizenship in the country which had been the scene of his grandfather's first experience in war, and having relatives in St. Louis, the family of Karst, the head of which, Emile Karst, was then French consul at that city, he there took up his residence and commenced practice as a physician and has obtained a reputation worthy of his name. In 1881 he married Miss Georgine Schepp, of St. James, La., a lady of French descent, by whom he has two children, Genevieve, born 1884, and Robert, born 1887. Dr. Derivaux is a member of the St. Louis Medical Society, the St. Louis Gynaecological and Obstetrical Society, the Union Club, and of the Missouri Society of the Sons of the American Revolution, in which body he possesses the unique distinction of being the only representative of foreign birth of the French contingent who nobly aided us in our early struggle for existence as an independent people.

FUNKHOUSER, Robert Monroe, physician and surgeon, was born in St. Louis, Mo., December 10, 1850, son of a prominent merchant of the same name, who is mentioned in several biographical works of St. Louis. His ancestors, on his father's paternal side, came from Berne, Switzerland, two brothers, Christopher and John, emigrating in 1692 to Holland, remaining there until 1698, when they went to England, from whence they proceeded to New Amsterdam about 1700, in which year they left for Virginia, one settling at Fredericksburg, the other at the "Neck." A descendant, Christopher, his great-grandfather, was a soldier in the Revolution; he laid out Morgantown, W. Va., and Morgantown, Ky., naming them after his kinsman, Gen. Daniel Morgan. His grandfather, Robert Roland Funkhouser, was a member of the first legislature of Illinois. On his father's maternal side, the family came from England in 1646, Zachariah Cross, a descendant and his great-grandfather, was born in Baltimore County, Md., March 25, 1761, and died in Wayne County, Ill., February 27, 1833. While still a school boy in Maryland, sixteen years of age, being fired with patriotism by the example of his father and brothers (one of the latter being Lieut. Jos. Cross, mentioned in history), he joined the company of soldiers (in which were two of his brothers) when they passed his home; he was discovered by his brothers, and being unable to take him with them, sent him to their cousin, Gen. Francis Marion, known as the "Swamp Fox," of North and South Carolinas, for whom he acted as scout; and it is said that with many thrilling adventures he served during the remainder of the Revolution and was promoted to the rank of corporal. March 25, 1777, he offered his services to the colonies for nine months as a volunteer in Capt. Wm. Hicks' Company, North Carolina troops, and at various times he served in the companies of Captains Maxwell, Thomas Wallace, and Hubbard till the close of the war, under Gen. Nath'l Greene's command, his services covering North and South Carolina, Tennessee, Georgia, and Alabama. On February 8, 1833, while residing at St. Louis, being then 72 years of age, he applied for and obtained a pension for services in the Revolutionary War as a private in the North Carolina troops. His grandmother was a sister of Lord Cole. Zachariah Cross married Easter (Hetty) Johnston, whose father, Nathan Johnston, was of the "Clan Johnstone:"—

"On all the banks of Annandale
  The gentle Johnstone rides,
He has been there a thousand years,
  A thousand shall he bide."

Easter Hetty Johnston was the daughter of Dan'l Boone's eldest sister, whose ancestor was one of the colonists who came to Jamestown with Jno. Smith in 1607, or immediately thereafter. On his mother's side, he is connected with the Spencer and Russell families of England, his mother, Sarah Johnson (Selmes) Funkhouser, being a daughter of Tilden Russell Selmes, who was a Colonel in the late Civil War, being injured at the battle of Vicksburg. The subject of this sketch received his early education in private schools and under the tutelage of the late Bishop Dunlap. He is an alumnus of the University of Virginia (1868-9), of Dartmouth College (1871), of the Columbia College Law School (1873), and of the University of New York (1874), having received the degrees of A. B., A. M., LL.B. and M. D. He has been admitted to the New York and St. Louis Bars. After attending the hospitals in New York, he returned to St. Louis and entered upon the practice of his chosen profession. He was one of the founders of the Beaumont Medical College, and for a number of years was Professor of Surgery; he also held the chair of Surgery in the St. Louis College of Physicians and Surgeons and has been consulting surgeon to a number of St. Louis hospitals. He has made original researches in Physiology, Psychology and Surgery and contributed papers on various medical subjects, but at present confines his practice principally to surgery and gynaecology. He is a member of numerous societies, scientific and otherwise, including the Sons of the Revolution. The Doctor is a great student, not only of his profession, but in all departments of knowledge; his chief aim is to do what he thinks right, under all difficulties. It is safe to assert that no physician holds, in a greater degree, the confidence and esteem of his patients, friends, and the public in general. Dr. Funkhouser has been twice married, both wives, Virginia C. and Alice M., being the daughters of Dr. A. M. Cantrell of Virginia, and the great-granddaughters of Leonard Daniel of Cumberland Co., Va., who at the age of 17 entered the Revolutionary Army; he was stationed first at Norfolk and later at Yorktown, and witnessed the surrender of Lord Cornwallis in his eighteenth year. His father, William Daniel, one of the early settlers of Cumberland County, served during the entire Revolutionary War.

IRWIN, James Harvey. In the county of Ayr, Scotland, sacred to the memory of Burns, is the vale of Irvine, whose beauties were sung by the immortal bard and which is the original home of the family, whose patronymic appears in various forms as Irvine, Irwine, Irwin, Irving, Erwin, Erwine, etc., but who all claim the same ancestor, William de Irwin, armor-bearer to King Robert Bruce, who received from that king a grant of the forest of Drum and his own arms when Earl of Carrick "Or, a saltire and chief gules." He took his name from the town of Irvine situated on the river of the same name, originally "Iar Avon" or west river. The crest borne by the family was also granted at the same time, "three holly leaves" with the motto "sub sole, sub umbra, virens" (growing in sunshine or shade). Two branches of this family have become prominent in this country; the founder of one, William Irving, who came direct from Scotland in 1763, who was the father of Washington Irving; and of the other, Richard Irwin, who was born in Ireland, County Armagh, in 1740, emigrated to America and settled in New London, Chester County, Pa. He was the son of David Irwin of Armagh, who was descended from the Irwins of Ayr, a branch of which family was among the Scotch Presbyterians who colonized the north of Ireland in the reign of James the First. The descendants of this branch of the family are entitled to the honor of record among the inheritors of the glory of the heroes of the Revolution, through the services to the cause of liberty of the Richard Irwin above referred to. Records show that on March 13, 1776, he was appointed 1st Lieut. of Capt. William Murray's Co. of the Committee of Safety for White Deer Tp., Northumberland, now-Union Co., Pa. When the cause of his country no longer needed his arm he settled down on his farm, and in 1812 closed a long and useful life at the age of 72 years. His son, Samuel Irwin, born August 17, 1765, married Jane Miller of Northampton and died in 1847 at Cherry Tree Tp., Pa., his widow surviving him until Nov. 4, 1865. He was one of the pioneer settlers of Cherry Tree, was appointed Postmaster of the township and was one of the foremost men in the community, owning an extensive farm. His brother, Judge Irwin, was also a prominent figure in the State. Of his ten children, William Irwin, father of the gentleman whose name heads this article, was born at Cherry Tree, January 9, 1811. He, like his father, devoted his life to agricultural pursuits, at the same time taking a leading position in the public affairs of the county, where his name commanded respect. He married, January 5, 1837, Eliza Stewart of the same place and died October 16, 1863. Nine children survived him, of whom James Harvey Irwin, the principal representative of the family in the State of Missouri, was born at Cherry Tree, August 5, 1846. He

(34)

was educated primarily at the public school of his native place and entered on a collegiate course at Alleghany College, Meadville, Pa., but the premature death from typhoid fever of his father in 1863, interrupted his academical career and the interests of the bereaved family demanded his first care. On the outbreak of the Civil War just after his entrance into college he volunteered for service, but was rejected on account of his extreme youth. His older brother, Samuel, joined Company E, 16th Pennsylvania Cavalry, and died on the march to Gettysburg, under circumstances which showed that he was no degenerate scion of the family tree. He was lying in hospital seriously ill when the news of the impending battle reached him and in spite of all efforts to prevent him, he left his bed of sickness, mounted his horse and galloped after his regiment, reaching it, however, only to fall back in his saddle and die in his comrades' arms. After being summoned home Mr. Irwin remained on the farm for six years, until, in 1869, he went to St. Louis to take charge of the interests of the Climax Mower and Reaper Company, as manager. His connection with this corporation lasted for fifteen years, and in 1885 he became treasurer of the Western Electric Company, of which he had been for some time one of the directors. On the absorption of this corporation by the present consolidation he disposed of his interest and entered the Beck and Corbitt Iron Company, of which he is now treasurer. Mr. Irwin was married September 20, 1877, to Miss Nellie Birchard, of Cambridge Springs, Pa., a descendant of an old Massachusetts family, and a relative of the late President Rutherford Birchard Hayes, whose mother was Sophia Birchard. The family of Birchard is also entitled to honor in our columns through the great-grandfather of Mrs. Irwin who was a commissioned officer in the British army, but resigned his commission rather than fight against the colonists. Following in the footsteps of his forefathers, Mr. Irwin is a staunch adherent to Presbyterian principles and is deacon of the Second Presbyterian Church of St. Louis. Of domestic tastes, he has not identified himself with societies, but spends his leisure in the bosom of his family, taking, however, a warm interest in the Missouri Society of the Sons of the American Revolution. He is a worthy descendant of the sturdy Scotch Knox Presbyterians who introduced the leaven of their principles into the North of Ireland and who have made the influence of their sterling qualities felt wheresoever they have planted their feet.

HADDAWAY, Walter Scott, is the descendant of a family whose name, with those of its principal alliances by intermarriage, the Dawsons and Impeys, has been prominently identified with the history of the State of Maryland since the early part of the seventeenth century. In this work he represents more than one of the heroes who fought for our independence in the War of the Revolution, being the great-grandson of Captain William W. Haddaway, who, in 1778, raised a company of volunteers in the Thirty-eighth Battalion of Maryland; great-grandson of Thomas Harrison, brother of Benjamin Harrison, one of the signers of the Declaration of Independence, and father of President William Henry Harrison; and great-grandson of John Impey Dawson, who held a commission from the Council of Maryland as Lieutenant in Captain Haddaway's company. The name of Haddaway (pronounced Haddawy) is of Scotch origin, and the founder of the family on this continent, Roland Haddaway, was born on the family estate, near Oldham, Lancashire, England; came to Maryland two years after its first settlement by Lord Baltimore, receiving a grant of a large tract of land on the western shore of Chesapeake Bay, known as the family estate of "Lancashire," and is still in the possession of his descendants. In 1812 the family became connected with the Dawsons and Impeys of Maryland by the marriage of William Haddaway, grandfather of our subject, to the granddaughter of John Impey Dawson, of Cromwell, a descendant of Henry Dawson, of Breedon, Leicestershire, England, two sons of whom came to America in 1631, and were grantees of land on Isle of Kent, Chesapeake Bay; and of Thomas Impey, of Delmore End, Hertfordshire, England, who was one of the founders of the city of Oxford, and of the family of Lord Chief Justice Impey of India, temp., Warren Hastings. The family estate, called Cromwell, which was purchased from Cromwell by Thomas Impey in 1664, is still held by descendants, and the homestead built about that time is in good preservation. Walter Scott Haddaway, who represents the family in Missouri, was named for Sir Walter Scott, one of whose line married Roland Haddaway above referred to. He was born in Talbot County, Maryland, September 28, 1854, and educated at St. John's College, Annapolis. In 1873 he went to the University of Maryland, where he studied law and was admitted to the bar in 1875. After practicing his profession for some time in Talbot County, he removed to Wellington, Sumner County, Kansas, where he practiced until 1880, when he returned to Maryland. In 1885 he went to St. Louis to look after his investments in coal mines, and in 1890 he joined the Consolidated Coal Company, with which he is now connected. On September 13, 1886, he married Alice Gordon Bull of St. Louis, daughter of Jas. R. Bull and Eunice Davis Chase, grand-daughter of William Davis of Freetown. Their family consists of four children: Thomas Sherwood, born 1887; Eunice Chase, born 1888; Walter James, born 1890, and Roland, born 1896. Though active in politics as a Democrat, and president of the South St. Louis Democracy, Mr. Haddaway has never sought public office. He is a member of the Missouri Society of the Sons of the American Revolution; of Granite Lodge A. F. A. M., St. Michaels, Maryland; the Protestant Episcopal Church Club of St. Louis; for ten years Senior Warden of St. Paul's Episcopal Church, and is identified with Carondelet Council, St. Louis Legion of Honor. Following is the line of descent from Roland Haddaway: 1st. Roland Haddaway, born, England, 1587; married, 1609, Jane Scott; died, Maryland, 1667. 2d. Peter Haddaway, born, England, 1627; married Eliza Barker, 1655; died, Bay Hundred, 1686. 3d. Thomas Haddaway, born, Bay Hundred, 1663; married Mary Larkey, 1688; died, Bay Hundred, 1709. 4th. Thomas Larkey Haddaway, born, Bay Hundred, 1690; married, 1716, Rose Kemp; died, Bay Hundred, 1761. 5th. William Haddaway, born, Bay Hundred, 1718; married first Mary Seers in 1740, and second Martha Ward, 1753; died, Bay Hundred, 1773. 6th. William W. Haddaway, born, Bay Hundred, 1758; married, 1783, Elizabeth Harrison, daughter of Thomas Harrison, died, Talbot County, 1818. 7th. William Haddaway, born, family estate called "Lancashire," Talbot County, 1793; married, 1812, Ann Dawson Kersey; died, Talbot County, 1827. 8th. Thomas Sherwood Haddaway, born, Lancashire, 1831; married, 1853, Sarah Catherine Thompson; died, Lancashire, Talbot County, August 28, 1876. 9th. Walter Scott Haddaway, born, Talbot County, 1854; married, 1886, Alice Gordon Bull, connected with the noble family of Gordons of England. The arms are: Haddaway, Scotch, Ar. 3 hunting horns, vert stringed sa. Ref. Burke's Encyclopedia of Heraldry. The crest borne is: An ostrich, wings addorsed; in mouth a horseshoe, ppr. Motto: Nil desperandum.

MAYFIELD, Stephen, grandfather of Dr. W. H. Mayfield, was of English extraction; the family settled in North Carolina in the early part of the eighteenth century. When seventeen years of age, and at commencement of the Revolutionary War, Stephen enlisted in the Light Horse Brigade of North Carolina, and served through the conflict which gave independence to Americans. At the close of the war he returned to North Carolina, lived there a few years and removed to Mayfield, Ky., being one of its founders. Shortly after he settled in Jackson, Mo., where he conducted a plantation; he married late in life, and had a family of seven children; he was of powerful physique and lived to a good old age. Of his sons, George Washington Mayfield, of Patton, Mo., is the only known surviving son of the Revolution in Missouri. He was born in Jackson, Mo., in 1820; married Mary Cheek, also of Revolutionary descent, by whom he had eleven children, five of whom are physicians of prominence. Mr. Mayfield has been a consistent Christian all his life, and was one of the organizers of the Baptist Church in Missouri; though nearly eighty years of age, "his eye is not dimmed," nor is his "natural strength abated." His wife was revered as one of the mothers of the church; she died in 1893, leaving a community in mourning. Dr. Wm. Henderson Mayfield was born at Patton, Mo., Jan. 18, 1852, and was reared on his father's farm; educational facilities were few, and it was not until his eighteenth year that he possessed more than the bare rudiments of knowledge. In 1870 he entered Carrollton Institute, where he obtained a good education; afterwards he qualified for teaching at the Fruitland Normal Institute. He taught school eight terms; during this time he purchased an interest in dry goods at Sedgerwickville, retaining his interest until coming to St. Louis; during this period he entered upon the study of medicine under Dr. H. J. Smith, and completed his medical course at the St. Louis Medical College, from which he graduated as M. D. in 1882. He devoted great energy to the cause of Christian education in Missouri, resulting in the establishment of the Mayfield, Smith Academy, at Marble Hill; named in their honor. After practicing his profession for a short time at

George W. Mayfield.

Sedgerwickville and Mayfield, he was called to St. Louis to fill the chairs of Materia Medica, Therapeutics and Diseases of Children, which he occupied until he resigned to personally conduct the Mayfield Sanitarium, being one of the finest of its kind west of the Allegheny mountains; with a resident staff of four surgeons, and a consulting staff of 102. Dr. Mayfield has been spoken of as a God-made surgeon. His skill in performing delicate operations is wonderful, especially in cases of perineal and uterine laceration, which has made him famous. For twelve years Dr. Mayfield's name was prominently connected with the Missouri Baptist Sanitarium, of which he was founder, superintendent and surgeon-in-chief, up to spring of '96, when he resigned and at once began the building of the Mayfield Sanitarium. Dr. Mayfield was married May 10, 1874, to Miss Ellen C. Sitzes, of Marquand, Mo. Mrs. Mayfield inherits the business acumen of her father, and to her co-operation is largely attributed the success which has attended the Doctor in the great enterprises he has undertaken. Dr. Mayfield is editor and proprietor of the "Surgical Retrospect," a valuable journal to the profession. He is a member of the St. Louis Medical Society, Missouri State Medical Society, the Tri-State Medical Society, the Mississippi Valley Medical Society, honorary member Southern Illinois Medical Association, and of the American Medical Association. In Freemasonry he is a member of Marble Hill Lodge. Dr. Mayfield follows the teachings of his youth, never taking important steps without prayer. His practice of this principle especially in the operating room has brought its reward in the hearty co-operation and appreciation by his patients. Dr. Mayfield is also president of the Mayfield Brothers' Sweet Springs Sanitarium, at Sweet Springs, Missouri, a corporation with a paid-up capital of $50,000. The ground consists of twenty acres of beautiful grove, upon which the Sanitarium stands, together with ten buildings, owned by Drs. W. H., A. J. and R. L. Mayfield.

MAYFIELD, Eli Burton, M. D., another member of the noted Mayfield family of Missouri, and a descendant of Revolutionary ancestry, whose useful and honorable life is a part of the history of Missouri, and whose ability as a physician and surgeon forms an important link in the medical history of St. Louis. He is also a grandson of Stephen Mayfield, who was of English origin, the family emigrating to North Carolina in the eighteenth century, and served throughout the Revolutionary war. The full history of this distinguished soldier appears in the family genealogy of the Mayfield family. Stephen Mayfield left seven children, the most conspicuous of whom is George Washington Mayfield, the youngest son, who is supposed to be the only living son of the Revolution in Missouri. Our subject is also the son of Mary Cheek, who, as before mentioned, was a Revolutionary descendant. Her death occurred in 1893, leaving a community in mourning. Eli Burton Mayfield, youngest son of George Washington Mayfield, was born in Bolinger County, Mo., January 6, 1862. His education was received at the Mayfield-Smith Academy, and at the State Normal School, Cape Girardeau, Mo. Afterward he engaged in teaching, himself, and was recognized as one of the ablest in his county. In the spring of 1884 he began the study of medicine, and graduated from the College of Physicians and Surgeons, in St. Louis, Mo. He began practice in St. Louis, then went to Grubville, 35 miles south of St. Louis, where he was engaged in the practice of his profession for seven years, and was recognized as the leading physician of his county, and of the three adjoining counties of Washington, Jefferson and Franklin. In 1893 he went to New York City, where he took a post-graduate course at the New York Polyclinic College. He returned to St. Louis, and accepted the position of assistant surgeon of the Missouri Baptist Sanitarium, which position he resigned, in 1896, to accept the position of assistant surgeon and house physician at the Mayfield Sanitarium. September 17, 1890, he was married to Miss Ida M. Conrad, daughter of Jacob J. Conrad, a prominent farmer, and Judge of Bolinger County. She is a granddaughter of David Conrad, a prominent State Senator of Missouri. Miss Conrad graduated from the State Normal School of Missouri. Fraternally, Dr. Mayfield is a member of the A. O. U. W. In religion, a Baptist, like his family before him. He is a polished and pleasant gentleman, and able and learned in his profession. He is also a prominent member of the Masonic fraternity.

BRINSMADE, Hobart, has proven himself a worthy representative of the heroes who gave to Americans a priceless heirloom to hand down to their descendants. The Brinsmades are of English origin, family seat being Somersetshire, England. Our subject

(37)

is a great-grandson of Abraham Brinsmade, who was a Captain in the Connecticut militia in the Danbury alarm in April, 1777; and took an active part at the battle of Ridgefield. Mr. Brinsmade has in his possession two Revolutionary relics of great value, a writing desk used by Captain James Bebee, originally brought from England, also a flintlock musket, formerly owned by Captain Abraham Brinsmade, and used in the Revolution. Our subject's line of descent is as follows: John Brinsmade, who came to America from England previous to 1650; John Brinsmade's son, Daniel, born 1696. Daniel's son, Abraham, born February 27, 1726, married Mary Wheeler January 14, 1745. Abraham's son, Daniel, born September 22, 1752, married Mary Bebee May 4, 1777. Daniel's son, Ali Brinsmade, was the grandfather of our subject. He was born in 1793 at Trumbull, Connecticut, formerly North Stratford, and was a man of prominence in public affairs; was also a deacon in the Congregational Church, being appointed in 1826. Lewis, son of Ali Brinsmade, the father of our subject, was born at Trumbull, Connecticut, in 1823. He engaged in agricultural pursuits and is still living (1897) at the old home. Rev. James Bebee, great-grandfather of Mr. Brinsmade, was pastor of the Congregational Church at Stratford for thirty-eight years, being ordained May 6, 1747; he was often spoken of as the "fighting preacher." He was chaplain in the French and Indian Colonial wars, also a Captain in Gen. Washington's corps of sappers and miners. He died September 8, 1785. Abraham Brinsmade was also a deacon in the Congregational Church. Hobart Brinsmade, the son of Lewis Brinsmade and Elizabeth Fairchild, was born at Trumbull, Conn., Nov. 20, 1845. His mother came from a distinguished family of Revolutionary fame who settled in Stratford, Conn., about 1639. Our subject received his education at the Easton and Stratford Academies in Connecticut, and completed his studies at the age of seventeen. He taught school four years at Durham, N. Y.; Fairfield, New Canaan, and Bridgeport, Conn. He then engaged in the book business at the last-named place. After continuing in that line for about four years, he disposed of his interests and entered the employ of the Howe Sewing Machine Co. as resident manager for Western New York, being located at Elmira for six years. He was then transferred to St. Louis as their general Western manager, where he remained until 1885, when he went to Europe in the interests of the Wheeler & Wilson Sewing Machine Company, with headquarters at London, as general European manager. After remaining abroad for several years, he returned to St. Louis in 1891 and engaged in the wholesale millinery business under the firm name of King, Brinsmade & Co., and is president of that company. He married Miss Ella M. Lyon, of Bridgeport, Conn., in 1872. Two sons blessed their union. Mr. Brinsmade is prominent in religious circles, being a deacon in the Congregational Church, superintendent of its Sunday-school, director of the Missouri Sunday-School Association and of the St. Louis Sunday-School Union. He is a director in the Y. M. C. A., secretary of the Missouri Society of Colonial Wars, and a member of the Mercantile Club.

ALBAN, George, great-grandfather of Charles Willis Alban, was born in Winchester, Va., in 1758. At the early age of 18 years he joined the patriots of the Revolution, enlisting under Capt. Berry, in the Eighth Virginia Regiment, commanded by Col. Muhlenberg. In the following year he was transferred to Gen. Washington's Body Guard, under Capt. Gibbs, in which he completed two years' service, at the end of which time, being disabled by wounds, he received his discharge and returned to his native State, where he resumed farm life. In 1797 he removed to Jefferson County, Ohio, settling near Steubenville, where he died at the age of 82. Of his family of ten children William Alban was the eldest son. He was born in Virginia, in 1786, and followed agricultural pursuits until the War of 1812, when he raised a company on the then frontier, and was commissioned a Captain in Cotgreave's regiment of Ohio militia. At the close of the war he returned to his farm, where he remained until 1818, when he removed to Canal Fulton, where he was elected Justice of the Peace, and until the close of his life was prominently identified with public affairs. He died in 1845, leaving nineteen children, having been married three times. Of the children, Joseph Patterson

Chas W. Alban.

Lieutenant-Colonel Samuel Hopkins.

Alban was born April 19, 1842. He chose the medical profession, and was a student when the Civil War broke out. He at once enlisted as a private in the 102d Ohio Volunteer Infantry, but did not serve, being appointed assistant surgeon by the Surgeon-General, and did noble work in the battles of Athens, Decatur, and other noted actions, serving until the close of the war, at which time he was in charge of a hospital at Decatur, Ala. After the war he settled at Huntsville, Ala., where he practiced dentistry for a year or two, then established a drug business in which he continued until 1871, when he sold out and traveled until 1877, when he established in Memphis, Tenn., a dental and surgical instrument supply house. He married first Jemima Bollman, also a descendant of Revolutionary heroes through her great-grandfathers, Asa Cook and Abraham Bollman. His second wife was Blanche Gantt, daughter of Col. George Gantt, a L't-Colonel in the Confederate army. Charles Willis Alban was born in Millersburg, Ohio, January 30, 1862. His early education was obtained at Huntsville, Ala., and at Ontario and Findlay, Ohio, graduating from the Normal School. He began teaching at the early age of 16. After one term he entered his father's business at Memphis in 1878, remaining there until 1885, when he went to St. Louis and was connected with several prominent business houses until January, 1897, when he established a surgical instrument house in St. Louis. Mr. Alban was married in 1885 to Myrah Blanche Collins, daughter of the Rev. Chas. F. Collins, formerly of Tennessee, now pastor of St. Matthew's Church, Clifton Heights. This family is also of notable descent, its first American ancestor being Thomas Rogers, one of the Pilgrim Fathers, descended from the martyr, John Rogers. The Collins are also related to the Kidder family, whose genealogy is traced to 1492. Mr. Alban resides at Clifton Heights. Proud of the patriotism of his ancestors, he is an enthusiastic member of the Missouri Society of the Sons of the Revolution.

BROWN, James Newton, is a descendant on his mother's side from Revolutionary stock. He is the great-grandson of John McLaughlin, private in Captain Patterson's Company, of Colonel Erwin's Regiment, Pennsylvania troops, and served from 1776 to 1777. He was also a trooper in Colonel Marlberry's Regiment, North Carolina troops, 1780, and a trooper in Captain Samuel Hart's Company of Colonel Dixon's Regiment of North Carolina during the same year. This hero of the Revolution took an active part in the battles of Trenton, Princeton and Ramson's Mills. His son, James McLaughlin, was the maternal grandfather of our subject; he also saw service during the revolutionary period, 1814, as a private in Captain Krider's Company of Colonel Pearson's Regiment, North Carolina troops. His daughter, Mrs. Rebeca Hallworth, nee McLaughlin, is the mother of Mr. James Newton Brown. She is now a resident of the State of Illinois, and notwithstanding her age, 80 years, she is still in the possession of fair health and sound mental faculties. Her son has inherited the warrior spirit of his ancestors and in the early part of the war of the rebellion enlisted in the Tenth Illinois Volunteer Infantry and subsequently re-enlisted as a veteran in the same regiment. His terms of service in behalf of the perpetuation of the government which his forefathers helped to create, cover a period of four years. Our subject was born in Randolph County, Ill., in 1843, and is the father of an interesting family of children and an amiable wife. Mr. Brown is one of St. Louis most energetic and capable Insurance men. He holds the responsible position of special agent and adjuster for the American Central Insurance Company. Socially, both himself and family are held in high esteem among the "West End" residents of St. Louis. In manner and speech Mr. Brown is the ideal gentleman, as well as the patriotic citizen. He is a member of the G. A. R. and a Past Commander, and held the position of Aide-de-camp on General Veasey's staff, Commander-in-chief of the Grand Army of the Republic in 1891. He has been 31 years a member of the I. O. O. F. and also affiliates with the Legion of Honor. He is an active and influential member of the Presbyterian Church, and at one time was a ruling elder of Lafayette Park Church.

HOPKINS, Innis, dates his ancestry back to the year 1660, through James Taylor, who emigrated from Carlysle, England, to the then American colonies, now the United States, and settled in Caroline County, Virginia. In 1700 Dr. Arthur Hopkins emigrated to this country and settled in Culpepper County, Virginia, where he married Miss Isabella Taylor, from whom descended Innis Hopkins' branch of the family. He is a member of the Missouri State Society of the Sons of the Revolution through his great-grandfather, Lieutenant-Colonel Samuel Hopkins, who entered the Revolutionary War as captain of the Sixth Virginia Regi-

(39)

ment, February 26, 1776; was wounded in the battle of Germantown, October 4, 1777, and was for gallantry promoted to Lieutenant-Colonel of Fourteenth Virginia Regiment, June 17, 1778. He was taken prisoner at Charleston, May 12, 1780, and exchanged and transferred to First Virginia Regiment, February 12, 1781, and served with distinction to the close of the war. In addition to Lieutenant-Colonel Samuel Hopkins' services in the Revolutionary War, he was commissioned a Major-General in the war of 1812-15 with England, and commanded a division in the Northwest, with his headquarters at Vincennes, Indiana. He was a graduate of William and Mary College, of Virginia, a lawyer, and also represented his district in the United States Congress from 1800 to 1815. Innis Brent Hopkins, the father of Innis Hopkins, was born in Kentucky, and was a practicing lawyer for thirty-five years, living in Louisville, Kentucky, where he died and is buried in the famous Cave Hill Cemetery. The mother of Innis Hopkins was a Miss Virginia Caroline Taliaferro, named after the State and County of Virginia, where her parents lived, and is a descendant from the distinguished family of Taliaferros from that State. Innis Hopkins, the subject of this sketch, was born in Kentucky and finished his education at Transylvania College, Lexington, Kentucky. He came to St. Louis in 1878 and entered service in the freight traffic department of the O. & M. Railroad as clerk and received promotion until he now has charge of and looks after the entire Southwestern territory of the freight traffic interest for the Erie Despatch, which operates over the seven Eastern roads from St. Louis in connection with the Erie Railroad system. April 15, 1885, he married Miss Mary C. Lake, of St. Louis, a descendant through her father of the Lake family who settled in Rhode Island, and on her mother's side from the distinguished family of Fylers from Natchez, Mississippi. Mrs. Hopkins on paternal side is fourth in descent from Pardon Lake, third in descent from Pardon Anthony Lake and Mary Terry, his wife, second in descent from James R. Lake. On the maternal side she is fourth in descent from Francis McLean and Roxie McKinney, his wife. Third in descent from Otis McLean and Clara Munsell, his wife. Second in descent from James Hamilton Fyler and Clarissa McLean, his wife. Mrs. Hopkins is the daughter of Charles Dillingham Lake and Louisa Fyler, his wife. Mr. and Mrs. Innis Hopkins have one daughter, Innis Russell, who is a member of the Children's Society of the American Revolution. Mr. Hopkins, while always a busy man, is approachable, and has a kindly smile for all; his wife is a cultured lady, and occupies a prominent position in social and religious circles in St. Louis.

GREGG, Norris Bradford. Among the younger members of the Sons of the Revolution, none stand higher than our subject. He is one of the prominent young business men of St. Louis and has gained the confidence and esteem of all with whom he has come in contact. He is by his integrity and manhood carefully carrying out the principles for which his gallant forefathers fought. Our subject is a great-grandson of Samuel Gregg, Major of the 23d New Hampshire Militia, who marched with his command to the Lexington Alarm, April, 1775, also marched to the Alarm at Walpole, 1775; was a member of the Committee of Safety, 1779, having been a sergeant in the British Army in the French and Indian Wars. On the breaking out of the Revolution, he was offered a commission in the British Army which he refused. Samuel Gregg's brother, Col. Wm. Gregg, was a U. S. officer and held a very important command under Gen. Stark at the battle of Bennington. Our subject is of Scotch and English descent, being a lineal descendant of Captain James Gregg, who in 1690 emigrated from Ayr, Scotland, to Londonderry, Ireland. In the year 1718, he with sixteen other families emigrated to America and founded the town of Londonderry, New Hampshire, first called Nutfield. Norris Bradford Gregg was born in St. Louis, Mo., Nov. 8, 1856, is the son of Wm. H. Gregg, a prominent citizen and manufacturer of St. Louis, Mo., who married Miss Orian Thompson of St. Louis, mother of our subject, in 1855. Mr. Gregg received his education at Hon. Edward Wyman's Academy and at the Washington University, he also took a course in chemistry at the Chemical Laboratory of Chauvenet and Blair, St. Louis, Mo. At the age of nineteen years he completed his studies and entered the employ of the Southern White Lead Co., as chemist and assistant in manufacturing, afterwards traveled for the company, covering all territory from St. Paul to New Orleans, being engaged in that capacity until Nov. 1, 1880, when he entered the service of W. A. Thornburgh & Son, which firm incorporated soon after as the Mound City Paint and Color Co., Mr. Gregg becoming its secretary, and in 1887

(40)

was made president of same. He was mainly instrumental in building up the business of the company, having been its most active and successful manager previous to the retirement of Mr. Thornburgh. Mr. Gregg is also president of the Gregg Varnish Co. In the younger social circles he is prominent among the leaders, being a member of the Noonday, University, Country and St. Louis Clubs. He was married Dec. 26, 1884, to Miss May Hawley, daughter of Captain Geo. E. Hawley, of St. Louis. Mrs. Gregg was formerly of Alton, Ill.

EDGAR, Timothy Bloomfield. Four hundred years have elapsed since the discovery of a new world, and now, as the dawn of the fifth century breaks upon the American nation, a disposition has arisen among the inhabitants of the land to peer intently into the past, to scan old manuscripts, and records sere and yellow with age, to search among the ruins of fallen dynasties for the origin of the existing circumstances amid which they find themselves, which circumstances, the outgrowth of the battling of various elements, have built up a new and unique nation. The student of genealogy must inevitably realize that the building of the American nation was no haphazard work; but in the weaving of the web of the nation's life, an All-seeing Eye penetrated the distant future and a powerful and unseen Hand guided and controlled the everflitting shuttle. In tracing the various and far-reaching lines of the typical American family of Edgar we find the elements which enter into the ethnology of the American nation; as in the transition from its Saxon origin to a powerful Scottish House, of the Boyce family of Norman origin anglicized from the time of William the Conqueror, later allied with a line of Holland ancestry and with the ancient Welsh-English family of Harrell, thus combining in the veins of the American family of to-day the blood of Saxon, Scottish, Norman, Welsh and English.

Of the different Saxon families that became identified with the Scottish nation at the period of the Norman Conquest, some are more prominent than others. The history of the well-known line of Edgar the Ætheling, the fourth remove from Ethelred II, and the heir to the Saxon line of kings, as well as that of his sister, the Princess Margaret, afterwards as the wife of Malcolm III of Scotland, the Scottish Queen, is familiar to all; but not so, perhaps, is that of the Saxon-Scottish House of Dunbar. An ancestress of this house was the Princess Elgiva, daughter of Ethelred II, king of the Anglo-Saxons and granddaughter of Edgar, the Saxon king of England, and the wife of Uchtred, Prince of Northumbria, England. Their daughter and heiress, Algetha or Algitha, was given in marriage to Maldred, grandson of Malcolm II of Scotland and brother to the "gracious King Duncan" of the same country. The first Cospatrick, Earl of Northumbria, son of Maldred and Algitha, was confirmed in the Earldom of Northumbria by William the Conqueror in 1067. He (Cospatrick) received a grant of Dunbar, Scotland, with the lands of Lothian, from his kinsman, Malcolm III, in 1072; probably a portion of the same territory wrested from his ancestors by Malcolm II, in 1018. The following bit of history gleaned from "Genealogical Collections Concerning the Scottish House of Edgar" (Grampian Club, London, 1873), may be of interest to the descendants of that ancient house. The second Cospatrick of Northumbria was the first Earl of Dunbar, and the fourth Cospatrick the third Earl of Dunbar; Edgar, third son of the latter (temp. about the middle of the 12th century), appears to have been ancestor of those of the surname of Edgar. (Verstigan derives the name from Ead, an oath, and gar, to keep.) The name of Willielm, filius Edgari, appears among the witnesses to a charter granted in the reign of King William of Scotland by Earl Patrick, son of Waldeve, Earl of Dunbar, to the monks of Durham. This William, son of Edgar, seems to have been one of the progenitors of Edgar of Wedderlie (temp. probably about the close of the 12th century).

The armorial bearings of the House of Wedderlie (or Wadderlie) are found sculptured among the ancient ruins of the old manor house of the estate; and are portrayed in this volume, being copied from an old engraving in the possession of Mr. T. B. Edgar, which was bequeathed to him by his uncle, William Edgar, Esq. The heraldic blazon is: "Quarterly, sable and azure; in the first and fourth quarters, a lion rampant, argent; in the second and third quarters, three water bougets, or." Supporters: "two grey-hounds, proper." Crest: "a hand, in pale, holding a dagger in bend sinister." Mottoes: "Salutem disponit Deus" (God administers salvation. Vide: "Fairbairn's Crests," Vol. 2, page 581), and above the crest "Man do it."

(41)

The first quarterings denote kinship with the Royal House of Scotland, and the second, service in the crusades; the waterbouget being a vessel used by the crusaders for the carriage of water in the desert. Heraldic supporters were in ancient times only granted to the highest ranks of nobility. The Edgars were among the few families which disobeyed the act of 1672 in not having their arms matriculated in the Lyon Register then established.

The territory of the Edgars, Barons of Wedderlie, extended from the coast of Berwickshire to the Solway Firth, of which remained at the date of its final alienation from the family, by sale in 1733-6 to Lord Blantyre, only the ancient manor-house or fortalice and about six thousand acres of land extending towards the Lammermoor Hills. Striking coincidences of family history and locality point to the identity of Edgar of Wedderlie with Edgar of Ravenswood in "The Bride of Lammermoor." Among other baronies held by the family, when at the zenith of their power, which was during the reign of King Robert the Bruce, with whom they seem to have been closely allied, were those of Sanquhar, Dumfries, and Kirk Andrews. The House of Keithock, a cadet of the House of Wedderlie, seated in Forfarshire, was established in the 17th century when the family of Edgar acquired this portion of the ancient possessions of the noble House of Lindsay. The Edgars of Keithock were, though Episcopalians, devoted adherents of the House of Stewart, whose fortunes they followed through all reverses; suffering for them imprisonment, exile and loss of possessions. John and James, sons of David Edgar, Laird of Keithock, were prominent in the rebellion of 1715, when the former was taken prisoner and immured in Stirling Castle, dying in captivity; the latter succeeding in escaping to Italy where he became private secretary for fifty years to the Chevalier de St. George, styled by the Scots, King James VIII. Secretary James Edgar was repeatedly approached by Sir Robert Walpole, Prime Minister of England, with inducements to betray the trust reposed in him, all of which he spurned with contempt, until Sir Robert, imagining that he had not bid high enough, placed the sum of £10,000 to his credit in the Bank of Venice, of which he informed him by letter; when the Secretary, after consultation with the Chevalier, replied thanking him for the money, which he had lost no time in drawing from the bank, and informed him that he had "laid it at the feet of his Royal Master, who had the best title to gold which came, as this had, from *his own* dominions." In token of his gratitude for this service the Chevalier presented his faithful adherent with a valuable souvenir which is now in the possession of the head of the House of Keithock, the Hon James David Edgar, M. P., of Toronto, Canada.

John Edgar, nephew of the secretary, also followed the fortunes of Prince Charles Edward, was Postmaster-general to the Prince during his brief occupation of Edinburgh, and fought under his banner at Culloden. After that disastrous battle, he arrived a fugitive at Keithock, and sought the protection and aid of the same farmer who had assisted his uncle's escape thirty years before. To his surprise he was told that he could be accommodated with the identical clothes in which his uncle had found safety. Finding it impossible to escape to the Continent, he took passage to America, intending to join his uncle Thomas, who had settled in New Jersey; but the vessel was captured by a French privateer, and on discovering his identity he was landed, with his property restored, at a French port, whence he proceeded to Paris, where he obtained a commission in the Scottish Brigade, later joined his uncle, the Secretary, at Rome, and in 1756, on the publication of the Act of Indemnity, returned to Scotland.

Secretary Edgar's eldest brother, Alexander, succeeded to the estate of Keithock, which remained in the family until 1790. A younger brother, Henry, was third and last Bishop of Fife. Thomas Edgar, fifth son of David Edgar of Keithock, came to America in 1715-8 and purchased an estate near the city of Rahway, New Jersey, which he styled Edgarton after the family name and which remained in the family until 1885. By the marriage of his great-grandson, Alexander Edgar, to Sarah Crowell, in 1808, two important American families, the Bloomfields and the Crowells, became allied with the House of Edgar. The founder of the Crowell family in America was Edward Crowell, who was born in England or Wales in 1680 and who sailed from Scotland in the ship "Caledonia," landing at Perth-Amboy, N. J., in 1705. The family was originally Cromwell, presumably descended from Sir Henry Cromwell, grandfather of Oliver Cromwell, the Protector, but on the voyage to America the "m" was dropped. According to tradition, this change of name was recorded on a parchment, which was in the posses-

sion of the Crowell family of North Carolina until 1781, when it was carried off with other valuables by a party of Tarleton's Legion. (Vide: Edwin Salter, Washington, D. C., 1886, also "American Ancestry," Vol. IV, page 218. Sarah Crowell, wife of Alexander Edgar and great-granddaughter of the founder of the family in America, also mentioned Cromwell as the original family name.) Edward Crowell settled at Woodbridge, N. J., of which place he was town clerk for twenty-five successive years, was elder of the Presbyterian church there for thirty-nine years and died there October 27, 1756. His son James Crowell, by his third wife, Christian, widow of Dr. David Stewart, married Frances, daughter of Joseph Fitz-Randolph, a native of Virginia, who held a captain's commission in the Monmouth County, New Jersey, militia, in the War of American Independence. In 1777 Joseph Crowell, eldest son of James and Frances (Fitz-Randolph) Crowell, who was born December 8, 1759, thus only a stripling of 17, was seized with the heroic spirit of the times and enlisted as a private in the first battalion of the Second Establishment New Jersey Continental Line, with which he served until the spring of 1778, when he joined a troop of Light Horse of the New Jersey militia under command of Captain Nathaniel Fitz-Randolph. He saw much hard service, took part in the battle of Monmouth and, later, in an engagement with an overwhelming force of British, was taken prisoner with his captain and many others and confined for some months on the "Old Jersey Prison-ship" moored in one of the harbors of the New Jersey coast. Among the many prisoners whom he found already immured on this ship were Timothy Bloomfield and his son Charles, a lad of 18, who had both served in the American army. Timothy Bloomfield, a type of the stern, fearless patriot, had twice been strung up at the yard-arm, in the effort to extort from him a pledge not to bear arms against the British, but he held bravely to his principles, declaring that he would fight for his country as long as there was strength in his arm to use a musket. Joseph Crowell was the first of the prisoners to be exchanged and, once at liberty, cast about to secure the release of his captain and the two Bloomfields, whom the British would not exchange for any of less conspicuous bravery.

At this time a number of British officers were quartered in the neighborhood and among them a certain Captain Jones, who stood high in the esteem of the British. He conceived the plan of capturing this officer for the purpose of offering him as a ransom for his friends, and enlisted in the hazardous enterprise several others, including one Peter Terrat, a fearless man of gigantic stature and strength. Under cover of darkness and disguised as laborers they made their way to the British quarters where Captain Jones was confined to his room by sickness, while the rest of the officers were suffering from the effects of a carouse. Noiselessly Terrat slipped into the room where the sick captain lay upon his bunk and, presenting a pistol at his breast, bound and gagged him, then throwing him across his shoulder started for their boat and safely escaped with their captive to the New Jersey shore. The successful execution of Crowell's plan resulted in the desired exchange and Captain Fitz-Randolph and the two Bloomfields were again free. Unknown to himself the Bloomfields were intertwined with the life of Joseph Crowell otherwise than as brothers in arms, for he was ignorant of their relationship to a beautiful young maiden whom he had met when on his way to join his first command, the memory of whom was imprinted on his heart and had remained with him and nerved his arm through all his dangerous adventures. He had exchanged no word with her except bashfully to inquire the distance to his destination. Later in the war he was quartered with others at the house of Timothy Bloomfield, who was overjoyed to meet the young friend of his prison days, of whose share in his release, he was, however, ignorant. In the course of the evening, while the old warrior was fighting his battles over again by the fireside he incidentally wondered who it was that had been instrumental in securing his release, when young Crowell told him the story. The veteran was deeply moved and calling his family about him introduced them to their benefactor. In the person of one of the daughters, Eunice Bloomfield, the young soldier recognized the maiden of his dreams, and it was not long before she became the partner of his life. Her name is associated with an interesting episode of the war, of which a rare old Bible, now in the possession of Colonel R. C. Crowell of Kansas City, is a memento. During the absence of father and sons in the army, the British made a raid on the Bloomfield farm near Metuchen, running off the stock and plundering the homestead. Among the valuables carried off was the

(48)

family Bible, which was dearly prized and which Eunice determined to recover if possible; depending for success on the chivalrous deference, with which as a rule, the British officers treated the women of the country. She accordingly, accompanied by a young lady friend and a negro servant, set out on horseback for the British headquarters on Staten Island, 12 miles distant. Arriving at Blazing Star Ferry, the negro remained behind with the horses, while the young women crossed the bay and walked the distance of three miles to the British camp. Here they were received with courtesy by the commandant, and in response to his inquiry as to their mission, Eunice, with engaging simplicity, told the story of the raid, asking the return of nothing but the family Bible. The officer was touched, and after providing for the comfort of his fair visitors, made inquiry and found that the treasured book had been taken on board a transport then lying in the harbor. He took boat for the ship and in a short time returned with it and placed it in the hands of Eunice Bloomfield, who received it with joy.

The kindly commandant then inquired if there were anything else taken from them which they especially valued, expressing his willingness to make restoration if it were possible. Eunice, who had not thought of requesting the return of aught save the Bible, then bethought herself of her pet brindle cow, which had been captured with the rest of the stock and, informing the officer of it, he asked her to walk through the pasture adjoining the camp where large numbers of cattle were grazing, and see if she could find it among them. On doing so the faithful animal recognized its mistress and came bounding to her side to receive its wonted petting. After expressing their gratitude for the restoration of their treasures the young ladies were escorted by a guard of soldiers across the water and reached home with hearts overflowing with thankfulness. (Vide "Morris County Chronicle," N. J., March 29, 1895, extracts from history of "Eunice Bloomfield's Ancestors.") The old volume was but little defaced except by marginal scribblings of rude sketches and uncouth jests referring to Timothy Bloomfield and his boys. These still remain to recall the memories of those days and the heroine of its recovery to the family. On December 7, 1780, Joseph Crowell and Eunice Bloomfield were united in marriage and passed a long life of happiness together on his estate near Woodbridge, un-

til her death, on January 14, 1832. He survived her until March 18, 1834, when he too passed away. Their third daughter, Sarah Crowell, born in New Jersey, March 6, 1787, became the wife of Alexander Edgar, in 1808. He was the great-great-grandson of David Edgar of Keithock, was born in New Jersey, April 18, 1787, and died near St. Louis, Mo., April 1, 1851, his widow surviving him until February 19, 1870, when she died in St. Louis, Mo. Timothy Bloomfield Edgar, their third son, whose heroic lineage we have thus traced, was born on his grandfather Crowell's estate near Woodbridge, N. J., hard by Blazing Star Ferry, on January 20, 1815. Soon after his birth his parents removed to Rahway, N. J., where he grew into manhood. When of age he left his native State and entered commercial life in April, 1836, at St. Louis, where he became a successful man of business and was actively interested in various forms of philanthropy. At an early period in his career he became identified with banking interests and was one of the leading spirits in the Exchange Bank of St. Louis, into which had been merged the Dollar Savings' Institution of which he was a director. As a banker he won the unqualified confidence and esteem of his fellow-citizens. In 1860, he withdrew almost entirely from commercial life, having acquired a modest fortune and preferring to devote his remaining years to philanthropy and mental culture. He was, however, destined to soon enter upon the most active and important period of his life, when his time and talents would be engaged in sustaining a nation amid the throes of a civil war. He was contemplating a European tour when the clouds of war appeared on the horizon of his country, and as they grew more and more threatening and finally broke over the land and the city and State of his adoption, he bade farewell to all thoughts of pleasure and took his position with firmness among those who were ready to sustain the National Government in its hour of peril. In 1861 he was instrumental in furnishing the sum of $80,000.00 in gold, requested by General John C. Frémont to pay for ordnance; maintaining that it was the duty not only of private citizens, but of banking institutions also, to strengthen the hands of the Government. During the Civil War he applied himself by every means to relieve the burdens of the people and with rare single-mindedness refused to avail himself of the many opportunities presenting themselves to add to his

Edgar of Keithock.
Male Representative of
Edgar of Wedderlie.

From original bequeathed to
Mr Timothy B. Edgar,
by his uncle William Edgar Esq.

private fortune. He was one of a committee of two, appointed by the Merchants' Exchange of St. Louis, to proceed to Washington, D. C., and endeavour to secure payment of the government vouchers, amounting to about fifteen million dollars, which had accumulated in St. Louis and were at a discount of from eight to ten per cent; while the community was suffering from a lack of currency. It was a delicate and difficult mission but it was brought to a successful issue. He was President of the War Relief Committee, in which capacity he managed the large disbursements of the War Relief Fund to universal satisfaction, and with a degree of accuracy that seemed impossible to attain. In 1863 he was appointed by Governor Gamble a trustee of the "Missouri Institution for the Education of the Blind," to which institution he devoted much time and thought for many years. In 1864 he was elected a member of the Board of Corporators of the Soldiers' Orphans Home of which he was treasurer until its purpose was fulfilled and no further need for the institution existed. He was also a member of the Board of Public Schools of St. Louis for several years, trustee of the Public School Library Association, a life member of the Missouri Historical Society, one of the leaders in the St. Louis Provident Association, and is a member of the Missouri Society of the Sons of the American Revolution.

In 1865, relieved of the great responsibilities and many cares entailed upon him by the Civil War, Mr. Edgar yielded to his taste for travel, which has made him familiar with his own country, and accompanied by his wife, a daughter and a son, made the tour of Europe. In 1867 he organized the Continental Bank, of which he was the first President, and in 1873-4 was President of the Missouri Pacific Railway, of which great corporation he became a director on his return from Europe. In 1880 he resigned the Presidency of the Continental Bank, thus severing the last link in his active connection with the business world. We now turn to his domestic ties. On August 22, 1837, Mr. Edgar married Miss Mary Ann Boyce, who was born in Huntsville, Ala., Nov. 5, 1819. Mrs. Edgar is descended from an old family of North Carolina with which are allied in that State the Colonial families of Hardy, Gardiner and Harrell. William Hardy Boyce and his wife, Mary Eliza Harrell, parents of Mrs. Edgar, were children of neighboring planters in Bertie Co., N. C., the former born in 1796 and the latter in 1798. Mr. Boyce served in the War of 1812, married in 1816, and in 1818 removed to Huntsville, Ala. In 1828 he removed to St. Louis, Mo., where he became a successful lumber merchant. From 1840-9 he built several steamers, placing them on the Mississippi and Missouri rivers. He died at St. Louis in 1849, at the age of fifty-two years and some months, leaving behind him memories of a remarkable Christian character and of a Southern gentleman of the old school, which are still cherished in the hearts of his descendants. As far as known, the male line of the Boyce family is extinct.

His widow lived to mourn his loss until 1876, sorrowing over many loved ones gone before. Intense in her feelings, she suffered as only such natures can suffer, over the devastation of her beloved South-land by war. Deft in the use of her needle, many skillfully wrought pieces of her handiwork have been carefully preserved and are highly prized by her children and grandchildren. Mrs. Edgar was educated at the St. Louis Institute, where she developed talents for music, drawing and painting in water color. When the horrors of the Civil War came upon the nation her decisive character and executive ability were called into action. Though a Southern woman by birth, she sustained the Federal Government, realizing that in union alone was strength. She, like her husband, was foremost in all good works and devoted a large portion of her time and strength to the welfare of the nation; though at the same time her watchful eye and guiding hand were not withdrawn from her young children. She organized the Frémont Relief Society, aided in establishing the New House of Refuge Hospital, visited hospital camps in various parts of the State, opened her house for the reception and preparation of hospital stores, and was unrelaxing in her incessant care for the sick and wounded, until the organization of the Western Sanitary Commission and other kindred bodies relieved her of the strain; but she continued, through the entire period of the war, to extend a helping hand as occasion required, and in every way sacrificed herself for the benefit of her suffering fellow-beings.

She was one of the incorporators in 1868 of the St. Louis Woman's Christian Association, and was for a number of years a member of the Board of Managers of the St. Louis Protestant Orphan Asylum. Eight children have been born to Mr. and Mrs. Edgar: Frances Harrell (Mrs. Edward Parker Rice of St. Louis, formerly resident in Chicago for 20 years), William Boyce, Emma Crowell (Mrs. Oliver F. Garrison of Carthage, Missouri), Joseph Alexander (died in infancy), Selwyn Clay, Clara Rowe (died in infancy), Clara M. (Mrs. Charles Derickson McLure of St. Louis), and Robert Harrell. Mr. and Mrs. Edgar's living descendants number altogether twenty-seven, including seventeen grandchildren and four great-grandchildren. Three of their grandchildren died in infancy, and the eldest grandson, Edgar F. Garrison, died March 29, 1889, aged eighteen years and nine months. On August 22, 1897, Mr. and Mrs. Edgar celebrated the sixtieth anniversary of their marriage at Rye Beach, N. H., which has been their summer home for a number of years. They are still in the enjoyment of a hale old age, though their united years number over one hundred and sixty, and enjoying the quiet of their delightful home they look out upon the surging world, but care not to mingle with its strife and bustle; for they have already nobly served their generation.

The following is the direct line of descent from David Edgar of Keithock, Scotland, representative of Edgar of Wedderlie: (1) David Edgar, Laird of Keithock; (2) his fifth son; Thomas Edgar (founder of the family in America); (3) Alexander Edgar, second son of Thomas; (4) William Edgar, fourth son of Alexander; (5) Alexander Edgar, second son of William; (6) Timothy Bloomfield Edgar, third son of Alexander, the senior representative of the family in America, whose portrait with his grandson, Master Park McLure, son of Mr. and Mrs. Charles D. McLure, appears in this section.

Note. For the greater part of this most interesting historical and biographical record, we are indebted to the eldest daughter of Mr. and Mrs. Edgar, the authoress of the copyright work on the subject, printed for private circulation in 1893, which she most kindly placed at our disposal.

GREENWOOD, Moses Jr.—The founders of the family of Greenwood in America were Nathanael, Thomas and Samuel, sons of Miles Greenwood of Norwich, England, whose arms with the family descent are to be found in the College of Arms, London. The origin of the family is traced by Thoresby in his "Ducatus Leodiensis" to Guiomar or Wyomarus de Grenewode, achator or purveyor in the household of Maud the Empress, mother of Henry II., A. D. 1154 (vide E. de Vermonts "America Heraldica"). Miles Greenwood was baptized

(46)

in the parish of St. Peters, of Mancroft, Norwich, England, Sept. 1, 1600, and was buried in the church of St. Michael, at Pleas, Sept. 3, 1658. Nathanael, the eldest son, was born in 1631, Thomas in 1643 and Samuel in 1646. All came to America and settled in Massachusetts, where, in Copp's Hill, Boston, the family tomb erected in 1722, is to be found, on which is carved the armorial bearings of the family thus emblazoned: Argent, a fess between three mullets, pierced, of the field, in chief, and three ducks passant, in base: all sable. Motto, "Ut prosim" (may I be useful). An engraving depicting these armorial bearings appears in this work.

The subject of this sketch was born in New Orleans, La., May 30, 1862, son of Moses M. and Mary (Whittelsey) Greenwood. He is the great-great-grandson of Moses Greenwood, a soldier of the Revolutionary War and a member of Captain John Leland's company, Col. Pierce's regiment, Massachusetts militia, at Lexington Alarm, 1775; member of Captain Miller's company, Col. Doolittle's regiment, 1775; member of Captain John Boynton's Company, Col. Sparhawk's regiment, 1777; served from town of Hollister, Mass., in the Continental Army, for six months, 1780-81.

Moses Greenwood, Jr., obtained his elementary education at the University High School of New Orleans and afterwards attended Roanoke College, Salem, Va., from which he was graduated in 1881, with degree of Bachelor of Science, and afterwards obtained the degree of Master of Arts from the same institution. After graduation he resided at Salem until 1882, at which time he was appointed U. S. Assistant Civil Engineer, and assigned to duty on the Mississippi River Commission with headquarters in St. Louis, the "Commission" placing him in charge of the hydrographic surveys of the lower river. After serving the Government for three years, he resigned his position, feeling that the scope of his ambitions was too limited in that branch of the public service. In 1885, he formed a partnership with Mr. Alfred Carr of St. Louis, engaging in the real estate business under the firm name of Carr & Greenwood. The partnership was dissolved in 1889, when he became associated with his father, Moses M. Greenwood, the firm doing business under name of Greenwood & Company, being one of the leading real estate firms in St. Louis, transacting an enormous business, and engaged largely in interesting outside capital in St. Louis investments.

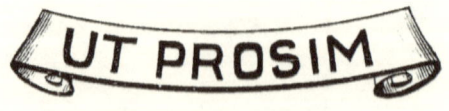

GREENWOOD.

GREENWOOD.

Mr. Greenwood is recognized as one of the most brainy, determined, energetic and successful young business men of St. Louis. As a Christian worker and churchman no young man in the West is more prominent, and few have accomplished more good than Mr. Greenwood. While notedly broad-gauged in all religious undertakings, he is a member of the Presbyterian Church, and is greatly interested in the Sunday School cause, and has become nationally known as a Sunday School worker. When but eighteen years of age he was superintendent of a Sunday School, and has always surrounded himself by christianizing influences. While president of the St. Louis Sunday School Union in 1892–93, he had supervision and charge of all arrangements for holding the Seventh International Sunday School and Second World's Sunday School Conventions, which convened in St. Louis, September, 1893. Before these conventions, Mr. Greenwood delivered one of the most forcible and eloquent addresses, upon the subject of "House to House Visitation," which was widely and favorably commented upon. This modern method of promoting Sunday School interests was conceived and perfected by him, and the Sunday School workers of the world gathered in the great Exposition building, were greatly interested and enthused by the presentation of the subject, by its gifted author. Since 1891 he has been a member of the Executive Committee of the Missouri Sunday School Association, and at this time, 1897, he is associate editor of the *International Evangel*. Mr. Greenwood was for four years a deacon in Rev. Dr. Jas. H. Brookes' church, and superintendent of the Sunday School of same; was also a deacon and superintendent of Sunday School of the West Presbyterian Church for seven years. Mr. Greenwood is known for his philanthropy, and his charity work is too numerous to mention. Most notably, the East End Industrial Church — known as the People's Church — which has received his best efforts and energies for years.

Fraternally he is a member of the following organizations: Masonic, Royal Arcanum, Legion of Honor, and Sons of the Revolution. Politically he is a Democrat, and gave his support in the campaign of 1896 to Palmer and Buckner and the Indianapolis Platform.

In 1884 Mr. Greenwood married Margaret F. Woods, daughter of Robert K. Woods of St. Louis, one of the founders of the Mercantile Library of St. Louis.

Following is the line of descent of Moses Greenwood, Jr.: 1st. Miles Greenwood. 2d. Thomas Greenwood, born in England, came to America, settled in Newton. Mass.; married Hannah Ward, July 8, 1670; died intestate, Sept. 1, 1693. 3d. Rev. Thomas Greenwood, born in Newton, Mass., Dec. 27, 1673; graduated from Harvard in 1690; married Dec. 28, 1693; died Sept. 8, 1720; wife died Jan. 24, 1735. 4th. Thomas Greenwood, born in Newton, Mass.; gave large tracts of land to his sons, who settled in Holden, Mass. 5th. Joseph Greenwood, born 1752; was town clerk of Holden, Mass.; married Sarah Stone. 6th. Major Moses Greenwood, born in 1752; married Betsy Dunlap, March 22, 1779. He died March 8, 1827; his wife died Dec. 9, 1826. 7th. Moses Greenwood, born Nov. 4, 1785; married Polly Brown, Jan. 9, 1806; he died Sept. 26, 1828; his wife died Jan. 14, 1859. 8th. Moses Greenwood, born May 23, 1808; married Adeline Ayres, August 31, 1831. 9th. Moses Merritt Greenwood, father of our subject, born in Hubbardston, Mass., June 20, 1834; a merchant and real estate broker of St. Louis, Mo.; married Mary Mulford Whittelsey, Sept. 16, 1858, the subject (Moses Greenwood, Jr.,) being their eldest son.

Four children have been born to Mr. and Mrs. Moses Greenwood, Jr.; Mary W., Annie Lou, Moses M. Jr., and Margaret Greenwood; three are living, Moses M. Jr., having died in 1892.

O'FALLON.

O'FALLON, Mrs. Anna M. Harris, a descendant from distinguished Colonial and Revolutionary ancestry, was the first State Regent of the Daughters of the American Revolution in Missouri, and organized its first chapter, being appointed Regent by the National Organization of Washington, D. C. She is a lineal descendant of five ancestors of the Revolution, being the great-granddaughter of Col. James Taylor of Caroline County, Va., who served with Gen. Washington in 1775; he was principal Surveyor of his county, and twice High Sheriff; also Lieutenant-Colonel for the county, and one of the Committee of Safety at the time of the rupture with Great Britain; he was a member of the Virginia Convention which formed the first constitution of the State, and in the one to ratify the Federal constitution; he served forty years in the councils of his State, and never lost an election, and was one of the earliest patriots who labored for political and religious liberty. Judge Edmund Pendleton, the distinguished jur-

(47)

1st, another ancestor, whose mother was Mary Taylor, and whose descendants were President James Madison and Zachary Taylor, father of Maj. Richard Taylor. Gen. Zachary Taylor, hero of the Mexican War, was the second President in her family. The fifth in descent was General James Taylor, of Newport, Ky., the financier of the War of 1812, whose vast influence was noted by Henry Clay; devoted his large individual fortune for his country's needs — Gen. Taylor equipped this regiment of volunteers, assumed the government obligation by paying all the indebtedness of the 1,200 or 1,500 volunteers, organized by Governor Meigs, with exception of arming them, and at the earnest solicitation of the Governor and other prominent men, consented to act as Quartermaster-General. In speaking of this act of heroism, Henry Clay said: "He devoted his individual fortune and credit to the supplies of the armies of his country, when there were no funds to reimburse him." Mrs. O'Fallon's great-grandfather, Col. John Harris, was a member of the Revolutionary Committee of Safety in 1775-76, in Cumberland County, Va., who fought at Yorktown, and received land warrants for his services. She is also granddaughter of Maj. Jordan Harris of the Continental Line, who served until the close of the war, February, 4, 1784; he was a member of the Virginia Society of the famous order of the Cincinnati; great-great-granddaughter of Col. Littleberry Mosby, High Sheriff of Cumberland Co., Va., in 1753, and a member of the Revolutionary Committee of Safety for that county, 1774-75; great-granddaughter of Maj. Hugh Moss, of Goochland County, Va., who served at Brandywine, and died from effects of wounds received at Valley Forge; last but not least in her category of renowned Revolutionary ancestors on the Harris family tree, appears the name of the third President in her genealogy — the immortal Thomas Jefferson.

Colonial ancestors of Mrs. Jas. J. O'Fallon as accepted by the Colonial Dames Organization, New York City, with references for services:

1. Henry Soane, speaker of the House of Burgesses, to whom large gifts in tobacco was granted for his fidelity.

2. Capt. Thomas Harris, member of the House of Burgesses, 1623-1639, and 1646; came to the colony in 1611. Settled in Henrico county, received grants of land in 1635-38. Member of the Virginia Company 1609. Reference, Chart of Descendants of Captain Thomas Harris by W. G. Stannard consisting of wills, deeds, marriage bonds, land grants and office documents, also Historical Magazine, Virginia, Vol. III, No. 3, January, 1897.

3. Major William Harris, died 1678, son of the above Justice of Henrico county, member of the House of Burgesses, 1652-56-7-8, appointed by the assembly 1656, Major of the Regiment of Henrico county and Charles City. References as above.

4. Major John Harris, born in Cumberland county, Virginia, member of the Committee of Safety, 1775-6. References as above.

5. Lieutenant Jordan Harris, Lieutenant in the Continental Line.—See Bounty Warrants, Harris Chart, issued for 2666 acres — allowed for serving to the end of the Revolutionary War.

6. Captain Anthony Savage, citizen of Gloucester county, Virginia. Justice in 1660 and had large landed estates on the Rhappahannock. The county records style him captain in 1660. References, William and Mary Quarterly, Vol. IV., No. 2, October, 1895.

7. Major Peter Field, born in Henrico county, Virginia, 1640, was a citizen of New Kent county in 1700, Justice, High Sheriff and member of the House of Burgesses, 1668. References, William and Mary Quarterly, Vol. IV., No. 2. October, 1895. Letter of Wilson Miles Cary — Member Genealogical Committee Maryland Historical Society; Alexander Brown's "Cabells and Their Kin."

8. Colonel Littleberry Mosby, born in Cumberland county, Virginia, 1729, died Powhatan county, Virginia, 1809. High Sheriff in Cumberland county, 1753; member of the Revolutionary Committee of Safety, 1774-1775; Captain of Militia in Goochland county, 1747; Colonel of Militia, 1777. Held the first court in Powhatan county at his private residence July 17th, 1777, Justice of the court; Chairman of Trustees of Academy in Powhatan county, 1792; "In council May 21st, 1823. It is advised that the heirs of Littleberry Mosby be allowed land bounty for three years' service as a captain in the Continental Line." References, Virginia Historical Magazine, Vol. 4, April, 1897.

9. James Taylor, the second of this name on this line of descent, was born in King William county, Virginia, March 14th, 1674, died in Orange county, Virginia, January 23d, 1729. Burgess in 1702-1714;

Mrs. Anna M. H. O'Fallon.

Gen. William Clark.

Justice for King and Queen county. This James Taylor was great-grandfather of two Presidents — General Zachary Taylor and James Madison. References, Slaughtors, St. Mark's Parish; The Taylor Family — Virginia Hist. Mag., Haydens' Virginia Genealogies.

10. James Taylor, the third son of the above, born in Orange county, Virginia, March 20th, 1703, died March, 1784; Burgess 1768; Representative of the Assembly in 1768 for Orange county. Virginia Magazine, Vol. III., No. 4, April, 1896.

11. Colonel James Taylor of Caroline county, son of the above, the fourth in line of this descent of whom mention is made in the Revolutionary Record, was a member of the Convention of Privilege and Election, 1778, of which the historian, Dr. Robert Brock, of Richmond, Virginia, says: "So distinguished a body I annex their names with the remark that such an array of genius, talents, and public and private worth had not before, nor has it been seen since, on such a commitee in Virginia." Virginia Historical Collection, Vol. 9, page 67.

12. Francis Thornton, born in Stafford County, Va., Jan. 4th, 1682; citizen of Spottsylvania, died in Caroline county, 1726; one of the first Justices of Caroline county; Justice of Esse county and Burgess for Spottsylvania, 1723-1726, settled at Snow creek, 1703; References, The Thornton Family, by W. G. Stannard, William and Mary Quarterly, Vol. 4, No. 2.

13. Christopher Branch, born in York county, England, 1595; citizen of Henrico Co., Va., died in 1681, Patentee in 1634. See Patent 157; Justice of Henrico, 1656; First Burgess of Henrico county, 1659. References, The Branch Family, by William G. Stannard.

14. Captain Thomas Jefferson, born in Henrico Co., Va., 1678, died 1731; Justice of the Peace, 1706; High Sheriff of Henrico, 1718-19. This Captain Thomas Jefferson was grandfather of the President. References, Letters from Mr. Wilson Miles Carey, member Genealogical Committee, Maryland Historical Society, Va., Mag., Vol. 1, No. 2.

15. Colonel Thomas Turpin, born in Cumberland Co., Va., May 19, 1708, died in Powhatan Co., June 20th, 1790; Lieutenant-Colonel of Militia in Cumberland Co. A delegate from Powhatan Co., Va. Burgess, 1741, 1748. First Justice Court of Cumberland, May 22, 1749; Colonel 31st August, 1754. Reference, Commission to Colonel Thomas Turpin, from Governor Dinwiddie. See Chart, Harris Family, by W. G. Stannard, and photograph of original commission, Va. Hist. Collection.

16. Major Hugh Moss, commissioned Captain of Militia in Goochland Co., Va., 1760; Major, 1770. Was married by the father of Henry Clay, a Baptist minister, to Jane Ford, a daughter of Thomas Ford and Returah Wynne. References, "Cabells and their Kin," Goochland Records, certified copies, P. G. Miller, circuit clerk for Goochland County, Va.

17. Benjamin Hubbard, citizen of Caroline county, Va., member of Committee of Safety, 1774-75. Certified copy of services in MSS. Book in possession of Robert Brock, secretary of Va. Hist. Society.

18. Major William Cannon, member of Committee of Safety, 1775; Captain in Revolution; County Lieutenant and Colonel of Cumberland Co., in 1780; Sheriff, 1790. Ref., Goodes Virginia Cousins, also will of Littleberry Mosby, in which he mentions daughter, Sarah Cannon.

19. John Netherland, born in Goochland Co., Virginia; died in that county in 1740; High Sheriff of Goochland Co., Virginia, 1736-40; Justice, 1728-84. References, Goode's Virginia Cousins, Alexander Brown's "Cabells and their Kin." Marriages, 3 and 4; certified copies, also marriages, 5 and 6.

Gen. William Clark, one of the Revolutionary heroes, whose portrait appears in this volume, was the uncle of the late Col. John O'Fallon, one of the most prominent men of his day, who gave large sums of money in endowing institutions, among which were the O'Fallon Polytechnic Institute, Washington University and others. Col. John O'Fallon was the adopted son of Gen. George Rogers Clarke, who was known as the "Hannibal of the West." Gen. William Clarke was placed in command of the troops of the Lewis and Clarke expedition, by President Jefferson, to act in conjunction with Merriweather Lewis in an expedition for "Exploring the river of Missouri and the best communication from that to the Pacific ocean." The party was composed of forty-three members including a black servant belonging to Gen. Clarke. The result of this expedition is a matter of history. President Jefferson referring to it said: "The expediion of Messrs. Lewis and Clarke for exploring the River Missouri and the best communications from that to the Pacific ocean, has had all the success which could be expected. They have traced the Missouri nearly to its source; descended the Columbia to the Pacific Ocean, ascertained with accuracy the geography of that interesting communication across the Continent, learnt the character of the country, its commerce and inhabitants, and it is but justice to say that Messrs Lewis. and Clarke and their brave companions, have by this arduous service deserved well of their country."

NAPTON, Charles McClung, is the worthy descendant of illustrious ancestry, being the great-grandson of Colonel Joseph Williams, who, with his brothers, General Robert Williams and Colonel John Williams, were foremost in the struggle for liberty, which resulted in our independence. Colonel Joseph Williams, of Welsh descent, was one of the earliest settlers of Surrey County, North Carolina, and was elected delegate to the Hillsboro convention in 1775. He commanded a regiment of militia at the outbreak of the war and did distinguished service in the cause of liberty. In civil life, after the cause for which he fought was won, he took a prominent part in the affairs of the new-born nation, and ended a well-spent life at a good old age, loved and respected by all. His son, Thomas Lanier Williams, was a wealthy scion of a distinguished family, who settled in Tennessee and became a prominent citizen of that State, holding the position of Chancellor for over forty years. From his marriage with Mary Lawson McClung, descended Melinda Williams, who married William Barclay Napton, the father of our subject. He was born March 25, 1808, at Princeton, New Jersey, where he was educated, and was graduated from the University there with first honors, at the age of sixteen years, the youngest graduate in the history of the institution with one exception. He adopted the profession of law, and after completing a law course at University of Virginia, moved to Missouri in 1834, and settled at Fayette, Howard County. His talents soon placed him in a leading position. In 1836, he was secretary of the State Senate, Attorney-General of the State in 1837, retaining same until his appointment as Judge of the Supreme Court in 1838, when he had barely reached the required age-qualification for the office. He occupied the bench up to 1852, when he returned to private practice, and in 1856 was again elected to the Supreme Court Bench, and held the position until ousted by the convention of 1861, on his refusal to take the oath of loyalty to the Union. Fearless in the carrying out of his convictions, he was an active upholder of the Confederate cause, in the armies of which four of his sons fought with distinction. Up to 1863, Judge Napton resided on his farm at Elk Hill, Saline County, Missouri. From 1863 to 1873, Judge Napton practiced in St. Louis, and on the death of Judge Ewing, was appointed by Governor Woodson to fill the vacancy on the bench of the Supreme Court for the unexpired term. In 1874 he received the Democratic nomination for the same office and was elected, serving until 1880, when he retired to his farm in Saline, where he died January 8, 1883. Of his family of ten children, nine of whom were sons, five adopted their father's profession, and of them our subject was born, on the farm at Elk Hill, Saline County, December 2, 1847. He was educated at St. Louis High School, Westminster College, and the University of Virginia. After graduation in 1869, he took up the study of law reading successively under Judge Strother, Colonel Samuel Boyd and Lewis W. Miller of Marshall, Missouri, at the same time undertaking the education of his four younger brothers. In 1871, while in Marshall, he received his license to practice and removed to St. Louis, where he formed a partnership with his father, which continued until the latter's elevation to the Supreme Bench. In 1877 he was appointed Assistant Attorney of the St. Louis and San Francisco Railway, which appointment he held until 1880, when he resumed general practice in partnership with B. R. Davenport, which continued two years, when he associated with him R. Graham Frost, until the retirement of the latter, since which time he has practiced alone. In the course of his legal career, Mr. Napton has attained eminence as a constitutional lawyer, and has been retained in many important cases argued before the Supreme Court, notably on the constitutionality of the Double Damage Law; the Oleomargarine Law; the law regulating the practice of Medicine, and the validity of the ordinance concerning Street Reconstruction in St. Louis. He has never been a candidate for public office. In 1888, he was chairman of the State Judiciary Convention for the nomination of Judge of the St. Louis Court of Appeals; is a member of the St. Louis and the Mercantile Clubs, the Missouri Society of the Sons of American Revolution, and of the order of Elks; having been Past Exalted Ruler of Lodge

COMSTOCK.

T. Griswold Comstock

No. 9, of that order. With a strong personal resemblance to his distinguished father, Mr. Napton also inherits his pronounced individuality and force of character, which, backed by his commanding talents, has placed him in the front ranks of the leading lawyers in the land.

COMSTOCK, Thomas Griswold, M. D. Of the distinguished descendants of the Revolution in the State of Missouri who so honorably uphold the dignity and great achievements of the Revolutionary heroes, none are more deserving of mention than our subject. The Comstocks are of German origin, and descended from Mayflower stock, Dr. T. Griswold Comstock's mother being the seventh generation in direct line from same. Her father was Dr. Daniel Calkins, of Lyme, New London County, Conn., the most polished and highly educated physician of that day.

Samuel Comstock, the Revolutionary hero, was a private in Captain John Ely's company of Col. Parsons' regiment, Connecticut Militia, from May, 1775, to January, 1776; also a private in Captain Martin Kirtland's company of Col. Huntington's regiment from March, 1777, to March, 1780, and in the same company in Col. Butler's regiment, from March, 1780, to the close of the Revolutionary War. The home of the descendants on his mother's side (the Calkins) was at East Lyme, Conn., which was used as an inn for 100 years; here General Lafayette and General Washington were entertained. The old residence which was the inn is still standing and in a good state of preservation, being visited from far and wide as a relic. Dr. Comstock's grandfather on both the maternal and paternal sides lived at East Lyme, Conn., and were slave-owners. His father, Lee Comstock, was born in Lyme, Conn., and died in LeRoy, N. Y., January, 1853. He was a prominent agriculturist. His mother, whose maiden name was Sarah Calkins, was one of the most beautiful, and accomplished ladies in New London County, Conn.

Dr. Thomas Griswold Comstock was born in LeRoy, N. Y., July 27, 1829. His classical education was received at the High School in his native town. His first step in life was as a drug clerk in New York City. Continued in that capacity three years; during this time he studied chemistry, pharmacy and medicine. Dr. Comstock came to St. Louis in 1847, and studied medicine under Dr. J. V. Prather, the founder of the St. Louis Medical College which was then the medical department of the St. Louis University, now known as the St. Louis Medical College of the Washington University. Dr. Comstock graduated in medicine as M. D. from the St. Louis University, continued his studies in medicine and subsequently went to Philadelphia, Pa., and attended the Homeopathic Medical College of Pennsylvania, now known as the Hahnemann Medical College, from which he also graduated. He afterwards went to Europe and spent some years in Vienna, graduating from the University of Vienna as Master in Obstetrics (Doctor in Midwifery). He traveled over Europe and attended lectures in London, Prague, Berlin and Paris, making a general tour through Italy and Switzerland, completing his tour in Scotland. From Glasgow he sailed for America, returning to St. Louis where he began the permanent practice of medicine and has continued it ever since.

Dr. Comstock was appointed Military Surgeon of Volunteer Union Regiment, under Gen. John B. Gray, during the Civil War, which position he held for a short time and resigned. Was for several years professor in the Homeopathic Medical College of Missouri, occupying the Chair of Obstetrics, and is still Emeritus Professor in the same college. Was formerly Professor of Obstetrics in the St. Louis College of Homeopathic Physicians and Surgeons. Dr. Comstock has been honored by the St. Louis University with degrees of Master of Arts and Doctor of Philosophy, and for twenty-five years has been a member of the American Institute of Homeopathy, and one of its vice-presidents. He held the position of attending physician, (Primarius) at the Good Samaritan Hospital over twenty-five years. Was married October 22, 1862, to Miss Rillie H. Eddy, of St. Louis, Mo.

In the muniment office in Frankfort-on-the-Main, in Germany, is the pedigree of the Comstock family, there spelled indifferently, "Komstohk" and "Comstock," which gives nine generations previous to 1547 A. D. The Comstock arms are, Or (gold), two bears rampant sable (black), gules (red) in chief and in base; a sword issuing from a crescent, the point downwards, all of last color, viz., (gules) red. Upon the arms a baronial helmet of the German Empire. Or, gules (gold and red) surmounted by a baron's coronet. Jeweled proper, issuing therefrom an elephant rampant, also proper. The bears imply courage, the sword issu-

(51)

ing from the crescent shows that some of the family fought against the Turks. The elephant in crescent was given as an indication of personal prowess and sagacity. Motto: "Non divitiae verum felicitas." (Not wealth but contentment.) Tradition says that William, Samuel, and Christopher Comstock came from Wales to America. Christopher had three sons: Daniel, Samuel and Moses. The Comstock name dates from 1330; sword and crescent given in 1400; elephant bestowed in 1400; motto in 1530 to 1550. Jno. Comstock came from England in 1639, settled first in Weymouth, Massachusetts, and moved thence to Saybrook, to what is now known as Lyme, New London, Connecticut. Samuel Comstock, of Hartford, 1848; Christopher Comstock, of Fairfield, Connecticut, 1661; William Comstock, of Wethersfield, 1649; Daniel Comstock, of New London, 1652; Daniel Comstock, of Fairfield, 1672. The name appears in the early records of Rhode Island.

HUSE, William Lee. The family of which this gentleman is the principal representative in the State of Missouri, is entitled to rank among those descended from the heroes of the American Revolution, through the services to the cause of the patriots, of Thomas Colby, grandfather of Mr. Huse, and one of the gallant band known as the "Green Mountain Boys" who served under Ethan Allen at the capture of Fort Ticonderoga.

Thomas Colby was born at Hampton, N. H., in 1759, but passed the greater part of his life at Danville, Vt., from which place he enlisted under Ethan Allen and where, after the storm of war had passed, he settled and, in 1844, passed away at the ripe age of over 85 years. He was pensioned in 1832, at the age of 74 years. He married Lydia Webster, who was of the same stock as the celebrated Noah Webster, and a daughter of this marriage, Sylvia Britt Colby, married John Huse, who was born in Danville, Vt., in 1801.

The Huse family is descended from one of the old baronial families of England; the first on record being Henry Hosatus, who was sheriff of the county of Oxford, in 1199, and from whom descended the Barons Hoese or Huse of Surrey, whose titles became extinct, from failure of direct heirs, in 1349 and 1361 respectively. The name, like many others, has passed through several changes; being spelled as Hoese, Husee, Huse and Hussey, of the latter there being several families holding rank among the landed gentry of England and Ireland, the principal line being represented by the Earls of Portsmouth. The armorial bearings of the family are blazoned as "Barry of six, ermine and gules" with crest "In dexter hand, proper, a cross patteè, in pale, or."

Mr. William L. Huse, son of John Huse, was born at Danville, March 9, 1835. In 1842 his parents removed to Chicago, then only a small town of 5,000 inhabitants. Here he passed his early life, gaining his education at the public schools, and at the age of 17 years entered the grocery business of H. G. Loomis. His ability and industry while in this employment, during which he attended Bell's Commercial College of Chicago, from which he was graduated in 1854, attracted the notice of I. D. Harmon & Co., a forwarding and commission firm with headquarters at Peru, Ill., who, recognizing his business talent, gave him the entire charge of a steamer running on the Illinois river. After four years he had saved enough money to enable him to acquire possession of a steamer and enter upon the transportation business on his own account. Continuing to prosper, he, at the age of 25, was owner of three steamers and doing an extensive forwarding business which, in the fall of 1860, he disposed of at a good profit and organized the firm of Huse, Loomis & Co., which commenced business on a large scale in ice and transportation.

In 1880, the immense interests of the firm rendered it advisable to incorporate, and it was merged into a joint-stock corporation as the Huse & Loomis Ice and Transportation Company with a capital of $550,000, with Mr. Huse as president and holding a controlling interest. He resided at St. Louis from 1861 to 1868, when he removed to Peru, Ill., of which city he was mayor in 1869 and 1870, during which period he was instrumental in the bridging of the river at that point. While there he also interested himself in the breeding of horses, having a large stock farm adjoining the city, and was also president of the Peru Trotting Association for six years, and director of the Bank of Peru.

Previous to his return to St. Louis in 1879, he sold out the stock farm in order to concentrate his attention on the large interests he possessed in other enterprises under his control.

In 1893 Mr. Huse was appointed by the U. S. District Court of Nashville receiver for the Paducah, Tennessee and Alabama

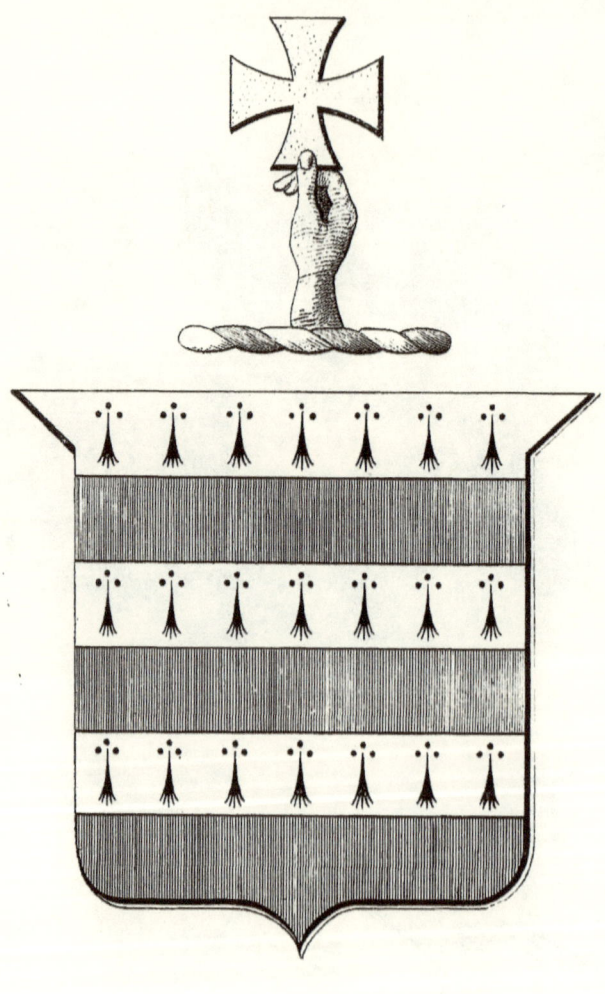

HUSE.

Railway Company, and the Tennessee Midland Railway Company, whose affairs he administered until the property was disposed of to the Louisville and Nashville Railway Company. Mr. Huse was also President of the Chicago, Paducah and Memphis Railway Company, and built 100 miles of the road from Altamont to Marion, retaining the presidency until the fall of 1896, when the line was sold for nearly $2,000,000, to the Chicago and Eastern Illinois Railway Company. He was also one of the incorporators of the Mississippi Valley Transportation Company and served on the directorate from its organization until 1885.

He is president of the Union Dairy Co., the Creve Cœur Lake Ice Co., the Crystal Lake Ice Co., Director of the Crystal Plate Glass Co., of the Boatmen's Bank, the St. Louis Trust Co., the Peru City Plow and Wheel Co., and principal owner and director of the Bohler, Huse Ice Co., of Memphis, Tenn., of which he was the originator. He was also for eight years trustee of Lafayette Park, is now President of the Board of Trustees of Westmoreland Place, where he resides, and has been for ten years on the Board of Control of Washington University.

His manifold business interests have not prevented him from cultivating social life, as he is a member of the Commercial Club of St. Louis, of which he is Past President, of the St. Louis Club, the University Club the Legion of Honor, and the Society of the Sons of the American Revolution.

In 1865 he married Martha E., daughter of the Reverend Harvey Brown, of New York, a prominent divine of the Methodist denomination and also a veteran of the War of 1812.

In the winter of 1896, Mr. Huse, accompanied by his wife, daughter and nephew, left St. Louis on an extensive tour of travel, in the course of which the party visited Palestine, penetrating as far as Damascus, Egypt, Turkey, Spain, Italy, Central Europe, Norway and Sweden, but were prevented from visiting the classic scenes of Greece by the war then in progress between Greece and Turkey. In August, 1897, they returned to St. Louis with minds fraught with interesting memories of foreign lands.

Supplementing his natural ability with acquired and steady habits of industry and economy, Mr. Huse has, unaided, attained rank among the merchant princes of America, and his career furnishes a lesson of inestimable value to young men starting out in life.

BARRET, Richard Aylett.—The Barret family are of Druidic Celtic origin and are traced through Gallic, French, Welsh and English history, to the Roman province, Limivoces, valorously doing their part at Gregovia, to beat down Cæsar's sword.

The tribes between the Garonne and Loire, with genuine refinement of manners and feeling, like the modern French, lacked capacity for political organization, and therefore gave way before the more practical Roman and Teuton. Division brought ruin, desperation and dismay at Alesia; they fled from Gallia to British West-Wales, where on the "Shaggy top of Mona high, in oak woods, their sacred rights might lie," and to the highlands of Scotland, thence in part, back to Normandy.

The Celtic Cavalry was proudly eminent in prowess of arms and dauntless courage; imitating their tactics, Cæsar won Pharsalia: Arthur's round table, begirt with British and Armoric Knights and peerage, and Jousts, as told in Geoffery of Monmouth's Historia Britanum and Roman de Brut of Wace, resounds in fable, romance and feats or high courage.

The barons of Limoges, Poitu, Breton and Maine, led the attack at Hastings. William Barret and other powerful barons in the Welsh Marches — Baddlesmere, Giffard — Walter Giffard — brought the good horse called for by Duke William, at Hastings: "the Duke stretched out his hand, took the reins, put foot in stirrup, and mounted"; the good horse sent by a Spanish King, pawed, pranced, reared himself up and curveted. Ref. Wace; Cheney, and about eighteen of the most notorious offenders were executed in 1322, in the rebellion of Thomas, Earl of Lancaster, prince of the blood, and one of the most potent barons that had ever been in England. Ref. Ed. 11, Hume: Vol. 11: p. 160.

The Barrets, relatives of the Gilberts, Raleighs and Leighs, associates in enterprises of adventure, gain and discovery, among the gallant spirits of a gallant age, ventured and strove for England's "best glory" the Atlantis, in the Occident.

Robert Barret; wife Penelope Gilbert; master of admiral Sir John Hawkins flag ship, Jesus of Lübeck, squadron sailing from Plymouth, Oct 2, 1567, encountered labyrinths of dangers, difficulties and vexations, especially in the harbor of Vera-Cruz, Mexico, where the Spanish plate ships incautiously sailing in, Sir John could have seized many millions worth; Spain and England being at peace, he hesitated. Master Barret, who spoke Spanish fluently, was invited aboard the admiral's ship under a flag of truce, was "traitorously stayed" by the treacherous Spanish Viceroy. Master, subsequently the renowned world circumnavigator, Sir Francis Drake, with the "Judith escaped. Ref. Hakluyt; Sir John's account, Vol. IV.

His sons, Charles and William, wives, Edith Leigh and Dorothea Payne, among "ye valiant adventurers and generous spirits. Ref. Hakluyt, Sir John's report, Vol. IV. Hakluyt, Vol. 3, p. 239; Alex. Brown, Vol. I, p. 6. Kingsley — p. 210; "personall possessors of the new found territories" the knowledge and tidings of which, gave the curious and busy multitude of the old world fresh impulse and new hope, with other "the Nobilitie, Gentrie, marchants," bought Sir Walter Raleigh's Va. patents, the one, with "diuers other gentlemen came ouer in the Starre", was copartner of Earl Plowden in the Palatinate, Novo Albion. Ref. Smith: Hazzard: Charter: Chs. 1: June 21, 1634; the other, William, Warden of the East India and London Companies "an office of high trust and responsibility", with the Court of Wardens and Asst. Wardens, at Trinity House, London, the architectural wonder of the day — a row of wooden Indians crowned the peristyle, burnt in the great fire of 1666 — India House fills the site — " governe here execute there " Va.— with more authority than King James his realm. His graphic and vivid pen, in the true declaration, 1610, " of eminent authority", paints the Isle of Bermuda, and wreck there, the on-hastening future glories of America, the shame of abandoning the venture, the correct causes and wherefore of previous failures. Wm. Barret, Gent, May 17, 1620, sells one share of the London Co. to Sr. Henry Crofte. Colonial Record Vol. 2. No. 33, also Va. Magazine No. 3, Jany. 97. p. 303. Smith: p: 150: Vol. II. p. 45: Force, p. 21: Force, Vol. III. No. 1: Burks: Vol. I, p. 340: Bancroft: Alex. Brown, Genesis, U. S. Thomas, his son; m. Edith Gilbert, enthused by the zeal of his father as to the dawning glories of the new world — master-ship-wright, embarked for the plantations 1622, " came ouer in the greate Abigale, along with him Lady Wyat, the Governor's wife, to superintend the building of ships and boats": Capt. Smith, Capt. Barick. companions in his survey of the Atlantic coast: Ref. Smith Vol. II. 65: Stith: p. 229. List of London Co.; Va. Magazine:

" Men, not other waies to be employed", settled at Appomatox, the confluence of the Bristol, and the broad and beautiful James, amid scenery of unrivalled magnificence, and established Barrets' Ferry, over which, Lieut. Col. Simcoe's, Queen's Rangers, crossed, 1781, p. 192.

Wm, succeeded, wife Ann Ludwell, a grant recorded; Land office, Richmond, Va., 700 acres, — head rights — Warranty, old town 1648, then Charles, Burgess and member of the Loyal Land League — land grants, 1730-32-34, his seat, the Hermitage, Louisa Co. Va., wife Mary Chiswell — Ref: Burk, Vol. III. p. 134. Will probated, Feb. 24, 1746, Louisa Court House: then, Reverend Robert, his younger son, wife, Ann Lee or Leigh; — Rector of St. Martin's Parish — Ref. Bishop Meade, Vol. I, pp. 420-30, Vol. II. pp. 42-4-5-72. Ref. old families and churches of Va. Presided 1754, in charge until 1785. Ref. Hawks, History and Journal of the Convention, p. 3; and V. C. H. 2. Dashields Digest: Councils of Va.

Chiswell, his son, — wife Ann Dangerfield, along with gallant young Virginians, rallied around Washington at Cambridge; at Trenton, his Colonel, Baylor, riding up to Washington, reported: " Sir the Hessians have surrendered" (Ref. Bancroft). Chiswell accompanied his Colonel to Philadelphia to deliver the flags, (trophies of Trenton and Princeton) to the Continental Congress; was Cornet the weary winter at Valley Forge, was at Monmouth, and through the Gates and Greene Campaigns of the South, as Captain of Light Horse — Ref. Army and Navy Journal. Va. Magazine of History and genealogy.

William, his son, Lieutenant, in Lieut Col. Wm Washington's, 3d Continental Cavalry, participated in the battles — Fair Forest, Cowpens, Guilford, and other engagements of that able corps. Capt. Robert Barret, his cousin, of Lieut Col. Wm Washington's Brigade, at Guilford, gallantly fell at the head of his dragoons — Ref. *Burk. Vol. III p 487.* Wm. was transferred Captain to Baylor's dragoons — Ref. Heitman, Va, Magazine. Dorothy, his wife, daughter of Lieutenant William Winston of the French and Indian wars, brother to Sarah, Patrick Henry's mother, was gifted with marvelous and effective elcquence; (*sample*) *Wirt, p. 21.* Dr. Thomas Winston, one of his ancestors, was of the London Co., *June 7th 1619;* Ref. *Va. Magazine* — Virginia's claim to the Ohio and Mississippi Valley, the sword only could arbitrate.

Gov Dinwiddie by proclamation granted

(54)

Rich'd Aylett Barret

200,000 acres of land in the fertile regions of the Ohio to be divided, pro rata, according to rank, among the officers and soldiers who voluntarily entered the service of the Colony for the armed expedition of 1754, fitted out to erect forts so that the Crown of Great Britain might assert and maintain its claim to the Ohio country, a gratuity so honestly and faithfully earned, owing to legal defects in the act, came near being lost to the soldier, entitled to the bounty land. Washington a champion of the wronged soldier, awakened a sense of justice among the State officials, laid before Gov., Botetourt, a concise history of the origin of the claim, visited the region 1770, where the pledged land lay.

"Patent — 16 — granted to Wm Winston wife Mary Overton — and others — 50,000 acres being at old Fort between Ohio and Missippi rivers, running up the Eastern Side of Missippi, and Western side of Ohio, in one or more surveys, between s'd rivers [west of Ohio]": *Va Magzine of History — Vol. V: No. 2 | 97:*

In the Revolution, from start to finish, Wm. Winston was Adjutant and Captain in Major Lee's (Light Horse Harry's), famed Legion: Heitman; Exploits, White's, Wm. Washington's, Bland's, Moylan's, originally Baylor's Rg'mts; *Lee, Vol. 1, p. 161.*

Isaac, his father's pedigree, Browning's genealogical record, traces to Robert Bruce.

Mary Howitt writes, of Winston, "England: Hall tenantless." Woud ha"; high antique brick, number of gables, well grouped massive chimneys" —Winston, old church, no new one in the village; in the church sculptured figures of Sir, John Winston and his lady Penelope, in full court dress of queen Elizabeth's day, in kneeling attitude, with upturned eyes, and holding prayer books in their hands," "the tomb was erected by their son, Sir Christopher Winston."

Jack Churchill, duke of Marlborough; "who never fought a battle that he did not win, and never beseiged a place that he did not take." Ref: Creasy, p. 223; is of this, the Yorkshire branch of the family.

Col Jno Campbell's W. Va. Memoirs, says: Winston name most brilliantly, illumes the record of the Revolution." The fiery spirit, breathing thro' the burning words of Patrick Henry, lighted the flame of rebellion through the colony; the love of liberty glowed in the souls of other of kin, who also devoted fortune and sacred honor to the country's cause, his cousin, Sam'l Winston's, seven sons, being ardent patriots, and actively personally in the contest against Farmer George"; one of them, especially, Col Joseph Winston winning great renown for gallant services thorought the revolution." Col Wm Overton Winston, May 4, 1775, trained, at South Anna bridge the 1st Va, Volunteer Company of the Revolution, Hanover, Co; assembled at new New Castle and elected Patrick Henry Capt; Saml Meredith, his bro-in law, 1st Lieut; Richd Morris, a relative, 2d Lieut; Park Goodall, a relative, Ensign: Burk. Vol IIII. p.

Wm Winston Seaton, son of his sister Mary, late Editor of the Washington D. C. *Intelligencer,* p. 13: "In the unique affair of Kings Mountain Col Winston played a very conspicuous part; he led the right wing of the American forces and bore a distinguished part at the Bunker Hill of the South, contributing greatly to that momentous victory, of which, the battles of Cowpens, Guilford, were among the consequences." "Jefferson's letter" before me: "he remembered well the deep and grateful impression made by that memorable victory; it was the joyful enunciation of the first turn in the tide of success that terminated the war with the seal of our success." His wife, formerly Miss Gales, daughter of his co-partner, writes from Stokes Co; "this is the most magnificent place I ever saw"— a most beautiful Estate, and hedged about with reverential pride by the old North State, whose adopted son (uncle) is". He was then representative in Congress; "he is so obliging and attentive in endeavor to make my visit agreeable that it almost distresses me"; his mansion is near the mountains, and I sitting, enjoy the full view of them, a sight so grand, so sublime, I never witnessed; it seems as if the "cloud-capped summits" were within a squrrel jump of heaven".

Prof and Dr Richd Ferral Barret, one of the founders of Kemper Medical College, St Louis; Fund Commissioner of Ills; President of the Burlington Land Co, 1836, Black-Hawk territory; with Rev. Perry, brother to the Cmmodore, owner of Stonington Colony; with Col. Goode, proprietor of Taylorville, both in Christian, Co, Ills; city physician 1849-50, during the Cholera, establisher of quarantine consulting physician at the Hôtel des Invalides, with Col John O'Fallon, judge Walter, V. Scates, and Gov. Zadoc Casey, builder of the 1st rail-road in Ills, terminating at St Louis; viz: from Caseyville coal banks to the Mississippi,— son of Wm Barret, of Lieut Col. Wm; Washington's Brigade, and Bay-

(55)

BARRET.

lor's cavalry, and Dorothy Winston; married, Maria Lewis, daughter of Judge Richd. Aylett Buckner and Elizabeth Lewis Buckner — mother to Richd. Aylett Barret. Ref. History of Des Moines Co, Iowa; Scharf's History of St. Louis; Hyde's Encyclopedia; Congressional reports.

Judge Richd Aylett Buckner's father and mother — the paternal, was, Aylett Buckner, Major of Fauquier Co. Va. battalion, who married Judith Presly Thornton, daughter of Col Anthony Thornton; the maternal; Elizabeth Lewis Ro-Bards, who married Master Wm Buckner, of the Va, Navy, Surveyor General of Ky, judge of the Court of Quarter Sessions, Greene, Co, Ky; Ref. *Archives; Magazine of History List of Navy; Wm B Allen's, Ky.* Her brother Captain George Ro-Bards, a valliant soldier in the battles of Brandy-wine, Germantown, Monmouth; of the chosen few — picked men — that made the gallant daring successful bayonet charge on Stony Point, at Camden and at the surrender of Cornwallis, died in 1833, on his Cane Creek farm, Mercer, Co, Ky; his brother, Captain Lewis, married Rachael Donaldson, Old Hickory's, aunt Rachael. Ref. Year book Sons of the Revolution.— *War Dep't Records.*

Aylett, was the son of Richd Buckner, justice of Westmoreland Co Va, and Elizabeth Aylett, daughter of Wm Aylett; clerk and Burgess, of King Wm Co Va; *Archives; bishop Meade's old families and Churches.*

Richd. son of Richd, of Nominy Bay, Westmorland, Co, Va. Burgess, justice, vestryman, signer of protest against the stamp act 1665, and Elizabeth Cooke, daughter of Mordecai Cooke; patentee 1174, acres and other lands; seat Mordacais Mount. Mob Jack-Bay, Gloster, Co. ; sheriff 1698; Burgess, 1702-14 ; Ref. *Archives; Meade's, old families and churches.*

Richd Buckner's will directs, that a "double tombstone with an humble inscription" be erected over himself and Elizabeth,, his wife; *Va Magazine, History and biography Vol. No. 4, p. 452;*

Col Anthony Thornton, will recorded in Stafford, Co, among other things, bequeaths to his son, Presley, Lieut Col, Baylor's Dragoons, and chief of Washington's staff " the negroes"; to his " son Anthony ", County Lieutenant, and Col Va. Militia, Yorktown,— " all the land he had at the mountains "; his wife" only daughter and heiress of Col Peter Presly, of " Northumberland House," burgess, of Northumberland Co— Winifred "— mother of Presley, Anthony, Judith Presley, aforenamed — the former, of " Northumberland House ", " member of the Council 1760-69: " *Va Magazine of History and geneology and biography Vol. 1: p. 255.*

Col Peter Presley of Northumberland House, married Winifred Griffin, daughter of (Col Leroy of Rappahannock, born 1646). Col. Leroy Griffin, married, Winifred Corbin, daughter of Henry Corbin: Wm. Presley, of Northumberland House; burgess 1647-60, father of Peter, married, Jane, daughter of Charles Barret, of the Palatinate aforenamed, — New Jersy, Staten and Long Islands: Ref; Bishop Meade Vol. 2 p. 144 W. G. Stanard.— *Colonial book.*

W. G. Stanard certifies, " I have examined the will of Winifred Griffin, now on record in Richmond Co Va, which is dated Sept 10: 1709, and proved in Richmond Co Mar 15th, 1711, in which she gives legacies to her grand-daughter, Winifred Presley, daughter of Col. Peter Presley, and to her son-in-law, Col Peter Presley, and her son Thomas Griffin ".

" I also certify that I have examined the will of Corbin Griffin, now on record in Middlesex, Co, Va, and proved in that county in 1701, in which he makes bequests to his brother Thomas, his sister Winifred and his mother "Madam Winifred Griffin ".

" I also certify that the Richmond Standard of Vol III, 20, contains " a Pedigree of the' Corbin Family ", on the original of which is printed, this pedigree, down to the match of Garvin Corbin with Jane, daughter and co-heir of John Lane of York river, in Virginia, is extracted from the records of the College of Arms, London, by Sir, G C. Young, King at Arms, 1889 " ; contains the following:

Henry Corbin, the emigrant, married July 26th, 1645, Alice daughter of Richard Eltonhead, of Eltonhead, County of Lancaster, England". " She married secondly Captain Henry Creek of London, and died about 1684, having had issue by her first husband, three sons and five daughters; viz: VI. Winifred married Le Roy Griffin, of Virginia ; she died about 1709 ".

" I also certify, that the Volume of Maryland Archives, 1636-67 contains the following in a letter dated 1663, from Governor Berkeley of Virginia, to the Lieutenant Governor of Maryland :"I and the Councell here have authorized the Gentlemen of the Councell, Coll. Richd Lee, Coll.

Robert Smith, Coll. John Carter, and Mr Henry Corbin our Commissioners, to communicate our results to you"; and that in Henning's Statues at Large Vol. ii 320, in an Act passed Sept. 1674, is the following: "A grant, bearing date the nineteenth day of Aprill, in the six and twentieth yeare of the reigne of our Sovereigne Lord King Charles the second, under his Majesties seal of this colony and under the hands of Henry Corbin, Esquires, his Majesties now Councell of Virginia":

Richd. Aylett Barret, born June 21st 1834, at his grand-father's seat — Cliffland, Ky, Greene Co, conspicuous from afar, of various neighboring view; a lovely rural landscape, where Green river under craggy cliffs, ledge to ledge, crowned with cedar, and with thicket o'er grown; and mantling vine luxuriant, foams along its rocky bed, through irriguous valley, and shaggy hill, under pendent shades of trees of gigantic growth, whose venerable trunks and branches rise aloft, wearing the livery of centuries; was primarily instructed by private tutors at the old farm, near Barret's Station Pacific railroad, and at Rock Springs, the old mansion still standing, south side of Sarpy Ave; formerly Barret Avenue, just west of Sarah Street, at Wyman's, at St Louis University, at Phillips Exeter Latin Academy, at Harvard, at Heidelberg. Rec'd diploma of M. D. at Missouri Medical college, 1854, and was admitted to the St Louis Bar 1858.

The crisis of 1857 destroyed all values, and cut down incomes; his father's income of $20.000 per annum, dwindled to almost nothing; he died 1860, seeing life time struggles swept away, and left to Mr Barret to care, and provide for, and educate, a young family that had lived in extravagance and luxury — thought themselves rich, and knew not, that aspiring beggary is the height of misery.

The war came, and, war taxes, hardest on unimproved property; "to take up arms against a sea of troubles — was vain.

Mr. Barret had a divided duty — his family and the Union. A set of fanatics, brought on the crisis, but was the Union Tree, under the shadow of whose boughs, millions sat with delight, and whose fruits generations yet unborn should taste, to be up-rooted, or deeper planted? He gave gratis stores under the Barret House for recruiting purposes and some of Iowa's finest Regt's were recruited there. In 1861 he was sworn into the Company of Capt Thomas. W. Newman, Recruiting Officer, and Military Commander at Burlington, Iowa; Genl F. P. Blair gave him a Captain's commission in the 1st Mo, July, 1862; also was offered command of the 1st Battery, Iowa Light Artillery, Aug. 1861. Fortune so ordained that his ruling star of destiny pointed not to the sword and deeds of military daring, but to the pen and official business.

He was successively Government Attorney in the office of Confiscated and Contraband property, Genl B. G. Farrar; in the office of Col James O Broadhead, City Provost Marshal, and three years in the office of the Provost Marshal of the United States:

STATE OF MISSOURI.
OFFICE OF ACT'G ASS'T PROVOST MARSHAL
GENERAL, U. S. A.
ST. LOUIS, April 21st, 1866.

Richard A. Barret Esq.

Dear Sir:—

At the close of the long and arduous duties of this Office, permit me to express to you my kindest regards to say, that all our relations have been most agreeable, to testify my acknowledgement of your services and to wish for you, success in your future career.

I have the honor to be, Sir,
Very Respectfully
Your Ob't. Servant,
(Signed)   C. B. ALEXANDER.
B'vt. Brig. Gen'l. U. S. A. and Act'g Ass't.
Pro. Marshal Gen'l for Missouri.

Mr. Barret's parts played on the world's stage are briefly set down; in the history of Des Moines Co, Iowa, 1879; in Scharf's History of St Louis 1881; in the Bench and Bar of Missouri cities 1884; and in Hyde's Encyclopedia of the history of St. Louis. After having "ventured like little wanton boys that swim on bladders this many summers on a sea of glory" — Mistakes and Errors — faults of the head not of heart — forgot, and "a still and quiet Conscience, above all earthy dignities" — and sins forgiven — he hopes to creep unburdened towards the grave.

Rev Robert Barret, Rector St Martin's Parish — also married, Elizabeth Lewis — Captain, Wm Barret, of Lieut Col, Wm. Washington's, Brigade, and Baylor's Cavalry — her only son; her father, Robert Lewis, of Louisa and Albemarle; burgess 1744; mother Jane, daughter of Nicholas Merriwether, burgess 1744; burgess 1710–16, New Kent, 1748, Hanover; will proved Gouchland Co, 1744; names his son-in-law Robert, and grand daughter Jane.

(57)

John Lewis, son of John and Isabella, father of Robert Lewis, for years a member of the Council, married Elizabeth — with her acquired the Warner Hall Estate, daughter of Augustine Warner Jr. Speaker of the House of Burgesses Mar. 1675-6 and Feby 1676-7, and Mildred, daughter of George Read — her sister Mildred, married Lawrence Washington, and was grandmother of George Washington. Augustin Warner, Sr., burgess York and Goucester Counties 1652-8; member of the Council 1659 till death, wife Mary—settled in Elizabeth City Co., 1628. Ref, Wm. and Mary Quarterly, 11. 226-7.

Henings Statutes at Large 1-11
Journals of the Council 1715-25
" " " House of Burgesses 1744.
Will of Robert Lewis proved 1765; date March 27th 1753, recorded Gouchland Co, from Robert Lewis of Louisa Co, Gent, to Rev. Robert Barret of Hanover, husband of his daughter Elizabeth.

George Read settled in Va. in 1637, Secretary of State pro-tem 1640, burgess, James City 1649-56, and until death 1671, married Elizabeth, daughter of Nicholas Martian, an early settler in the Plantations, burgess, Kiskyacke, and Isle of Wight 1623-31-2; will proved, York Co, Apl. 24th, 1657.

Ref: Virginia Historical Magz. I:425-6
" " " " IV: 204-6
Henings Statutes at Large I: VIII-483.
Virginia Historical Register.

BURNHAM, Reverend Michael, D.D.
The family of which this eminent divine is a lineal descendant has been seated in England since the days of the Norman conquest, and was founded by William Le Veutre, who accompanied William the Conqueror on his invasion of that country, and, for his services, was ennobled and enfeoffed of several towns of the manor of Burnham. From this manor he took the territorial title of De Burnham, which subsequently became the family name; the prefix "de" denoting nobility being afterwards dropped by his descendants. The armorial bearings of this old family are heraldically emblazoned thus: "Gules, a chevron between three lions' heads, erased, argent;" with the crest: "a leopard's head, erased, proper."

Of this stock came Lieutenant Thomas Burnham, one of three brothers who settled in this country in the first half of the seventeenth century. He was born in England in 1623 and was one of the earliest settlers of Ipswich, Mass., where he died in 1694, leaving a family of twelve children. His great-great-grandson, Westley Burnham, whose services to his country in the War of Independence entitle his descendants to honor in this record, was born at Chebacco, Mass., August 27, 1747, and was the son of Westley Burnham and Deborah, his wife, daughter of Deacon Zachariah Story. Coming from a race of seafaring men and "vessel builders" as they were called in those days, he took to the sea in early life and gained reputation as a skilled navigator, no vessel commanded by Skipper Westley, as he was called, ever having been wrecked or dismasted. In 1776 he threw himself into the struggle for liberty, enlisting in Captain Daniel Giddings' Co. of Colonel Forbes Regiment of Massachusetts Troops. At the end of his term of enlistment he entered the privateer service, in the course of which his ship was captured and he with the rest of the men was taken to England, where he was confined in the Old Mill Prison. After some time of imprisonment he accepted an offer made by the British Admiralty to the American sailors to take service on board a royal vessel as seaman but not to do any fighting, and accordingly entered on board the "Preston" of 74 guns. On this vessel he sailed for the West Indian station and on the cruise was struck down by smallpox and sent ashore to hospital in Jamaica. Here he lay at the point of death and in fact his death was reported to his family by a man who had returned to America from Jamaica. He, however, recovered his health and took ship for Boston, whence, on his arrival, he walked to his home in Chebacco, where his return was hailed by his wife and friends as that of one from the dead. By this time the struggle for freedom had been brought to a victorious termination and he resumed his sea-faring life, and later engaged in the hereditary occupation of ship building, living to a good old age, for a considerable time of the latter part of his life being totally blind. He was a consistent Christian and in every way set a bright example of probity and well doing to his numerous children, of whom he had ten by his wife Molly, daughter of Robert Woodbury of Beverly Farms, whom he married in 1771, and who survived until April 27, 1830, when she died at the age of nearly 81 years. The family has always been noted for longevity, some reaching nearly their century. Dr. Burnham's father, also named Michael, one of several children, also lived beyond four score and died at the age of 81. He married Patience Andrews, who

was also descended from a long-lived ancestry.

Coming from such a vigorous stock, noted for great strength of body and mind, the reverend gentleman whose name heads this section has added luster to an already honored name. He was born in the town of Essex, Mass., and spent his early life on the farm and in mechanical pursuits. With no advantages of educational training other than those afforded by the country school, which he attended only in summer until twelve or fourteen, and in winter only until sixteen, he, in December, 1860, entered the English department of Phillips Academy, Andover, Mass., and in the following spring joined the third junior class of the classical department in which he remained one term, when, by means of hard vacation study, he succeeded in passing from the third junior to the second middle class and made such brilliant progress as enabled him to be graduated in two years and two terms with an English oration and to enter Amherst College in good standing. Here in his Freshman year he gained the first prize in oratory and, never relaxing in his efforts, though being forced to devote his vacations and part of his terms to teaching, was graduated with honors, receiving his degree A. B. in 1867. He immediately entered upon his professional studies at Andover Theological Seminary. During his Andover days, both in Academy and Seminary, he was actively identified with Mission School work and was twice Superintendent of the Mission Sabbath School in Abbot, a factory village. In the autumn of 1867 he entered the Andover Theological Seminary, was licensed to preach in his middle year and developed such powers in the pulpit as at once placed him in the front rank and made him the object of attention of numerous influential congregations who were seeking rising talent. In May, 1870, two months before his graduation, he received, and in due time accepted, a call from the Central Congregational Church at Fall River, where, after his graduation in July, he was ordained and installed Oct. 25th. In this field of labor his efforts were distinguished by a great ingathering of membership and increase of prosperity of the body; which was marked in his fifth year by the erection of a fine Gothic church building at a cost of some $260,000.00 which at the conclusion of his pastorate he left practically free from debt, a condition due to his ever unfailing energy and the loyalty of his loved people. During his labors here he received several calls from other congregations and was approached by Dr. Stearns, President of Amherst, with reference to the Chair of English Literature, but remained in the field of usefulness in which he had made such signal success. In May, 1882, he decided to accept a call from Immanuel Church, Boston, where he remained until 1885, when he was called to a wider field by the First Church of Springfield, where he spent nine happy years, which were referred to in the *Advance* of May 16, 1895, as among the most memorable ones in recent Congregational history. In February, 1894, he was called to Pilgrim Church, St. Louis, to succeed Rev. Dr. Stimson, when the question as to his acceptance, involving so many important church interests, both fields being of great responsibility, was referred to a council which was composed of representatives from the strongest churches in the East, including leading educators, and in which the interests of Pilgrim Church were represented by Deacon A. W. Benedict, a leading business man of St. Louis, and Clinton Rowell, a leading St. Louis lawyer, members of that church, who presented the claims of the Southwest. In accordance with the decision of the council, Dr. Burnham accepted the call and was installed June 1, 1894. Again quoting the *Advance* of May 16, 1895: "Both in his local work and in general church enterprise Dr. Burnham is recognized as one of the strong men of the denomination. In his preaching he is vigorous, spiritual and evangelical. In his pastoral work and association with his ministerial brethren he is tender and winning, yet strong and manly. In differences that have arisen he has taken pronounced ground, yet without bitterness. He has had opponents, but no enemies. He fills a most important place among the churches of the interior, who rejoice greatly at his record for long pastorates."

In 1887 he was distinguished with the degree of D. D. by Beloit College, has been a corporate member of the American Board of Commissioners for Foreign Missions since 1885, and in 1888 was elected to the Board of Trustees of Amherst College, and has served several years on the Board of Trustees of Wheaton Seminary for girls, and of Hartford Theological Seminary. Dr. Burnham always having had large and influential churches and fields of labor has never devoted himself to writing and publishing books, but a large number of his ser-

(59)

mons and addresses have been published, and among the latter, that delivered on Memorial Day, 1895, at the tomb of Lincoln in Springfield, under the auspices of Ransom Post, which was listened to by thousands, is described as one of the grandest tributes to Lincoln ever heard from any public speaker. In the same year Dr. Burnham was elected on the Board of Trustees of Drury College, Springfield, Mo., and in 1896 was made one of the Directors of the Chicago Theological Seminary. In 1897 he was elected Chaplain of the Missouri Society of the Sons of the Revolution, and in 1898 was re-elected to the same office.

On February 8, 1871, he married Cassandra V. Washburn, daughter of James Washburn of Abington, Mass., who was born in Middleboro, and Christiana Washburn Bailey, who was born in Kingston, of the Washburn-Bailey stock. Mrs. Burnham is therefore a descendant of the Washburn family on both sides and on her father's side is descended also from the Terrys of Revolutionary fame. She is a graduate of Mt. Holyoke Seminary of 1869 and was afterward associated for a time as teacher of music with what is now St. Margaret Institute, Waterbury, Conn. She is a woman of strong mind, great personal attraction and wields great influence in her position as pastor's wife. As a teacher of young men she has been remarkably successful, having at one time in the old First Church of Springfield, Mass., a class numbering over 130. She was for two years, until her removal to St. Louis, a Trustee of Mt. Holyoke College, served on the Nat. Home Missionary Board of Massachusetts, was an officer in the Woman's Branch of Foreign Missions in the same State; and is now President of the Board of the State of Missouri for Foreign Missionary work.

There have been born to Dr. and Mrs. Burnham five children, of whom two are now living: Edmund Alden, born May 3, 1872, a graduate of Amherst of 1894, from 1894 to 1897 a teacher in Smith Academy, St. Louis, and who held from 1896 to 1897 in addition the Chair of English in Eden College and Theological Seminary of St. Louis, and who is now a student of Hartford Theological Seminary; married Dec. 24, 1895, Miss Ruth Thayer, of St. Louis; and Mary Wesley, born April 12, 1874, a member of the class of 1897 of Smith College and now the wife of Mr. N. S. Kaime of St. Louis.

Dr. Burnham is one of eight brothers, five half-brothers and two own brothers, and has two half-sisters and one full sister. His brother by the same father, Geo. Washburn Burnham, was a member of the 39th Massachusetts Regiment; was captured with some 2,000 others at Petersburg, Va., August 18, 1864, and was confined until the 22nd of February of the next year. The history of that imprisonment is in the "History of Essex," page 410. At first and for a time, they (the prisoners), were allowed flour bread, but afterwards corn bread made of the corn and cob ground together. Once in four or five days, sometimes ten days, they were allowed a "bit of beef." "There were five days, not consecutive," says Mr. B., "when we had no food whatever." On one occasion our soldiers being driven to desperation by hunger, attempted to break out, but were fired upon by the guard; sixteen were killed and about forty wounded. There was no other attempt to break out. After a parole was finally ordered the soldiers were sent first to Greensborough, say fifty miles, the whole distance, except about fifteen miles, being performed on foot. The almost endless fighting at the Wilderness, the battle at Weldon railroad, and that at Petersburg, were the principal, if not the only battles, in which Mr. B. was engaged.

His brother, Leonard Burnham, was in the 48th Massachusetts Regiment, which was a nine months' regiment, with a war record as follows: He was with the regiment and followed its fortunes until April 11, 1863, when he was taken sick and went to the hospital. He remained at the hospital two months and three weeks, at the close of which term he joined the regiment before Port Hudson, on June 3d, and was with them through the remainder of that siege, also in a skirmish at Donaldsonville. He came home with the regiment and was mustered out of service September 3, 1863.

James Horace, the youngest brother, was also a member of the 39th Massachusetts Regiment. This regiment left the State September 6th, 1862, and were ordered to the defenses of Washington, where they remained until July 6th, 1863, when they joined the Army of the Potomac. Their first engagement was at Mine Run, Va., on the 29th and 30th of December, 1863, although they had had some skirmishes under Gen. Meade. At this time the command was taken by Gen. Grant. In the following spring they crossed the Rapidan, and attacked the rebel army at the Wilderness, Va. During this fight Mr. B. was

wounded in the abdomen on the right side by a rifle ball, which he carried till March 14th, 1865, when it was extracted at the Summit House hospital in Philadelphia. It was a remarkable escape, first from death by the bullet, and second from death by blood poisoning, but he was mercifully spared both. Up to the time of being wounded Mr. B. had never been away from the regiment, although he had had a typhoid fever, disqualifying him for duty some eight weeks. He never joined the regiment after the ball was extracted, and after the surrender of Lee, was discharged.

Dr. Burnham was prevented from entering the army himself by the fact of having started somewhat late in life in his studies and, by the advice of friends, was persuaded to keep on at his work, since so many of his brothers were in the ranks. But he sympathized deeply with those on the field.

Following is the full genealogy of the American family from its progenitor of Colonial days: 1. Lieut. Thomas Burnham, born England, 1623, married Mary Tuttle, 1645, died Ipswich, Mass., 1694. 2. John Burnham, born Ipswich, 1648, married, 1668, Elizabeth Wells, died 1704, his widow surviving until 1716; his tombstone is still to be seen in the old cemetery at Essex. 3. David Burnham, born October 20, 1698, married, 1711, Elizabeth Perkins, died Feb. 2, 1770. 4. Westley Burnham, born October, 1719, married, first Joanna Thornton, 1740 (d. s. p.), second, Deborah Story, 1743, died June 28, 1797; his widow dying nearly a centenarian in 1821. 5. Westley Burnham, born Chebacco, August 27, 1747, married Molly Woodbury, 1771, who died in 1830 at the age of 81, he surviving until Sept. 21, 1835. 6. Michael Burnham, born the 3d of April, 1781; died Oct. 28, 1862, married Nov. 27, 1808, Abagail Burnham, born 4th Nov., 1785; died April 6, 1828; married Nov. 19, 1828, Thirza Burnham, born March 28, 1793; died 26th, 1838; married Oct. 21, 1835, Patience Andrews, born Aug. 14, 1801; died Oct. 17, 1850; married March 23, 1859, Susan Burnham, born Nov. 25, 1795; died Apr. 23, 1883. 7. Rev. Dr. Michael Burnham, born Essex, Mass., married Cassandra V. Washburn.

CRANE, Charles Samuel, is another instance of the truth of the old adage, "blood will tell." He comes of a line that fought to make this country free; and he himself has fought — another kind of fight, it is true, but none the less worthy and noble, viz., the fight by which men build up and enrich countries by energy and business efficiency.

Among the best known men in the country, as also among the most useful, are the officials of the great railway companies. If the country is closely knit together in all its parts, East and West, North and South, forming one perfectly symmetrical, commercial whole, it is largely as the result of the pluck, enterprise and achievements of the men who preside over the great railway systems, which we justly consider the most extensive and perfect in the world. Mr. Crane, the subject of this brief sketch, is a typical railroad man of the best kind. He has worked his way up, step by step, until he arrived at his present proud position of general passenger and ticket agent of the great Wabash system. His record will bear enumeration, if only to teach afresh to youth the trite lesson that success comes only to the faithful and constant. For over thirty years Mr. Crane has been connected with railroading, and during all that time he has never swerved from his first and only business love. He has not been fickle; herein, perhaps, consists largely the secret of his success.

Charles Samuel Crane was born at Tecumseh, Lenawee County, Michigan, October 23, 1847; and received his early education at Tecumseh, graduating at the High School of that town in 1864. Immediately after graduating he began life on his own account by accepting an appointment as yard clerk with the Toledo and Wabash Railroad, at Toledo, Ohio. In this position he continued for two and a half years, when he entered, in similar capacity, the local freight office of the same railroad company. Here he served a further three years. An opportunity then offering, Mr. Crane joined the clerical staff of the Northern Transit Steamship Company; putting in two years of useful service, and acquiring information of inestimable value in the special line to which he had all along devoted himself. In 1872 he re-entered the service of the Wabash Railroad at Toledo, this time in connection with the general passenger department, in which he continued until 1880, in which year the Wabash consolidated with the St. Louis, Kansas City and Northern, making the Wabash, St. Louis and Pacific Railroad. At this juncture, Mr. Crane was promoted to the position of chief clerk in the general ticket department. This position he retained

(61)

until 1885, when he was made Assistant General Passenger and Ticket Agent, and so continued until 1889. In this year, the railroad with which Mr. Crane was for so long and honorably identified, went through another process of reorganization, and assumed its present short title of the "Wabash." Mr. Crane retained his old position in the reorganized system, until September, 1894; then fresh promotion came to him, and he was appointed General Passenger and Ticket Agent of the Wabash System; which position he still holds to-day (1898). As we have seen, Mr. Crane's record has been uniformly consistent. The fact is, he is a natural born railroad man. His tastes and his abilities and his interests are all centered in the great railroad in the service of which he has spent so many arduous and useful years. The Wabash is, we need scarcely say, one of the best conducted and most popular railroad systems of the United States, and it is so largely on account of the men who are connected with it, prominently among whom is Charles Samuel Crane, who is undoubtedly one of the most popular, energetic, efficient and successful General Passenger Agents in the West. Under his management the passenger service of the "Wabash" has attained the highest degree of merit and success.

Mr. Crane, in 1875, married Miss Jessie Beach, of Northfield, Mass., by whom he has a family of three children, Jessie B., Robert P., and Ralph L., all of whom are living.

Socially, Mr. Crane is among the leaders, and has hosts of friends. He is a member of the order of the Sons of the American Revolution, his paternal grandfather being Nathan Crane, who was a private in Captain Lyon's Company of the Second Regiment of the New Jersey (Essex County) militia.

CADLE, Henry, Secretary of the Missouri Society Sons of the Revolution, was born Muscatine, Iowa, December 25th, 1851, his parents being among the early settlers of that city. His father, Cornelius Cadle, born in New York City, was engaged in the importing and sale of mahogany and other fancy woods, previous to his removal to Muscatine, where he located in 1843, and where he built the first steam saw mill engaged in the manufacture of pine lumber and which industry has always been the leading one of the place. He continued his long residence of nearly forty-three years in Muscatine until his death in 1886; his father, also named Cornelius Cadle, was engaged in the mahogany business in New York, and with Gov. Dewitt Clinton and others organized the first free schools of New York. The mother of Henry Cadle was Miss Ruth Lamprey, previous to her marriage in 1849 to Cornelius Cadle. She was a native of Orfordville, New Hampshire, and moved to Muscatine in 1846, and died there in 1885. She was a woman of great force of character, and will ever be remembered in that city for her charitable and philanthropic work.

In 1871 Henry Cadle moved to Princeton, Missouri, where he was engaged in the lumber business until 1885, and has been a resident of Bethany, Missouri, since 1890, and is President of the Cadle Lumber Company of that town.

Mr. Cadle is an enthusiast on the subject of Patriotic-Hereditary Societies. He was admitted in 1893 a member of the Iowa Society Sons of the Revolution, there being no society of that organization in the State of Missouri, at that time, and by request of the committee on new organizations of the General Society he undertook the promotion of a society in Missouri, and succeeded so well that he organized, February 22d, 1894, in St. Louis the "Society Sons of the Revolution in the State of Missouri," with forty-eight charter members, a larger number than any other State Society had started with. The prestige thus gained has been all along maintained, and the Missouri Society is everywhere known for its influential and large membership, as well as its activity in useful patriotic work. He has been secretary continuously since the society was organized, and is also Assistant Treasurer-General of the General Society, and has devoted much time to promoting the society.

He is also the promoter of the "Society of Colonial Wars in the State of Missouri," and is the Registrar of the State Society, and Deputy-Governor General for Missouri of the General Society.

He is a member of the "Illinois Society of the War of 1812," and also a companion of the District of Columbia Commandery of the "Naval Order of the United States."

As Mr. Cadle's grandfather, Cornelius Cadle, emigrated from the parish of Westbury-on-Severn, Gloucester, England, to New York City in 1790, he therefore has no claims to membership in the Colonial and Revolutionary societies by reason of the service of any paternal ancestors, but the membership is derived from the service of the maternal ancestors who were among the early

Puritans of Masachusetts Bay Colony. Mr. Cadle has traced his maternal ancestry to the following emigrant ancestors, all of whom finally settled in the town of Hampton, New Hampshire.

Henry Lamprey (1616-1700), Edmund Johnson (1651), Thomas Marston (1615-1690), William Lane (1659-1749), Rev. Stephen Bachiler (1661-1660), Christopher Hussey (1595-1685), John Sanborn (1620-1692), Robert Tuck (1664), William Eastow (1655), Roger Shaw (1661), Thomas Ward ( ), John Knowles (1705), Francis Asten (1642), Robert Page (1604-1679). Samuel Fogg (1672), Henry Robie (1618-1688), John Mason (1696), Thomas Philbrick (1667), John Redman (1615-1700), John Cass (1675), Thomas Brewer ( ), Godfrey Dearborn (1686), Thomas Webster (bap. 1631-1715).

From his ancestor, Rev. Stephen Bachiler, descended the poet, John G. Whittier, and from the ancestor Godfrey Dearborn, descended Major-General Henry Dearborn, who commanded the American Army in the War of 1812, while from the ancestor, Thomas Webster, descended the illustrious Daniel Webster.

Mr. Cadle's membership in the Society of Colonial Wars is derived from the service of the following ancestors: —

Fifth in descent from James Johnson (1677-1752), Ensign of New Hampshire troops in Queen Anne War, 1705.

Fifth in descent from John Johnson (1694-1750) a private in Captain Week's Company, New Hampshire troops in the Queen Anne War, 1712, also private in Captain John Goffe's Company, New Hampshire troops in King George's War, 1746.

Seventh in descent from Thomas Marston (1615-1690), Representative to the General Court of New Hampshire, 1680-1684.

Eighth in descent from Roger Shaw (1661), Representative to the General Court of Massachusetts 1651, '52, '53.

Sixth in descent from Samuel Fogg (1659-1717), a soldier in King William's War from Hampton, New Hampshire, 1694.

Eighth in descent from William Eastow (1655), Representative to the General Court of Massachusetts, 1644, '48, '49.

Sixth in descent from William Lane (1659-1749), a soldier in King William's War from Hampton, New Hampshire, 1694.

Eighth in descent from Christopher Hussey (1595-1686) a member of the Council of New Hampshire, 1680; Representative to the General Court of Massachusetts, 1658-60.

Seventh in descent from Nathaniel Batchelder, Sr. (1630-1710), Representative to the General Court of New Hampshire, 1695.

Sixth in descent from James Fogg (1668-1760), a soldier in King William's War, from Hampton, New Hampshire, 1694.

Sixth in descent from Ephraim Marston (1655-1742), Representative to the General Court of New Hampshire, 1697-1709, '15, '16, '17.

Sixth in descent from John Redman (1672-1718), a soldier in King William's War from Hampton, New Hampshire, 1694.

Seventh in descent from John Redman, Sr., Representative to the General Court of New Hampshire, 1722.

Eighth in descent from Robert Page (1604-1679), Representative to the General Court of Massachusetts, 1657-68.

Sixth in descent from Stephen Batchelder (1676-1748), a soldier in King William's War, from Hampton, New Hampshire, 1694.

Seventh in descent from John Sanborn (1620-1692), Ensign and Lieutenant of the Military Company of Hampton, New Hampshire, 1679.

Mr. Cadle's membership in the Society Sons of the Revolution is through the service of the following ancestors: —

Greatgrandson of Daniel Lamprey, Private in the Company of Captain Henry Elkins, Colonel Enoch Poor, 2nd Regiment New Hampshire foot, 1775.

Greatgrandson of Ezra Johnson, Private in the Company of Captain Philip Putnam, Colonel Nahum Baldwin's Regiment of New Hampshire troops, raised for the reinforcement of the Army in New York, 1776; was in the battle of White Plains.

Great-great grandson of Simon Lane, private in the Company of Captain Henry Elkins, Colonel Enoch Poor, 2d. Regiment New Hampshire foot, 1775.

Great-greatgrandson of John Lamprey, member of the Committee of Safety for the town of Hampton, New Hampshire, 1775.

Mr. Cadle is a member of the "Illinois Society of the War of 1812," and a companion of the District of Columbia Commandery of the Naval Order of the United States through the service of his kinsman John Cadle, who was Surgeon's Mate of the frigate " Peacock " in the War of 1812, and afterwards Surgeon of the frigate " Macedonia."

(63)

Mr. Cadle had an uncle in the Mexican War, and also three brothers in the War of the Rebellion, and he has been accepted as a member of the "Society of the Army of the Tennessee" in right of the service of his brother in the War of the Rebellion, Colonel Cornelius Cadle, late Assistant Adjutant-General of the 17th Army Corps, in case he should survive his brother. As Mr. Cadle has been represented in nearly all the wars of this country he feels that since his kinsmen have performed such good service in doing the fighting that he can well afford to monument their memory by his association with the different patriotic-hereditary societies.

FOGG, Josiah.—In England at the close of the Norman conquest in the 11th century the name Fogg appears prominently in the county of Kent. During the reign of Henry I in 1112, they settled in the town of Ashford, Kent, about 54 miles from London. During the reign of Henry IV. Sir John Fogg founded a college at Ashford about the year 1450 and died there in 1490. His son John Fogg also resided at Ashford and left a will dated November 4, 1533.

Near the north side of the cathedral of Canterbury the figure of Sir Thomas Fogg with a shield of arms was carved in wood and hung on the pillar of the nave next to his place of burial. William Fogg was buried here in 1525. Sir John Fogg was a member of Parliament in the reign of King Edward IV. The ancestor of Josiah Fogg was Samuel Fogg, who was born in Kent county, England, in 1613, came to America in 1638 and settled in Hampton, New Hampshire. He was granted a tract of land which has remained occupied by his descendants to the present time and is now owned by John H. Fogg. Seth Fogg, a son of Samuel, was born in 1667; he took an active part in the colonial wars from 1695 to 1708. His son, Samuel Fogg the second, was born in 1700, and he took part in the colonial war of 1745. Josiah Fogg, son of Samuel the second, was born in 1728, was a lieut.-colonel in the New Hampshire militia and went with his regiment in the Rhode Island expedition under Gen. Sullivan in 1777-8. Stephen Fogg, the son of Josiah, was born in 1759 and served as private three years in the New Hampshire militia. He was at the battle of Bunker Hill; his last enlistment took him to the banks of the Hudson, where he was when the war closed. He drew a pension from 1832 to his death in 1842. His son, Isaiah Fogg, was born in 1789 and died in 1877.

Josiah Fogg, our subject, son of Isaiah Fogg, was born in the town of Centre Harbor, county of Belknap, New Hampshire, April 7, 1820. His father was a successful farmer and was enabled to give his son a good common school and academic education. On his mother's side Josiah Fogg was of good English and Revolutionary stock. His great-great-great grandfather, John Libby, was born in England in 1602, came to America in 1630 and settled near Portsmouth, New Hampshire, in the State of Maine. His great-great-grandfather, Anthony Libby, was born in Maine in 1649. His great-grandfather, Jacob Libby, was born in Hampton, New Hampshire, in 1695. His grandfather, Abraham Libby, was born in Rye, New Hampshire, December 29, 1739, died in Chester, New Hampshire, August 3, 1799. Abraham Libby was a member of the Committee of Safety of the town of Rye during the War of the Revolution and was also a sergeant in a company of New Hampshire militia.

In 1840, Mr. Fogg went to Boston, where he engaged as clerk in a store for four years; during this time he often saw ex-President John Quincy Adams, and Josiah Quincy, Sr.,—Josiah Quincy, Jr., the Mayor of Boston,—Daniel Webster, Rufus Choate, Abbott Lawrence, Robert C. Winthrop. He knew well W. F. Harnden, who established Harnden's express, the first in the United States. He also knew Mr. Harnden's young country clerk, who originated the much used initials O. K.

In 1840, he saw the Cunard, the first steamer that ever crossed the ocean, enter Boston Harbor on the 23d of July, 1842. He saw the capstone of Bunker Hill Monument raised and swung into its place, and on June 17th, 1843, he attended the dedication of that monument — and listened to the eloquent oration delivered by Daniel Webster. In 1846, he started west and arrived in St. Louis, January, 1847. He took a position as hotel clerk, and so continued several years. In 1850 he subscribed towards the purchase of the lot at the corner of Broadway and Locust street, for the Mercantile Library Association, and became one of its life members.

In 1852 Mr. Fogg formed a copartnership with Mr. Theron Barnum, and leased the new Barnum Hotel, corner of Second and Walnut streets, and it became at once one of the leading hotels of the country. In 1855, Mr. Fogg was elected a trustee in

Josiah Fogg

the First Congregational Church and Society; he served consecutively twenty-one years. In 1860, the Prince of Wales with a good representation of the nobility of England, visited St. Louis and stopped at Barnum's Hotel, and when leaving the Prince personally returned thanks to Messrs. Barnum and Fogg for the excellent manner he and his party had been entertained. During the War of 1861-1865, Mr. Fogg was a consistent Union soldier. In 1862 many Confederate prisoners were brought to St. Louis. Many delicacies were supplied them by Mr. Fogg through his friendship for friends of the prisoners in St. Louis. In 1862 he was elected a director in the board of public schools and served three years; during this time the present excellent public school library was founded and greatly aided by the vote and voice of Mr. Fogg, who at once became a life member. In 1868 he was elected a director in the old North Missouri Railroad, now the Wabash, and served four years. Two leading characteristics of our subject is unselfishness and integrity. No citizen of St. Louis ever had a higher compliment paid him.

Prior to the war a charter had been granted by the Mexican Government for a railroad, to run from the city of Mexico to Laredo on the Rio Grande river, also the Texas Legislature had granted a charter for the International and Great Northern to run from Laredo to Northeast Texas, on which some work had been done. The Illinois Central Railroad was completed to Cairo and had made much money during the war and Mr. Fogg thought that road might extend from opposite Cairo through Little Rock to Northeast Texas and connect with the Texas road and thus cut off St. Louis from that rich section. To protect St. Louis from this diversion of trade, he drew up a charter called the South East Missouri Railroad Company and had it incorporated by the legislature February 17, 1865. This charter authorized the extension of the Iron Mountain Railroad to Arkansas. He asked the late Hon. Thomas Allen to become the president of the new company, and after much deliberation he consented. After much negotiation, through the suggestion and personal efforts of Mr. Fogg, Mr. Allen on the 12th of January, 1867, became the sole owner of the Iron Mountain and Cairo and Fulton Railroads, from which he made several million dollars. The city of St. Louis was benefited thereby untold millions, and Mr. Fogg never received one dollar. Had the Iron Mountain Railroad not been extended, there might not have been any cotton compress or cotton exchange in St. Louis.

Among the personal and business friends of the late James B. Eads, no one had his confidence more than Josiah Fogg. In February, 1866, Mr. Fogg was one of fifteen to subscribe twenty thousand dollars to fulfill the requirements of the Illinois and St. Louis bridge charter which enabled Capt. Eads to commence work on the great structure.

For some years prior to 1871 a controversy had existed between Livingston County, Missouri, and the Hannibal & St. Joe Railroad in regard to the ownership of nearly ten thousand acres of land located in Livingston County. The county claimed them as swamp lands and the railroad as non-swamp lands. The prospect was that a long and expensive lawsuit would be the result, as the growth of the county was retarded; the officials sent their attorney to St. Louis to see if he could find a banker or some one who would secure a settlement of the difficulty. The attorney was advised to see Josiah Fogg. He sought an introduction and explained the situation. Mr. Fogg went to Chillicothe with the attorney, and in a short time found what was wanted. He then went to Hannibal to see the officials of the railroad, and in less than thirty days the railroad was the owner and had a clear title to nearly ten thousand acres of good land in Livingston County, and the county had received into its treasury over thirty thousand dollars in cash, and all parties were satisfied. Early in 1889 Congress passed an act declaring the 30th of April of that year to be a national holiday, it being the centennial anniversary of the inauguration of Gen. George Washington, as first President of the United States. This announcement suggested to several citizens of New York, New Jersey and adjoining States the desirability of forming State societies of Sons of the American Revolution and that delegates from these State societies should meet in New York on the 30th of April, 1889, and organize a National Society Sons of the American Revolution. A committee was appointed who drew up a circular explaining the object and sent a copy to the Governor of each State and Territory asking that they have societies organized. In March of that year Hon. D. R. Francis, then Governor of Missouri, received the circular. He sent it to Josiah Fogg and authorized him to

(65)

carry out its objects. Mr. Fogg at once called a meeting of Revolutionary descendants which was well attended, and on the 23d of April a society was duly organized and a delegate appointed to attend the meeting in New York, on April 30th, to organize a National Society Sons of the American Revolution. Through the efforts of Mr. Fogg and others the Missouri society has gradually increased so that the number, character and standing of its membership places it upon a solid basis. In 1858 Mr. Fogg married Miss Josephine Brooks, a charming lady of Rome, New York. They have two children, Mary Libby Fogg and James Eads Fogg, and all reside together at their pleasant home, 3964 Westminster place.

HUGHES, Charles Hamilton, M. D., is one of the most noted descendants of the American Revolution in the State of Missouri. He comes of royal Welsh ancestry. The family in English heraldry are known as the Hughes, of Gwercles, Edeirnion, County of Merioneth, Wales. The right to a coat of arms (two lions rampant), and the motto, "God and Enough," was granted to the Hughes family in 1619, Sir Thomas Hughes, a barrister at law, being at that time knighted, having his seat at Wells, Somerset and Gray's Inn. Richard Hughes, a member of this noted family and great-grandfather of Dr. Charles Hamilton Hughes, was a hero of the Revolution who served with Gen. Washington at Brandywine, Valley Forge, and in other battles of the Revolution, and was one of the minute men sent from Virginia to defend Washington City, when it was menaced and taken by the British in the War of 1812. He came from Archerstown, County of Tipperary, Ireland, in 1760, his father, Abram Hughes, having emigrated from Wales to Ireland about 1740. Richard Hughes served as a private in the Pennsylvania Line from the beginning to the end of the War of Independence. He received what was known as depreciation pay until 1781, that is, the State patriotically guaranteed pay to its volunteers in the Revolution, to make up deficiency by depreciation of Government money; after 1781 he declined further pay or pension. He owned an estate near to and embracing Harrisburg, Pa., and an island in the Susquehannah river. He married Elizabeth Scarlet and died in Rockingham County, Va. Richard Hughes, his son, married Nancy Davis, of Virginia and emigrated to West Virginia in 1829, settling near Camden. Soon after he moved into Ohio. Printed records of his history further appear among those of the pioneers of the Ohio valley. Harvey J. Hughes, second eldest of four sons of the aforesaid, was the father of Dr. Charles Hamilton Hughes, subject of this sketch. Elizabeth R. Stocker, mother of Dr. Hughes, was the daughter of Captain Zachius Stocker, the founder of Elizabethtown, Indiana, and an officer of the War of 1812. Dr. Charles Hamilton Hughes, subject of this sketch, was born in St. Louis near where the first reservoir was built. He obtained his primary education in the private and public schools of St. Louis and at the St. Louis University, and later he attended Denison's Academy, Rock Island, Ill., and completed his literary education at the Iowa College, Iowa. Dr. Hughes turned his attention to the study of medicine at an early age and under the tutelage of physicians of eminence, — Dr. T. O'Reardon, Dr. James Thistle of Davenport, Iowa, and of Dr. Cartwright of New Orleans, one of the most eminent physicians of the South, — perfected himself for college, and graduated as M. D. from the St. Louis Medical College in 1859. As a student, he acted for one year as assistant physician in the U. S. Marine Hospital of St. Louis; after graduation he visited the leading medical colleges and hospitals of the East and soon after entered the service of the U. S. Government at the outbreak of the Civil War, as assistant surgeon, and in July, 1862, was promoted surgeon and placed in charge of the Hickory Street and McDowel's College, leading military hospitals, St. Louis, and "Stragglers' Camp." Dr. Hughes' ability during the war called forth the praise of his superior officers in the service, one of his field hospitals having been declared the most efficient in the service. He was one of the youngest full commissioned surgeons in the army. In 1865 he was mustered out, and in 1866 was elected to the medical superintendency of the Missouri State Lunatic Asylum at Fulton, Mo., where he continued five years. Dr. Hughes is considered one of the ablest expert neurologists and alienists in America. In 1876, at the International Medical Congress at Philadelphia, he read the first American contribution before a public association on "Simulation of Insanity by the Insane," being then and still regarded, the first systematic treatise on this subject in the literature. His contributions since then have been too numerous to mention. Principally among these are his

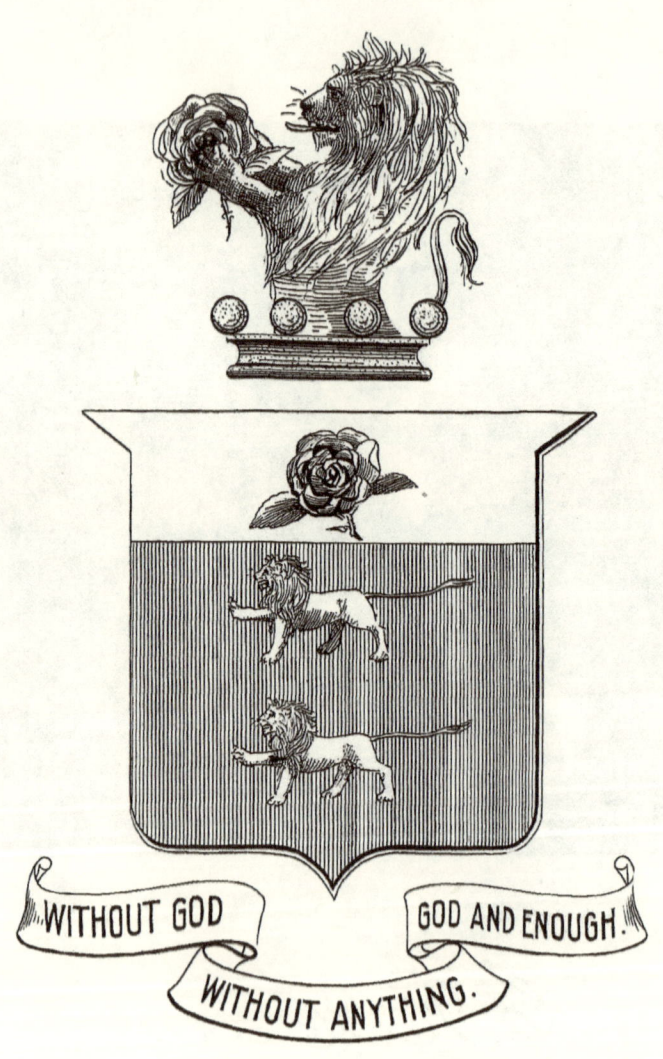

HUGHES.

contributions to psychiatry and neurology, which have acquired cosmopolitan recognition in his profession. He has besides edited and published for nineteen years "The Alienist and Neurologist," a journal of great value to the medical profession, devoted to scientific, clinical and forensic psychiatry and neurology. Since 1890, Dr. Hughes has been professor of psychiatry, diseases of the nervous system and electrotherapy and president of the faculty of Barnes Medical College. He is a member of the American Neurological Society; the Mississippi Valley Medical Association, having been its president in 1891; president of the Neurological section of the Pan-American College of 1893; vice-president of the Medico-Legal Congress of 1892; vice-president of the International Congress of 1873; a member of the St. Louis Medical Society, Missouri State Medical Society, a member of the judicial council of the American Medical Association and president of the Section on Neurology of the same association. He is also an honorary member of the Chicago Academy of Medicine, and of the British-Medico Psychological Society, and corresponding member of the New York Medico-Legal Society. He is a man of recognized literary as well as scientific ability and his financial prosperity has been commensurate with his professional success. This record is taken from the "National Encyclopædia of American Biography," "Stone's Biography of Eminent American Physicians and Surgeons," "Old and New St. Louis," and other printed records.

HOLMAN, John Beriah. Among the names of the heroes of the War of Independence, whose memory, whether as soldiers in the ranks or in command, should be held in everlasting honor by those who have inherited the fruits of their victory over tyranny and oppression, and who are indebted to their heroism for their glorious heritage of citizenship in the greatest Republic in the world, is that of Henry Rogers, great-grandfather of the gentleman whose name heads this section of the Missouri tribute to the founders of our liberty, and who perpetuates herein the record of his ancestor's share in the achievement of our independence and the birth of a great nation. Henry Rogers was born in Morris Co., N. J., in 1752, and was in early youth when he joined the ranks of the patriots at the commencement of the struggle, enlisting in the New Jersey Militia in the fall of 1775 in Captain Morris' Company of Colonel Lord Stirling's Regiment. He bore his part with honor throughout the conflict, was lamed by a wound in the hip, and lived to enjoy for many years the freedom which he had helped to win. He was by trade a weaver and early in the century settled in Hamilton Co., Ohio, dying in Cincinnati in 1840 at the great age of 88 years, having enjoyed the pension granted by a grateful country since September 13, 1826. His only son, Henry Rogers. a member of the Pioneer Association of Ohio, still survives at the age of over 81 years. He resides near Mt. Pleasant. One of his six daughters, Jemima Rogers, became the wife of Dr. Richard McFeely, a physician descended from an old Virginian family, whose daughter, Jemima McFeely, married John B. Holman, of Oneida County, N. Y., who settled in Cincinnati, Ohio, and who was the father of the subject of this sketch. The family of Holman is one of prominence in New York State and has given its name to Holman City. John Beriah Holman, the principal representative of the family in the State of Missouri, was born in Cincinnati, Ohio, October 11, 1854, and received his early education in the public schools of his native place. On the removal of his parents to St. Louis in 1865, he entered Washington University, where he took a scientific course, and in 1871, having determined to adopt a commercial career, he entered the employ of the Iron Mountain Railroad in the general ticket office in St. Louis. Here he remained until 1874, when, although but just out of his "teens," he embarked in business for himself as a commission merchant. In 1879 he went into the real estate business, which he conducted until the opportunity of his life presented itself and his foresight enabled him to take at its flood the "tide which led on to fortune," in the purchase of the inventor's rights in a patent machine for the manufacture of boxes, with which, in conjunction with his brother, William H. Holman, he founded the manufacturing business which has since attained such large proportions, and added by his enterprise another to the many important industries which have built up St. Louis to its present commercial standing in the front ranks of the cities of the Union. In 1885 the business was incorporated as a joint-stock company with William H. Holman as president and John B. Holman as secretary and treasurer. On the death of his brother in 1891, he was elected president of the corporation which position he still holds. The plant of the concern covers a large extent of ground at the corner of Eighth and

Walnut streets and employs nearly 200 operatives. Mr. Holman is also prominent in other important business enterprises, being president of the Missouri Fire Brick Company, and one of the directors of the Vincennes Paper Co., and of the National Bank of the Republic. He is recognized as a man of weight in commercial circles, but has never sought public office. As a member of the Missouri Society of the Sons of the American Revolution, he honors the memory of his Revolutionary ancestors. In the fraternity of Free Masons, is a member of Occidental Lodge No. 163; St. Louis Chapter No. 8, R. A. M.; and St. Aldemar Commandery of Knights Templar. An accomplished amateur of photographic art, he is vice-president of the St. Louis Photographic Society, and being an ardent lover of nature as well as a keen disciple of Isaac Walton, he delights in occasionally leaving the busy haunts of commerce with his fisherman's outfit and camera as an adjunct, to travel by lake and stream, returning not only with the evanescent trophies of his skill as an angler, but also reproductions of scenery, which will, in after years, serve to awaken memories of days spent in commune with the beauties of nature.

On December 20, 1876, Mr. Holman married Frances, daughter of the late Martin W. Wash and Margaret Jane (Humphreys) Wash of St. Louis, who was the daughter of Richard Lanham J. Humphreys and Chloe Eleanor Tippet. Mr. Humphreys was born in Alabama in 1780, held plantations there until his removal to Maryland, where he died in 1845. The Wash family was one of the most noted of Louisa County, Va., where they held extensive plantations and large numbers of slaves. William Wash, great-grandfather of Mrs. Holman, fought with the patriots in the War of Independence and his uniform was long preserved in the family, and together with his striking personality, is remembered by his oldest living representative, his granddaughter, the venerable Mrs. Bradford, widow of the late Sheriff Bradford, who resides in St. Louis County, and who, notwithstanding her four-score years, still retains her faculties undimmed and a memory overflowing with recollections of the past.

Martin Wash, son of William Wash and Dorothy (Lipscomb) Wash, also served his country in the War of 1812; holding a captain's commission at the siege of Richmond, Va. Martin W. Wash, born January, 1824, son of Captain Martin Wash and Sarah (Perkins) Wash, and father of Mrs. Holman, served in the Mexican War, in Colonel Doniphan's regiment and was wounded in action. He died in February, 1883. His brother, Judge Robert Wash, was one of the most prominent figures in the early days of St. Louis, where his name is perpetuated in street nomenclature, Wash street being named in his honor. He went to St. Louis from Virginia after the War of 1812, and began the practice of law, occupied many important public positions, and was one of the Judges of the Supreme Court of Missouri. He also served in the Indian War as aide-de-camp to General Howard.

John Edgar Holman, only son of Mr. J. B. Holman, who thus inherits Revolutionary blood on the maternal as well as the paternal side, was born in St. Louis, Mo., October 22, 1877, was a graduate in the class of '95 of Smith Academy, and is now connected with his father's company.

MANSUR, Alvah. The Mansur family is another of those represented in the State of Missouri, which are entitled to be recorded in the roll of honor, as descended from patriots who offered up their all in the cause of freedom.

William Mansur, great-grandfather of the gentleman whose name, as the principal Missouri representative of the family, heads this section, was one of the pioneer settlers of Wilton (now Temple), N. H., where he purchased land in what was then a wilderness. He was originally from Dracut, Mass., where he was born about 1742, and settled in Wilton before 1772. As recorded in the town minutes of April 19, 1775, he was one of fifty-six patriots, who marched from Wilton to Cambridge, on the "Lexington Alarm." In the same records we find names of those who enlisted in the Continental service from Wilton, serving in Captain Israel Towne's company, Colonel Reed's regiment, from January 7, 1776; and among them those of William Mansur and Peter Felt, the latter another great-grandfather of our subject. Subjoined to the list occurs the following which we extract from the town minutes:—

To show the determination of the above-mentioned gentlemen in defence of the lives, liberties and properties of the inhabitants, the following resolution was agreed to:— We, the subscribers, do hereby solemnly profess our entire willingness at the risque (*sic*) of our lives and fortunes, with arms to oppose the hostile attempts of British fleets and armies against the united American Colonies whenever and to such a

Yours very truly,
Alvah Mansur.

degree as such attempts of Britain may require. Then followed the signatures of 84 inhabitants of the town, the twelfth on the roll being that of Peter Felt and the thirty-eighth that of William Mansur; these two, with their company, formed part of the garrison of Ticonderoga when Burgoyne with his batteries forced its evacuation on the night of July 5, 1777.

An extract from the census of Wilton of 1775 shows the spirit of the inhabitants as exemplified in the return of the family of William Mansur, thus: Males under 16 yrs., 5; males from 16 to 50 yrs. and not in ye army, 1; females, 2; guns, 1; gunpowder, ¾ lb.

By his wife, Isabella Harvey, whom he had married at Dracut, Mass., William Mansur had a numerous family, among whom he died peacefully in 1814, leaving behind him the record of a man who had done his duty to his country and to his fellow-man. His son, Stephen Mansur, who was born at Wilton, Dec. 18, 1773, married Hannah, daughter of Peter Felt, who was his father's comrade in arms, and survived to the patriarchal age of over 91 yrs., dying at Wilton, May 11, 1865. His son, Alvah Mansur, father of our subject, was born March 25th, 1801, at Wilton, married, March 11, 1829, Elizabeth Wood of Littleton, Mass., and settled at Lowell, where he engaged in woolen manufacture, and became prominent in the early history of that city; he died there, November 1, 1840, his widow surviving him until Sept. 5, 1862.

Their son, Alvah Mansur, our subject, now one of the foremost citizens of St. Louis, was born in Lowell, Mass., December 5, 1833. He was educated at the public schools of his native place and at Phillips Academy, Andover. At the age of 20 yrs. he went to New York where he remained for three years employed in the wholesale hardware business; he then emigrated West to Moline, Ill., where he engaged in the same business until 1859, in the spring of which year, being smitten with the prevailing "gold fever," started for Pike's Peak, Colorado, teaming across the plains, then principally inhabited by Indians and overrun by countless herds of buffalo.

From the Rocky mountains he returned in the fall of the same year to Moline, where he made an engagement with John Deere, the pioneer plow manufacturer of the West, with whom he remained until the outbreak of the Civil War, when he assisted in raising a company in response to President Lincoln's first call for troops. The numbers offering being largely in excess of the call, this, with many other organizations, was not accepted by the Government; but on the second call for service for three years, was mustered, into Company H, 19th Illinois Infantry and attached to the Army of the Cumberland.

At the end of his first year's service he was commissioned First Lieutenant, and during his three years campaigning, a great part of which was on detached duty, he participated in many of the stirring episodes of the war. In 1864 he returned to Moline, but feeling averse to settling down after the excitement of army life, he went to Colorado where he spent some years in mining with fair success.

In 1869 he went to Kansas City and forming a partnership with his former employer, entered into the agricultural implement business under firm name of Deere, Mansur & Co., and in 1874 established a branch of the same concern in St. Louis.

In 1889 he retired from the Kansas City business and purchasing his partner's interest in the St. Louis branch, organized, in conjunction with his brother-in-law, Mr. L. B. Tebbetts, the Mansur and Tebbetts Implement Co., now among the largest general dealers in farm implements and machinery in the West, of which Mr. Mansur is President. He is also principal owner and Vice-President of the Deere and Mansur Company of Moline, manufacturers of agricultural implements, organized in 1876. He is one of the directors of The St. Louis Trust Co.; a director and Vice-President of American Exchange Bank; a director of the Charter Oak Stove and Range Co.; the St. Louis Fair Association, and the Merchants Exchange.

In social life he is a member of the St. Louis, Commercial and Noonday Clubs; Ransom Post G. A. R., and the Missouri Loyal Legion. In 1865 he was married to Miss Angeline F. Blackington of Pennsylvania, who died in 1870, leaving one daughter who married Mr. George J. Kaime of St. Louis; she died November 10, 1897. Mr. Mansur is one of St. Louis' most esteemed and enterprising business men and has contributed largely towards building up the city to its present high status in the Union.

McLURE, Charles Derickson. This gentleman, whose name is known and respected far beyond the confines of the city of St. Louis, of which he is one of the foremost citizens, ranks among the descendants of Revolutionary heroes in the Missouri Society of the Sons of the American Revolution, as the great grandson of Richard

(69)

McLure, who gave over seven years of his life to the cause of his country in the War of Independence. Richard McLure, a native of Pennsylvania, in 1775, enlisted at Carlisle, Pa., in Captain William Hendrick's company of the Pennsylvania Rifle Battalion under command of Colonel Thompson. His company left Carlisle on July 15, 1775, under orders for Cambridge, Mass., where they arrived on August 8; and in September of the same year, joined the expedition against Quebec under Col. Benedict Arnold. Arriving before Quebec in December they encountered the enemy on the 31st of that month, when Captain Hendrick was slain and his men taken prisoners. In August, 1776, Richard McLure, with other prisoners, was exchanged and at once re-enlisted under General Wayne, with whom he served in Georgia, participating in the victory at Sharon and the following triumphal entry into Savannah. He remained with the colors throughout the whole of the struggle and when the arms of the patriots were crowned with the laurels of victory, received an honorable discharge at Philadelphia after over seven years service. He afterwards settled at Wheeling, Va., of which place he became an honored citizen. His son, Harmar Denny McLure, married Margaret Hills, from whom descended William Raines McLure, father of Charles D. McLure, whose name heads this section. Mr. W. R. McLure's personality was well known in St. Louis, with which city he became prominently identified and where he died in 1852. He married Margaret A. E. Parkinson, a descendant of an honored Virginian family, who still survives him and whose name requires more than a passing mention, revered as it is wherever the memories of the struggle of the Southern Confederacy survive. Born of Virginia parentage and raised on the soil of the Old Dominion it was but natural that her sympathies should be strongly enlisted with the South. Parkinson McLure, brother of Chas. D. McLure, served in the Confederate army and in 1863 found a soldier's grave.

Mrs. McLure has been for many years the president of the Society of the Daughters of the Confederacy, of which "Margaret A. E. McLure" chapter has been named in her honor. Though past her 88th year, she is still in the full enjoyment of her faculties and able as ever to take an active interest in the welfare of her fellow-beings.

Mr. Charles D. McLure was born in Carrollton, Mo., February 22, 1846. He was educated in St. Louis, and when but fifteen years of age went to the Far West, where he engaged in the freighting business in Nebraska, Colorado, Utah and Montana. His knowledge of human nature and judicious business methods enabled him to handle men and property successfully and profitably, and when, later, mining attracted his attention as offering a larger and better field for his operations, success still attended him. He was the originator of the Granite and Bimetallic Mining and Milling Companies of Montana of which he is one of the principal owners and is largely interested in many other important enterprises. In 1881, Mr. McLure returned to St. Louis, where he still resides. He is a director and Vice-President of the Lindell Railroad Company, director of the Granite Mining Company and Vice-President of the Bimetallic Company of Montana, has been for several years director of the Bank of Commerce of St. Louis, and of the St. Louis Trust Company since its organization. Ranking amongst the wealthy citizens of the State he is to be honored as the architect of his own fortunes, built up by his own honorable exertions, the fruit of which he enjoys with a conscience untroubled and a character unblemished, and his success in life has redounded not only to his own credit but to the welfare of others. On November 10, 1885, he married Miss Clara M. Edgar, daughter of T. B. Edgar, Esq. of St. Louis, whose family history is recorded on pages 41 to 46 of this edition. They have been blessed with a family of seven children to inherit the priceless record of an unsullied name. Park McLure, whose portrait at the age of seven years appears with that of his grandfather, Mr. Edgar, was born May 5, 1887; T. B. Edgar McLure, born September 8, 1888; William R. McLure, born November 10, 1889; Marianne Edgar McLure, born August 12, 1891; Clara Edgar McLure, born October 31, 1892; Charlotte McLure, born March 17, 1894; and Charles D. McLure, Jr., born December 17, 1895.

SHAPLEIGH, Alfred Lee. Another link in the chain of descendants of Revolutionary heroes, and a member of the Shapleigh family of St. Louis, Mo., who so honorably uphold, as descendants, the grandest accomplishment of American history, is one of Missouri's most prominent young business men, who undeniably exercises a powerful influence in the great business world,

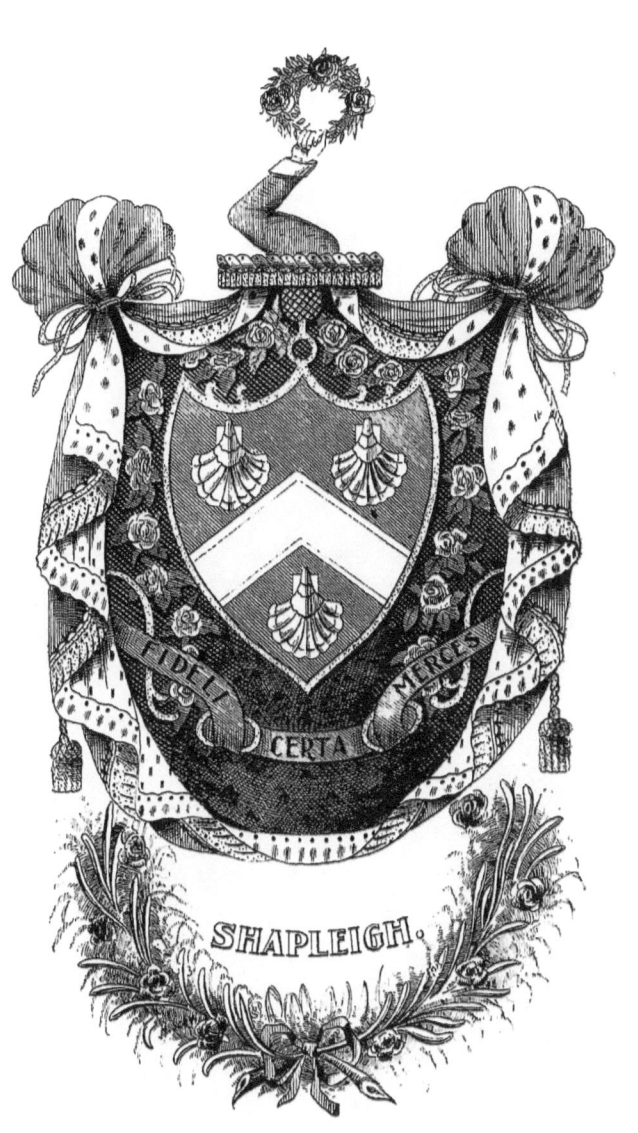

and is one of the many young men of the West whose brains and energies control many of the most important enterprises, directing the movements of vital industries, shaping the financial policy of banks, insurance and other important concerns. Our subject was born in St. Louis, Feb. 16, 1862. He was educated at the Washington University, from which he graduated with high honors in 1880. With the advantages of a liberal education he began his business career as a clerk in the Merchants Laclede National Bank; after leaving the bank he was for one year with the Hanley & Kinsella Company; later he became cashier for the Mound City Paint and Color Company. Since July, 1886, he has occupied the position of secretary of the A. F. Shapleigh Hardware Co. He is vice-president of the Merchants Laclede National Bank, director in the Union Trust Company, vice-president of the Imperial Building Company and also vice-president of the American Credit Indemnity Company of New York City. Socially he is a member of the Mercantile University, Noonday, Commercial and Country Clubs; of the former he has been its president; he is also a director of the Mercantile Library. Mr. Shapleigh married Miss Mina E. Wessel, Nov. 21st, 1888. Although Mr. Shapleigh is a very busy man he always has a courteous word and a pleasant smile for all.

LEMOINE, Edwin Spotswood, A. M., M. D. Among the descendants of the Revolutionary heroes in St. Louis, none deserve more conspicuous place in these columns than Dr. Edwin S. Lemoine, whose professional reputation and exemplary citizenship are of the highest order. He was born in Petersburg, Va., August 27, 1826. His father was John Estave Lemoine, born in Alexandria, Va., and was in later years a merchant and banker in Petersburg. His mother was Mary Bland Spotswood, born at Orange Grove, Orange Co., Va., daughter of John Spotswood and Mary Goode, of Whitby.

On the paternal side, Dr. Lemoine's grandfather was Jean Marie Le Moine, who came from Paris, France, about 1790, and located in Baltimore, Md., and Alexandria, Va., marrying the daughter of Captain Paul Estave, of East Virginia, whose godfather was Lord Dunmore, Governor of Virginia. His only brother, who never married, was an officer in the French army; the family in St. Louis have in their possession the portrait of this gentleman, and his uniform and table silver.

John E. Lemoine's children were William Haxall, John Bott Spotswood, Edwin Spotswood, Mary Goode, and Paul Estave. Mary Goode married Robert N. Nisbet, a banker in St. Louis. Dr. Lemoine is the great-grandson of John Spotswood, Captain 10th Virginia, organized February 20th, 1777. Captain Spotswood was wounded at the Battle of Brandywine, September 11th, 1777, and again at the Battle of Germantown, when he was taken prisoner October 4th, 1777. Subsequently his regiment was designated the 6th Virginia, September 14th, 1778. Captain Spotswood was exchanged November, 1780, and retired from the service February 12th, 1781. This Captain Spotswood was the grandson of Major-General Sir Alexander Spotswood, Governor of Virginia under Queen Anne. Governor Spotswood, when young, was Aide to the Duke of Marlborough at the battle of Blenheim, where he was badly wounded in the breast. His great-grandfather was John Spotswood, who was archbishop of St. Andrew's, author of the History of the Church of Scotland, and was buried in Westminster Abbey. The Archbishop's son, Robert Spotswood, was Lord President of the College of Justice of Scotland.

Major-General Spotswood was made Governor of Virginia in 1710, when thirty-four years of age. In a history of the times he is styled "A gallant cavalier, a brave and dashing soldier, a sagacious statesman, one of the most energetic, patriotic, and far-seeing that ever ruled Virginia." His son was John Spotswood, father of the above Captain John, and General Alexander Spotswood, both of whom were officers in the army of Virginia. This Alexander Spotswood married Elizabeth Washington, niece of General George Washington.

One of Governor Spotswood's daughters, Ann Katherine, was great-grandmother of Major-General Robert E. Lee. Governor Spotswood died at Annapolis in 1740, on his way to take command of the British expedition against Carthagena, and was buried at his country residence, Temple Farm, Yorktown, Va., in whose mansion Lord Cornwallis signed the "Articles of Capitulation." One branch of the family, on the Lemoine side, has in its possession an old punch bowl which was broken at the time of the capitulation. The workman who mended it, placed at the bottom of the bowl, as a clamp, a gold fish, bearing the inscription "Cornwallis and I, in captivity." Another punch bowl, belonging to Governor Spotswood, is in St. Louis and owned by Dr. Lemoine. When under nineteen years of age, Dr. Lemoine graduated from the College of New Jersey, now Princeton University, and at the present time is vice-president of the Princeton Club of St. Louis.

He attended lectures in the Richmond Medical College, and graduated from the Medical Department of the University of Pennsylvania, in 1848. He was then offered the position of "Interne" at the Blockley Hospital in Philadelphia, at that time the largest institution of its kind in the United States, but declined, and came to St. Louis in October, 1848. Dr. Lemoine was elected Secretary of the American Medical Association at its session in New York City, and served in that capacity in St. Louis in 1853 and 1854. He was sole medical director of the Life Association of America, during its entire existence. In 1890 he was a delegate from the American Medical Association to the International Medical Congress in Berlin. He has been a member of the St. Louis Medical Society from its reorganization in the 50's, till now; of the Medical Association of Missouri, and ex-president of the Obstetric and Gynecological Society; was also one of the original members of the medical staff of St. Luke's Hospital, which position he still holds, and also that of physician to the Memorial Home.

Dr. Lemoine was married in May, 1857, to Miss Kate P. Rice, daughter of Rev. N. L. Rice, D. D., of the Presbyterian Church, of which denomination Dr. Lemoine is a Ruling Elder. Their children were nine in number, two daughters dying in early infancy, and one son from accident in his sixteenth year. The eldest son, Louis Rice Lemoine, is married and living in Philadelphia; Edwin Spotswood Lemoine, married and living in New York; Katherine Bland, wife of Wm. E. Guy, of St. Louis; Eva Spotswood, Genevieve, and Adèle Goode, Lemoine.

ROBBINS, Alexander Henry. This gentleman, a Missourian by adoption, is entitled to the honor of descent from one of the Revolutionary soldiers, the perpetuation of the memory of whose services to their country is the object of this work.

The founder of the family in America, Richard Robbins, came from England in 1639, landing at Charleston and finally settled at Cambridge, Mass., and many of his descendants have contributed in no small degree to the intellectual eminence as well as the material prosperity of their country. Of this stock was Abner Robbins, great-grandfather of our subject, born at Brewster, Mass., in 1757, who, though but a youth of 18 years, showed that he inherited the same spirit which led his ancestor to face the perils of an unsettled country in order to secure the freedom of the American Colonies, being willing to sacrifice all the good that life might have in store for him on the altar of his country.

He enlisted in 1775, in Captain Harwood's company of Colonel Larned's Massachusetts Regiment, with which he served until the arms of the patriots were crowned with victory, when he returned to Brewster, where he married Judith Jenkins, a native of the same place, and where his long life, which closed in 1848, bore out the promise of his early years. His son, Alexander Robbins, who was a shipmaster and owner of coasting and fishing vessels, also drew the sword in his country's cause in the War of 1812. He married Eunice Sears, a descendant of Richard Sears, or Sayer, great-grandson of John Sayer, who was alderman of Colchester, England, early in the 16th century. He was driven from his native land by religious persecution, settled at Yarmouth, and founded a family, many of whose members, notably Captain Isaac Sears, leader of the "Sons of Liberty" in New York, bore prominent parts in the conflicts of the Revolution.

Their son, Captain Alexander Robbins, whose portrait and record appear on page 30-31 of this edition, married Eliza A. Chapman, daughter of the Reverend Nathan Chapman, of Dennis, Mass., a lineal descendant of Ralph Chapman, of England, founder of the American family, whose genealogical history was compiled and published in 1876 by Charles B. Gerard, a descendant in the sixth generation. Quoting this work:—

"Ralph Chapman was born in the parish of St. Saviour's Southwark, England, in 1615, and at the age of twenty years took passage for America on the ship 'Elizabeth' of London. On his arrival in Plymouth Colony he settled in Duxbury, where a grant of land is recorded in his name in 1640, and about 1650 became a resident of Marshfield, where he died in 1671. His oldest son, Isaac, settled in early life at Rochester, Mass., where he married the daughter of Colonel James Leonard, and in 1869 removed to Barnstable, where the records show him to have purchased a tract of land. He finally located at Yarmouth, in that part which is now the town of Dennis, where the house which he built, and the land which he acquired, has ever since been

in the possession of and occupied by his descendants."

The complete line of descent from the original settler is as follows: Ralph Chapman, born, England, 1615; married Lydia Wills of Duxbury in 1642; their eldest son, Isaac, born, Marshfield, 1647, married Rebecca Leonard, 1678, died, Dennis, 1737; their son Ralph, born, Dennis, 1695, married Elizabeth Wing of Sandwich, died, Dennis, 1779; their son John, born, Dennis, 1728, married Hannah Lincoln, died, Dennis, 1815; their son John, born Dennis, 1761, married Hannah Paine, 1788; died, Dennis, 1820; their son Rev. Nathan Chapman, born, Dennis, October 11, 1798, married, 1820, Eliza Hopkins of Brewster, who died September 11, 1883, aged over 85 years, surviving her husband exactly one month; their daughter, Eliza A. Chapman, was born at Barnstable, Mass., March 15, 1824, and married, February 25, 1845, Captain Alexander Robbins, before referred to, who attained his eightieth year on January 19, 1898. The venerable couple are residing in St. Louis, and are still young in all but years, so lightly has time laid its hand upon them. Their eldest son, Alexander Henry Robbins, whose name heads this section, was born February 22, 1846, in Boston, Mass., whence his parents removed to St. Louis in 1847.

He was educated at Davenport, Iowa, and in 1866 entered the business founded by his father, the A. Robbins Varnish Company, now a joint-stock corporation, of which he is Secretary and Treasurer.

In 1874 Mr. Robbins married Miss Annie Robinson, daughter of Mr. George W. Robinson, of St. Louis, steamboat pilot, and their union has been blessed with three children: Alexander Henry, born 1875, now a student of law at Washington University; Clarence, born 1877, now employed in his father's business; and Laura May, born 1879.

As a business man, Mr. Robbins has been active in extending the trade of St. Louis in his line of manufacture. He is one of the charter members of Alpha Council, Legion of Honor, and is also a member of the St. Louis Chess Club, of which he is past president.

He has a widely extended reputation as one of the masters of the science of chess. In his specialty as a composer of problems, his contributions have been sought for by the leading chess publications of Europe as well as America, and a selection of his compositions entitled "Robbins' Chess Problems" published some years ago, was hailed as a valuable addition to chess literature. As a tournament player he has measured his strength, and scored evenly, with some of the great masters, such as Lipschutz, Pollock, and others, against whom he was called upon to uphold the honor of St. Louis, in the tournament of the U. S. Chess Association, held there in 1889. In 1883 he was one of the players selected to meet Canada in the International Correspondence Tourney which opened in that year.

GREGG, William Henry, manufacturer, was born in Palmyra, N. Y., March 24, 1831. His father, John Gregg, having settled in that town, was married to Anne, daughter of William Wilcox, and granddaughter of Gideon Durfee, one of the first settlers of Palmyra, who had emigrated from Tiverton, R. I. He is of Scotch ancestry, and is descended from the Greggs of Aberdeenshire, the name there being spelled variously, Greg, Gregg, Greig, Grig, Griggs, Grag and Gragg. His original American ancestor was Capt. James Gregg, who, in 1690, emigrated from Ayr, Scotland, to Londonderry, Ireland, and in 1718 to New Hampshire, being one of the sixteen heads of families who settled at and founded the town of Londonderry, N. H. Maj. Samuel Gregg of Peterboro, N. H., his great-grandfather, was born in Londonderry, N. H., served in the Colonial army during a part of the French war, and took part in the Revolution as a major in the New Hampshire Militia. His brother, Col. William Gregg, was also an officer in the Continental army, and held an important command under Gen. Stark at the battle of Bennington. W. H. Gregg first came to St. Louis in 1846, after one year returning to Palmyra. In 1849 he took up permanent residence in St. Louis, where he has since resided. He was a clerk for Warne & Merritt in the hardware, woodenware, and house-furnishing business from 1850 until January 1, 1854, when he was made a partner, the firm becoming Warne, Merritt & Co. In 1856 he retired from that firm and became a member of the firm of Cuddy, Merritt & Co., owning and operating the Broadway foundry and machine shop, at that time one of the largest concerns of the kind in the country. In 1858 he retired from that firm, and formed a copartnership with John S. Dunham in the steam bakery business, and later, with Mr. Dunham and Mr. Charles McCauley, in the commission business, under the name of C. McCauley & Co., both firms being operated from the same office. In 1865, Mr. Gregg retired from business, and in 1867, with other parties, organized the Southern White Lead Company, of which he was elected president, holding the office until 1889, when the company was sold out to parties transferring it to the National Lead Company. The Southern White Lead Company was a very successful one, owning a factory in St Louis and one in Chicago, and selling its product in every State and Territory in the Union. Since 1889 Mr. Gregg has been out of business, devoting himself to travel and social life. During his business career he was a director in the Mechanics' Bank, the Mound City Mutual Insurance Co., and a member of the boards of arbitration and appeal in the Merchants' Exchange of St. Louis. He is a member of the Scotch-Irish Society; Sons of the Revolution; and Society of the Colonial Wars. In 1855, he was married to Orian Thompson, who is a descendant in the maternal line of the Lawrences of Groton, Mass. They have five children.

CATLIN, Daniel. The American family of Catlin, first represented in Missouri by the late Dan Catlin of St. Louis, father of the gentleman whose name heads this article, is descended from an ancient English family, of Norman origin, which ranked among the armigeri for many centuries. The name, like many others, has passed through numerous changes, having been variously written Cattelin, Cattelyn, Catling, Ketling, etc., and is probably derived from the Norman *Castellan* or *Chatelain*.

The founder of the family in America was Thomas Catlin, whose name appears also in Colonial records as Ketling and Catling. He was born in England, about 1612, and settled in Hartford, Conn., some time in the first-half of the 17th century. The exact date of his arrival in the colony is not known, as: (quoting Professor Edward Henry Tivining, in the Tivining Genealogy) " of the 20,000 or more, who emigrated between the years 1629 and 1640, the time of only a relatively small number can be ascertained from the passenger lists of the vessels on which they sailed. If any came after the proclamation prohibiting emigration without license (May 1, 1638), and prior to 1640, when emigration had practically ceased, it is not difficult to see why his name might not appear in the register. In the first place, although ships left England almost daily, Hotten's lists gave name of but one ship in 1638 and 1639. Further, these registers contained only the names of those who left England legally, *i. e.*, under license according to the proclamation, and doubtless thousands left secretly to avoid the oath of allegiance and supremacy and the payment of a subsidy to the Crown, as well as to escape the annoyance and disabilities which attended those who were disaffected to the Church. If he came over after 1640, in November of which year the Long Parliament assembled, he could perhaps have come without official registry."

The colonial records of Conneticut show Thomas Ketling, of Hartford, to have been successfully defendant in a case at court there on August 1, 1644. Soon after coming to Hartford, he was appointed constable of the town, a position which he held for many years. The office of constable at that time was one of the most honorable in the Colony. He held other places of trust in the Colony and town, and was repeatedly elected selectman. He was a landholder in 1646, received a portion in a division of lands in 1672, in 1684, with his son John, received a grant of ten acres from the town of Hartford and, besides, owned lands in other parts of the Colony, some of which, in South Meadow, is now in the possession of Colonel Julius Catlin. His first marriage seems to have taken place before his joining the Colony, as no record, either of the ceremony or of the births of his three children, is found. He was married a second time to Mary, widow of Edward Ermer. He died in 1690 at the age of 78 years. His only son, John, was baptized at Hartford on May 6, 1649; was made a freeman in 1665, and married July 27, 1665, Mary Marshall, by whom he had six children, of whom, Samuel, was born November 4, 1672-3, at Hartford; married (1st) January 5, 1702-3, Elizabeth Norton, by whom he had eight children; and (2nd) the widow, Sarah (Nicholls) Webster, who died without issue, December 12, 1762. He died towards the close of 1760, having passed his eighty-eighth year. His second son, Thomas, was born February 17, 1705-6; married, May 8, 1732, Abigail Bissell, daughter of Isaac and Elizabeth (Osborn) Bissell, who was born January 16, 1712, and by whom he had eight children. The third of these, Thomas, who was born June 18, 1737, at Litchfield, was destined to become one of the heroes of the War of Independence. He early entered the struggle, being commissioned Ensign on May 1, 1775. He was discharged in December of the same year, and in June,

1776, was commissioned Second Lieutenant in the Litchfield company under Captain Abraham Bradley, which formed part of six battalions ordered by the General Assembly to be raised and to march to New York, to join the Continental Army, and reinforce Washington. His company formed part of Colonel Gay's Regiment, 2nd Battalion, Wadsworth's Brigade.

In the retreat from New York, on September 15, 1776, Lieut. Catlin was taken prisoner and held by the British until near the end of the year, when he was sent to Connecticut for exchange. Among the "Wolcott Papers" is preserved a deposition which appears in the "History of the Town of Litchfield," by Hon. George C. Woodruff, published 1845, and which recites the hardships suffered by the captives.

The deposition, taken on May 3. 1777, before Andrew Adams, Esq., J. P. of Litchfield, gives this account, in substance, of the treatment of Lieut. Catlin and others by the British, viz. : —

"That he was taken a prisoner by the British troops in New York Island, September 15, 1776, and confined with a great number in close gaol for eleven days; that he had no sustenance for forty-eight hours after he was taken; that for eleven whole days they had only about two days' allowance, and that their pork was offensive to the smell. That forty-two were confined in one house, until Fort Washington was taken, when the house was crowded with other prisoners. After this, they were informed that they should have two-thirds allowance, which consisted of very poor Irish pork, and bread, hard, mouldy and wormy, made of canaille and dregs of flax seed. That the British troops had good bread. Brackish water was given to the prisoners, and he had seen $1.50 given for a common pail of water. Only between three and four pounds of pork was given three men for three days. That for near three months, the private soldiers were confined in the churches, and in one were 850. That about December 25, 1776, he and about 225 others, were put on board the "Glasgow" at New York, to be carried to Connecticut for exchange. They were on board eleven days, and kept on black coarse broken bread and less pork than before. Twenty-eight died during the eleven days. They were treated with great cruelty, and had no fire for sick or well. They were crowded between decks, and many died through hardships, ill-usage, hunger and cold." In 1777, a Thomas Catlin was voted one of a committee to purchase and provide clothing for non-commissioned officers and soldiers in the Continental Army, belonging to Litchfield. In 1780, Lieut. Thos. Catlin, of Litchfield, was appointed one of the inspectors of provisions for the army. Lieut. Catlin had assumed the responsibilities of matrimony before entering upon his military career, having married, December 25, 1763, Avis Buel, daughter of Deacon Peter and Avis (Collins) Buel, who was born January 26, 1744, and died June 24, 1807, leaving a family of six children. Her husband survived her until December 29, 1829, nearly reaching the age of ninety-three years. Their son, Levi, was born at Litchfield, November 11, 1772, and married, August 31, 1803, Anna Elizabeth Landon. He was a farmer and lived three miles southeast of Litchfield. He took a prominent part in public affairs, was a Whig in politics, and held several town offices.

He died, October 16, 1841. His son, Dan Catlin, was born at Litchfield, November, 24, 1806, and married Emily E. Merwin.

In 1844, he removed to St. Louis, Missouri, where he commenced the manufacture of tobacco, the pioneer of that industry in the State, and laid the foundation of the business which has since attained such vast proportions.

He died in St. Louis, universally respected and recognized as a citizen whose energy and enterprise had helped largely in the advancement of the city. His son Daniel Catlin, the eighth in descent from the original settler, was born in Litchfield, September 5, 1837. He commenced his education in his native place and when, in 1850, the family rejoined his father in St. Louis, he was educated in the free schools of that city. On leaving school he entered his father's business, of which he assumed the sole responsibility in 1859. In 1876 its expansion rendered incorporation desirable and it was accordingly chartered as the Catlin Tobacco Company. Mr. Catlin has also taken an active part in other enterprises of importance to the city, having been for twenty-eight years director of the State Bank, one of the founders and on the Board of Directors of the St. Louis Trust Company, Director of the Iron Mountain Mining Co., of the Art Museum, and others. In 1872, he married Miss Justina Kayser, daughter of Henry Kayser, of St. Louis, by whom he has three children: Daniel

Kayser Catlin, born March 21, 1877; Theron Ephron Catlin, born May 16, 1878, both men students at Harvard University, and Irene Catlin, born May 8, 1875. Mr. Catlin has never made himself prominent in public affairs, but has always quietly exerted his great influence in the direction of the advancement of the interests of his city and State. He has always been a liberal patron of the fine arts, and owns a fine gallery of paintings.

HUMPHREY, Frank Waterman, of St. Louis, Mo., was born in Weymouth, Massachusetts, June, 1852, and is a direct lineal descendant of that Jonas Humphrey, who departed from Wendover, Bucks, England, early in the seventeenth century, and settled in Dorchester, Massachusetts, about the year 1637. Of this early settler was born a son, also named Jonas, who established himself in Weymouth, Massachusetts, about the year 1645, and was the founder of Weymouth branch of the Humphreys, an account of which can be found in the "Humphrey Family in America," a work written by Fred K. Humphrey, M.D., in which the family records are brought down to date. The following shows the descent of the subject of this sketch: Jonas Humphrey, born at Wendover, Bucks, England, 1620; emigrated to this country and established in Dorchester, Massachusetts, 1635. Of issue of the above was Jonas Humphrey, who removed to Weymouth, Massachusetts, and founded the branch of the Humphreys of Weymouth, which has been honorably identified with the town of Weymouth since 1645 — or for rather more than two centuries and a half. Of issue of the above was the third Jonas Humphrey, born at Weymouth, Massachusetts, 1655. Of issue of the above was yet another Jonas Humphrey, born at Weymouth, Massachusetts, 1684. Of issue of the above was Samuel Humphrey, born at Weymouth, Massachusetts, 1728. Of issue of the above was James Humphrey, born at Weymouth, Massachusetts, 1754. This James Humphrey had a somewhat distinguished career. He was fitted for college at the age of eighteen, and with such excellent results that he was enabled to start as a teacher of others. His knowledge of the classics was at once wide and accurate, so that he obtained quite a reputation both as a Latinist and as a Grecian, which were regarded as rather rare accomplishments in those early Colonial days. For thirty years this ripe scholar held the highest offices in the gift of the town of which he was regarded as one of the brightest ornaments. In 1777, he married Deborah, daughter of Abel and Deborah (Loud) Tirrell, of Weymouth. He died 1819. This James Humphrey enlisted June 22, 1775, and appears with rank of private on muster and pay-roll of Captain Joseph Trufant's company, serving 6 months and 12 days. Enlisted again Jan. 1, 1776, as drummer in Captain Joseph Trufant's Independent Company, serving 4 months and 22 days. On June 5, 1776, he yet again enlisted under the same captain, Josiah Whitney's regiment, and served until December 1, 1776. Of issue of the above was Ebenezer Humphrey, born at Weymouth, 1781, and known in the family records as the "Colonel." Of issue of the above was Albert Humphrey, born at Weymouth, 1810. Of issue of the above was Frank Waterman Humphrey, the subject of this sketch, born at Weymouth, Massachusetts, June, 1852. The above particulars appear on the records of the town of Weymouth, Massachusetts, supplemented by the family records in possession of Samuel Humphrey, the son of James Humphrey.

Frank Waterman Humphrey was educated at Boston, Massachusetts. At the early age of sixteen, young Humphrey was on the lookout for a business opening. His opportunity soon came, and he commenced his career clerking in the Wool Commission house of J. C. Howe & Company, an old and wealthy concern held in the highest reputation. At the expiration of something like a year and a half he connected himself with the wholesale clothing house of Beard, Moulton & Company. Here his fidelity and ability were soon observed and rewarded by gradual promotion through every stage of the business; so that when he resigned his position in 1873, he was regarded as one of the best posted and most efficient men connected with the house.

Like every young man with energy, Mr. Humphrey was ambitious to engage in business on his own account, nor did he delay. Surveying the situation with keen and steady gaze, the embryo merchant recalled the advice — "Go west, young man." This advice, Mr. Humphrey determined to apply to his own case. So we find him at the early age of twenty-one, leaving his own great State of Massachusetts, a State which was hallowed by the remembrance of eight generations of ancestors, and turning his steps toward the growing West and the fullness of its promise. Arrived at St. Louis, Mr. Humphrey decided that he had struck the

(76)

HUMPHREY.

right location, and at once opened a retail clothing store. Business came to him from the very beginning.

In 1873, Mr. Humphrey married Miss Emma Henrietta, daughter of John M. and Catherine Walsh. She was born at South Braintree, Massachussets. Of this union four children have been born, of whom three survive, viz.: Frank Hackett (b. 1877); Brighton Walsh (b. 1879); and Adele (b. 1882), respectively. Mr. Humphrey is a man of great energy and persistency. By these qualities he has built up his considerable business, to which he devotes his constant attention. While looking after his own affairs, Mr. Humphrey takes a keen interest in all matters affecting the well-being of the community in which he himself lives and thrives. In private life he is sociable, and has gathered around him a host of warm friends.

Frank Waterman Humphrey enjoys the almost unique distinction of tracing back on the spindle side to good old Colonial and fighting Revolutionary stock no less than four times.

(1.) Through his mother Elizabeth Waterman Humphrey, daughter of Jacob (and Nabby) Bates. Jacob Bates (b. 1787) was the son of Alpheus Bates (b. 1759), of Weymouth, Massachusetts, by his marriage with Elizabeth, the daughter of Micah and Elizabeth Pratt. Alpheus Bates appears with the rank of private on the muster and pay-roll of Captain Joseph Trufant's Company, Colonel Josiah Whitney's Regiment. Enlisted first time, December 1, 1776; and served subsequently upon no less than three separate occasions, taking his final discharge, June 9, 1778.

(2.) Again, through his maternal grandmother, Nabby Lincoln (Waterman) Bates (wife of Jacob Bates), who was the daughter of David Waterman by his union with Elizabeth Lincoln (b. 1765), who was the daughter of Levi Lincoln (b. 1737–8) upon the Index to the Revolutionary War Archives, deposited at Boston, Mass. This Levi Lincoln is named with the rank of private on the Lexington Alarm Roll of Captain James Lincoln's Regiment, which marched on the alarm of April 19, 1775, from Hingham, Massachusetts. He subsequently appears with rank of First Lieutenant on muster and pay-roll of Captain Thomas Hersey's Company, Colonel Lovell's Regiment. Date of enlistment March 4, 1776.

(3.) Another strain of early Colonial and Revolutionary blood flows in the veins of Frank Waterman Humphrey through his maternal great-great-grandmother, Elizabeth Norton (b. 1743), daughter of William and Elizabeth Norton, who subsequently married Levi Lincoln of Hingham, Mass., in 1764. Elizabeth was the daughter of William Norton (b. 1718), of Hingham, the son of Captain John Norton, who married (January 12, 1715–16) Elizabeth Thaxter, daughter of Colonel Samuel and Hannah (Gridley) Thaxter. The record of these Nortons ascends to Rev. John Norton, born at Ipswich, Mass. (1651); graduated at Harvard College (1671); married Mary, daughter of Arthur and Joanna (Parker) Mason of Boston (1678); ordained colleague pastor in Hingham (1678), where he continued in the work of ministry until his death (1716).

(4.) Yet once again, Frank Waterman Humphrey traces his Revolutionary descent upon the spindle side, this time through his grandmother, Betsy (Pratt) Humphrey, the wife of Colonel Ebenezer Humphrey, the daughter of Benjamin and Betsy (Dyer) Pratt. Benjamin Pratt was born in 1756 and died 1818. Abstracts from the Record Index to the Revolutionary War Archives, deposited at Boston, Mass., show that Benjamin Pratt appears as private on Lexington Alarm Roll of Captain Jacob Goold's Company, Colonel Benjamin Lincoln's Regiment which marched on the alarm of April 19, 1775, from Weymouth and Braintree. He subsequently enlisted upon several occasions, taking his final discharge January 1, 1777.

The Humphreys of America, like their progenitors in the old country, have proved themselves a virile race, multiplying exceedingly and spreading themselves over most of the States of the Union, including Connecticut, Massachusetts, New York, Virginia, etc.

Frederick Humphreys, M. D., New York, historian of the family, in his monumental work, "The Humphreys Family," issued in 1883, states that there were at that time a total of 6,355 (recorded) descendants from Michael Humphrey, the emigrant, in the line of his youngest son, Samuel. At the same time, he gives the records of no less than 103 families claiming descent of Jonas Humphrey, of Weymouth, Mass. The historian evidently inclines to trace the American Humphreys to a common origin. That the family is one of distinction is admitted, and the deeds of its members in this republic indicate that, so far as achievements are concerned, they have not fallen short of the illustrious ancestry they claim.

To give a single illustration: of the male descendants of Michael Humphrey no less than thirty-three held high civic office prior to 1883, including two members of U. S. Congress, three State Senators and four County Court Judges; while no less than fifty-seven of them held high military titles, among them one major-general, two generals, two adjutant-generals, fifteen colonels and three lieutenant-colonels.

Summing up, at the conclusion of fifteen years of arduous labor in connection with his exhaustive work, the author of "The Humphreys Family" points out that though the records may fail to show connection yet the several branches "exhibit the distinctive family traits of character," viz.: "self-reliance," "readiness of acquisition" and "adaptation to circumstances." These traits are certainly characteristics of Frank Waterman Humphrey, who at the early age of twenty-one left the old family State of Massachusetts, to establish himself in business in the city of St. Louis, Mo., and by dint of his enterprise promptly acquired his present enviable position as head of one of the most substantial concerns in the West. The same authority has this further to say of the Humphreys: "The antiquity of the family, as such, cannot be questioned. Among the brave warriors who followed William the Conqueror from Normandy in 1066, we find Sir Robert de Umfreville, Knight, 'his Kinsman' Lord of Tours and Vian; Humphrey de Carteret, whose son, Regnaud de Carteret accompanied Duke Robert to the Holy Land; Humphrey, Lord of Bohun, who seems to have been related to the Conqueror, and whose descendants were Hereditary Constables of England; and subsequently Earls of Hereford, Essex and Northampton. There were also Humphrey of Tilleul, the Warden of Hastings Castle 1066-67; Humphrey, the King's Seneschal, killed in the storming of the Castle of Le Mans, 1073; and Humphrey, the Priest, who was living in the neighborhood of Battle Abbey prior to 1087.

"In the 'Doomsday Book,' one of the most ancient records of England, "the register from which judgment was to be given upon the value, tenure and services of lands therein described," the name 'Hunfridus' frequently occurs. There are mentioned: Humphrey, of Dover; Humphrey the Chamberlain, who held of the king lands in Leicestershire, Hampshire, Dorsetshire, Gloucestershire, etc.; Humphrey of St. Omer, 'a foreign follower of William;' Humphrey, who held of the king lands in Herefordshire; and several others. This serves to show that there were residing in different parts of England, soon after the Conquest, several bearing the name of Humphrey, some of whom had doubtless received, from the king, grants of land as a reward for their services.

"Members of the family were engaged in the crusades: Peter d'Amfreville, 1197; Le Sire d'Umfraville (related to Robert de Umfreville), and Le Sire d'Onfrei, 1091. The first-named was "a Norman noble, knight, or esquire," who bore arms which are thus described in Dansey's 'English Crusaders:' — *Argent; on eagle, sable, armed gules.* The arms borne by the other two are also there represented. Recurrence to these early dates discloses the fact that these arms borne by Humphrey families in England were brought from France by the companions of the Conqueror."

James Humphrey, the founder of the Humphreys of Massachusetts, was, as we have already seen, born in Wendover, England, in 1620, the date being fixed by a certain affidavit dated 2nd July, 1688, found in the Massachusetts archives (*Liber 129. Fol. 16*) and preserved in the State House, Boston; and confirmed by copy of an ancient warrant belonging to him, and ingrossed on parchment about eight by six inches in size, and still in possession of his descendant, in the eighth generation, Richard C Humphrey, of Dorchester, Mass., said warrant being addressed "to the Constables of Wendover, Burrough and to each of them"—and concluding "Hereof fayle not. Dated this 20th day of June, 1632, By me, Wm. Grunge." Having shown the antiquity of the Humphreys, as a family, and having traced through a period of over two centuries and a half the Massachusetts' Humphreys to the Humphreys of Wendover, in the county of Buckinghamshire, England, the further question here arises as to identity of these English Humphreys. There can be no doubt but that these Humphreys of Wendover, Bucks, England, were members of a cadet branch of the Humphreys of Farnham Royal of the same county of Bucks, England. Such has been the uniform family tradition, and, when a family can trace its ancestry in direct line for over two hundred and fifty years, such traditions are entitled to consideration, especially when we recall to mind the troublous times and the laxity in keeping

J. W. L. Slavens
& Grand Children

written records at a period when writing itself was regarded as a monopoly of the learned.

The Coat of Arms of the Buckinghamshire Humphreys — Humphrey (Umfrevile) Farnham Royal, Buckinghamshire, and Northumberland, England — are as follows: (Temp. William the Conqueror) gu. a cinque-foil arg., within an orle of eight cross-crosslets or. Crest: — out of a mural crown or., an eagle's head erm, Motto: — Cœlestem spero coronam.

SLAVENS, James W. L., was born in Putnam County, Indiana, August 3, 1838. His great-grandfather, John Slaven, a Scotch-Irish Protestant, settled in Virginia in early life, where he raised a large family. His son, Isaiah Slavens, the grandfather of the subject of this sketch, served in the Revolutionary War, and soon after its close, having married a Miss Stuart, of Maryland, he removed to Kentucky, and for a time engaged in surveying. Three of his sons having enlisted in the War of 1812, he determined to join them, and immediately volunteered and served out the term of his enlistment. He died in Putnam County, Indiana, aged eighty-six years. Hiram B. Slavens, the father of James, was born in Montgomery County, Kentucky, in 1802. He acquired a good education for the times, and for several years taught school in his native county. He removed to Putnam County, Indiana, in 1827, where he entered land on which he resided the rest of his life, engaged in farming. In 1829 he married Sarah Holland, daughter of William Holland. She was born and raised in Bath County, Kentucky. Her ancestors came from England and Scotland to Virginia. Her mother's maiden name was Susannah Grant. Hiram Slavens was widely known as a good citizen and an earnest friend of education. He gave active aid in the foundation of Asbury University, of Indiana.

James worked on his father's farm until he was old enough to attend college, when he entered the Indiana Asbury University, and taking a classical course he graduated with high honor in 1859. After his graduation he was married to Miss Mattie McNutt, a daughter of Collin and Mary McNutt, of Douglas County, Illinois, and immediately moved upon a tract of land which he bought in Douglas County, Illinois, there remained one year, getting his land fenced and securing a tenant. In the meantime he gave considerable attention to the study of law, which he prosecuted exclusively the ensuing year, and in the spring of 1861 began the practice in Tuscola with William McKenzie. He soon after enlisted in the 73rd Illinois Regiment United States Volunteers, and was commissioned quartermaster of the regiment, but soon after getting into the field was detailed into the subsistence department, where he continued until the close of the war, serving the last year on the staff of Major-General George H. Thomas, and was mustered out of the service in July, 1865.

He removed to Kansas City in the fall of 1865, living for a short time at Independence, and in the spring of 1866 began the practice of law at Kansas City with his brother, L. C. Slavens. He was elected Treasurer of Kansas City in the spring of 1867, and in the spring of 1868 formed a copartnership with E. W. Pattison and William Epperson in the beef and pork packing business. They built that season the first packing house in Kansas City where Jacob Dold & Sons' house now is, in West Kansas City — and in the fall of that year they packed four thousand five hundred head of cattle, which was the beginning of the large beef packing business for which Kansas City has become celebrated. The following year he became associated in the packing business at Kansas City with J. C. Ferguson and others, of Indianapolis, and built the brick packing house now occupied by Morris & Butt.

In political faith Mr. Slavens is a Republican, though never taking an active part in politics. He was elected Mayor of Kansas City on the Republican ticket in 1877 and was afterwards Mayor of Westport. He is a Mason, a Good Templar, and a member of the Methodist Episcopal Church. He was a lay delegate to the general conference of that church held in Baltimore in 1876. Mr. Slavens is one of the most enterprising and public-spirited citizens of Kansas City.

SLAVENS, Luther Clay, was born in Putnam County, Indiana, August 13, 1836. His parents were born and reared in Kentucky; his grandparents in Virginia. His great-grandfather, John Slaven, was born in the north part of Ireland and came to this country before he was twenty-one years old. He was in Pennsylvania for a while, but soon settled in that part of what was then Augusta County, Va., which is now Rockingham County. He married Elizabeth Stuart, of Scotch descent. While they resided in Rockingham County, there were born to them ten children — seven sons and three daughters. Several years before the Revolutionary War the ancestor John, and his family, removed to that part of Augusta County which is now Higland County, Va., and with two other families, settled on the headwaters of Jackson river, about six miles from Monterey. These three families were the first white people who settled in that valley. Here they obtained fine land. John Slaven's farm is still owned by his descendants, having remained in the family more than one hundred and twenty-five years.

The ten children, which John and Elizabeth Slavens took with them to this farm, all lived to be grown, and raised families of their own. They were as follows: William and Daniel, who settled in Tennessee; Reuben and Henry, who settled in Ohio; Isaiah, who settled in Kentucky; John, who settled on the Greenbrier river, in what is now called Pocahontas County, West Va.; and Stuart, who remained on the old farm. Of the daughters, Comfort, married a Higgins, Naomi, married a Galford, and Elizabeth, married Abraham Ingraham. Of the seven sons, three, *i. e.*, William, John, and Isaiah, served in the Revolutionary War. Isaiah was the grandfather of the subject of this sketch. He married Martha Stuart, after the war, resided a while in Greenbrier County, Va., and moved to Montgomery County, Ky., about 1792. From that State he went into the War of 1812, as he said, to take care of three of his sons, who had enlisted.

The father of the subject of this sketch was Hiram B. Slavens, who was born in Montgomery County, Ky., in 1802. He settled in Putnam County, Indiana, in 1827, and was married to Sarah Holland in 1829. Her parents were Virginians, of English and Scotch descent. Luther C. Slavens was reared on a farm. He was educated at Indiana Asbury University (now Depauw), graduating in the classical department in 1858, and in the law department in 1860. He was married in January, 1861, to Sallie B. Shelby, a daughter of Isaac Shelby, of Tippecanoe County, Indiana. Her grandfather, David Shelby, served in the Revolutionary War before its close, enlisting when only sixteen years old. His father was also named David, and was a brother of Gen. Evan Shelby, a revolutionary soldier, who was the father of Gen. Isaac Shelby, of Kentucky.

In the spring of 1866, the subject of this sketch settled in Kansas City, Missouri, where he continued the practice of the law, and justly ranks as one of the ablest lawyers at the bar. He is a man of strong character, great self-reliance, and possessed of a clear, logical mind. In 1889 he was appointed city counselor of Kansas City. The relations between the city and the waterworks company then supplying the city with water, had become complicated, and the company supposed it had matters in such shape that it could hold the works perpetually.

It was owing to Mr. Slavens' thorough investigation, and clear presentation of the situation in his legal opinions to the common council, and to the measures advised by him, that the city was enabled to obtain the ownership of the water-works, though this result was accomplished only after several years of litigation — during all of which time Mr. Slavens was retained by the city as one of its counsel, though he held the office of city counselor but one year.

When the city acquired the water-works, both he and John C. Gage, who was one of the leading counsel in the water-works litigation, consented to serve for a time, as members of the Board of Public Works, whose duty it was to operate the waterworks on behalf of the city. Their object was, not only to start the management of the water-works along prudential and conservative lines, but also to keep it out of city politics. This was successfully accomplished as long as they were on the board.

Mr. Slavens' first vote for President was cast for Abraham Lincoln; and while he has generally voted the Republican ticket for President, he has been independent in local elections, voting for the best man, regardless of politics. He is opposed to the gold standard, high protective tariff, and trusts; and might now be called a free-silver Republican. Both he and his wife are members of the M. E. Church, as were their parents.

TWISS, Stephen Prince. This gentleman, as a descendant of one who bore no unimportant part in his day in the councils of those who founded our liberties, is here recorded as one of those who honors himself in honoring his ancestry, and it can well be said of him that he has preserved unsullied the bright escutcheon which he inherited.

His great-great-grandfather, Amos Singletary, was elected to the Provincial

Luther Clay Slavens.

Congress from Sutton, Worcester County, Mass., on February 1, 1775, and was thus one of the counselors of the people when the first gun, whose echoes have not yet ceased to reverberate in the world, was fired in the cause of liberty, on the green at Lexington on the memorable nineteenth of April, 1775. That he retained the confidence of his constituents in that critical period, is proven by the fact that he was elected, on May 31, of that year, delegate from Sutton to a Provisional Congress at Watertown, on May 29, 1776, Representative from Sutton to the General Assembly, and re-elected in 1777-8-1780-1-3. His name also appears on the committee for Worcester County, appointed to raise men for the invasion of Canada. He closed an honored life at Sutton where he had so long enjoyed the confidence of the people. His daughter, Mehitable, married Peter Jennison, a descendant of English settlers, whose daughter Lucy married James Twiss. Their son, James Jennison Twiss, married Elsie Prince, parents of our subject.

Stephen Prince Twiss was born in Charlton, Worcester County, Mass., on May 2, 1827. He passed his early years on the paternal farm, and received such educational advantages as were afforded by the country schools of those days. From a father of no mean mental caliber he inherited the judicial mind which, in later life, raised him above his fellows, and with a character, purified by the healthy moral atmosphere of a typical New England home, and moulded by the teachings of a Christian mother, he was well armored for the struggles of life.

After attending the country school and between terms working on the farm, he went to Southbridge to learn the trade of a carpenter; but, was fortunately diverted from that course by an injury to his hand. In September, 1845, he entered Leicester Academy, where he studied for five years, supporting himself in the intervals between school sessions by manual labor and teaching in the public schools. Thus, in study, manual labor, school teaching for three winters and, for a short period, employment in the store of his uncle, Stephen Prince, of Boston, the years passed until an overruling Providence directed him in the course in which his life was destined to run.

In May, 1850, he entered Dane Law School, at Harvard University, where he took his degree in 1852; and in March, 1853, he was admitted to the Bar of his native State. He commenced practice in the city of Worcester, where he soon made his mark; being elected in 1856 to the State Legislature. In 1863 he served in the city council and was later appointed city solicitor, which position he held for two terms.

At the breaking out of the Civil War, he raised a part of a company for service by authority of the city government of Worcester, which was, however, not mustered in. In November, 1865, he removed to Kansas City, where he continued the practice of his profession. Here he was soon selected for honors by the Republican party; and in 1872, was elected to the House of Representatives, to which he was re-elected in 1874 and 1876.

In 1878, notwithstanding his well-known strong Republican principles, he was appointed City Counselor by a Democratic Mayor, and his appointment unanimously confirmed by a Democratic council. His reputation as a constitutional lawyer extended beyond the confines of his city or State, and when it was recognized by the Executive that the affairs of the Territory of Utah required on the Supreme Bench a man of thorough knowledge of the Constitution and a reliable, impartial judge, who could not be swayed from a right and constitutional course by any influence which might be brought to bear upon him, Stephen Prince Twiss was chosen as the man of the hour, and in December, 1880, was appointed by President Hayes, Associate Justice of the Supreme Court of the Territory of Utah, taking the oath of office January 1, 1881, at Salt Lake City.

The wisdom of the selection was proven by the after-course of events in that Territory, then at a most critical period of its history, and the traces of his wise and impartial administration of the duties of his office, are indelibly imprinted on the judicial structure of the State. His integrity, uninfluenced by popular clamor, and his interpretation of the Edmunds law against polygamy, won him the confidence of all parties, either Mormon or Gentile, and when, at the expiration of his first term of office, he signified his intention to decline the tendered re-appointment, the feeling of respect entertained for him by all parties was shown in the following editorial expression in the *Southern Utonian*, of Beaver, Utah, which, after recapitulation of the good effects of "His Honor's" administration, stated: "If a petition signed by every person in his district will induce him to stay on the Supreme Bench in Utah, that petition can be secured." In 1885 he returned to Kansas City and resumed his law practice, which, after a few years, he relinquished for a well-earned leisure. Judge Twiss was married Feb. 16, 1870, to Miss Louisa Woodbury Clark, daughter of Rev. Nelson and Elizabeth (Gillman) Clark, of Somerset, Mass. She died in Kansas City soon after marriage; and on August 5, 1873, he married Mrs. Emmeline Bidwell, daughter of Samuel Conklin, of Tecumseh, Mich., and widow of Alonzo F. Bidwell. A child of this marriage died in infancy.

Judge Twiss has ever taken strong interest in the cause of Christian education and is President of the Board of Trustees of Kidder Institute, Caldwell County, Mo. He is a Freemason of high rank and also identified with many other social organizations. He is a member of the Society of the Sons of the American Revolution and at the last election the Kansas City Chapter honored itself as well as him by electing him President. Though past the allotted span of life, it can truly be said of him that "his eye is not dimmed nor is his natural strength abated," and it is hoped that for many years his kindly personality and imposing presence may remain familiar in the city of his adoption.

JEWETT, Erwin Scovell, is eligible to representation in this work, through the service in the cause of American Independence, of his great-grandfather, Thomas Jewett, a lieutenant in the Vermont Militia. He was born in Norwich, Conn., Aug. 17, 1736, died in Vermont, May 29, 1812.

Our subject is the grandson of Samuel Jewett and Lucy C. (Hungerford) Jewett, his wife. Samuel was born June 5, 1761, died Oct. 20, 1830. He was returned to the Vermont Legislature eighteen times. Our subject is the son of Charles Jewett and Catherine (Scovell) Jewett. Charles was born in Weybridge, Vermont, June 13, 1810; graduated at Middlebury College in 1834; where he received the degree of A. M. He went to Niles, Mich., in 1836, began the practice of law, and became one of the most learned and successful lawyers of his day. He was Prosecuting Attorney of Berren County four years; Circuit Court Commissioner four years; Judge of the Probate Court four years; and Justice of the Peace eight years. He died in Niles, Dec. 20, 1880.

Erwin Scovell Jewett was born in Niles, Mich., April 29, 1838. He was educated in the public schools of his native town, and at the Baptist College, Kalamazoo, Mich. He remained with his parents, assisting in farm work, until his twentieth year, when, in 1856, he went to California, via Isthmus of Panama, where in Yuba County he engaged in mining, until the spring of 1857, when he returned to Niles, and in the summer of same year became a clerk in the office of the Michigan Central Railroad. He then went to Galesburg, Ill., found employment as freight brakeman on the C. B. & Q. Railroad; was soon promoted to baggage man in passenger service, then to freight conductor, then to passenger conductor; all during an interval of about four years. In 1865 he accepted the position of passenger conductor on the Hannibal and St. Joseph Railroad, so continued one year, when he became passenger and ticket agent for the Hannibal and St. Joseph Railroad, Keokuk Packet Company, and the Atlantic and Mississippi Steamship Company, with headquarters at St. Louis, Mo., where he remained but a short time, the agency being closed on account of the cholera epidemic of 1866. May 15, 1867, he went to Leavenworth, Kansas, as local passenger agent for the Missouri Pacific Railroad, and in September of same year he was appointed passenger and ticket agent of that road at Kansas City, Mo., where he has resided ever since. Mr. Jewett married Amelia Virginia Cox, of Peoria, Ill., Nov. 26, 1862. Her grandfather was an officer in the Revolutionary War. They have four children, Charles, assistant ticket agent Missouri Pacific Railroad; Thomas Scovell, a paymaster in the United States Navy; Harry Erwin, assistant cashier for the Harvey Eating House Company at Kansas City, and their married daughter, Mrs. Albert E. Holmes. Mr. Jewett is a Republican in politics, and has always done all in his power to further the interests of that great party. He was a candidate for Mayor of Kansas City in 1874, and came within ninety-six votes of being elected, although the city was largely Democratic.

He has been prominently connected with the City, County and State Committees of the Republican party from the time of his residence in Kansas City. In 1886 he was appointed a member of the Examining Board of the Naval Academy, at Annapolis, Ind. Was a delegate to the National Republican Convention at Minneapolis, Minn., which nominated Benjamin Harrison for the Presidency, for a second term.

Margaret A. E. McLure

In 1890, he was elected to the Upper House of the City Council for four years; and was legislated out of office through the illegality of the extension of the city limits. In the spring of 1898 he was again elected to same position.

Very few railroad men have had so long-continued and successful experience in one city, representing the same road over 31 years, as Mr. Jewett. He has always been foremost in the ranks of those ever ready to advance the welfare of Kansas City. He and his estimable wife are prominent members of the Presbyterian church. They have an elegant home, far enough removed from the business center to insure quiet, comfort, and rest.

McLURE, Margaret A. E. — The name of McLure is well known far outside of the State of Missouri. Mrs. McLure was born at Williamsport, Washington County, Pennsylvania, March 24, 1811. The town of Williamsport may be said to have been created by her grandfather, Joseph Parkinson, who laid it out in 1792, and named it after his son, William Parkinson, the father of the subject of this sketch by his marriage with Miss Susan M. Wells. The early training of Mrs. McLure was surrounded with every care. The naturally heroic soul of the young girl bloomed in the security of a refined home, and breathed the pure reposeful atmosphere of a well ordered family. It may be supposed that it was at this critical and formative period of her life that Mrs. McLure laid in that vast fund of physical vitality, and moral and intellectual force, that she was afterwards fated to display throughout her long life, to the delight and admiration of all who had the honor of her acquaintance.

Mrs. McLure was educated at Pittsburg, at a private school of high reputation in those days and which was presided over by Professor Twyman. Here she was taught every accomplishment. In society, such accomplishments have their end and uses, but the glowing enthusiasm, the brave heart, the undaunted will power which this lady was destined afterwards to display upon the saddest, and most trying of all fields, that of civil war, were acquired in no school. Such qualities are innate, and for their full and noblest developments we must look to the home and family. Mrs. McLure describes her early career with noble simplicity as that " of a wife and mother left a young widow, I devoted myself to my children until the first gun was fired at Sumpter, since then I have given myself to the Confederate cause." Here we hear the cry of a great heart, and that heart a woman's. During the ferment attending the bitter, sad war, Mrs. McLure resided at St. Louis. Two of her sons were away, fighting for the cause, they with Robert E. Lee, held to be right; and for which William Parkinson McLure, the eldest son, was to give his life. Mrs. McLure never made any concealment as to where her sympathies were.

In the South, Mrs. McLure was received with the utmost respect and affection. After the fall of Vicksburg, the First Missouri Brigade sent Lieutenant Hall to Mrs. McLure with a courteous invitation to visit them at the parole camp of the Confederate army, encamped on the plantation of General Nathan Bryan Whitfield, at Demopolis, Alabama.

The cheery message, " The boys wish to see you," so brief and at the same time so full, went to the mother's heart. Yes, they were " her boys," for had not her own first-born son been one of them, and yielded his life for the cause? Mrs. McLure moved among the wounded as an angel of mercy, and many, who weakened and dispirited by reason of their wounds and sufferings, experienced a renewal of strength as they listened to the brave words of one who knew whereof she spoke. Mrs. McLure retained the happiest and proudest memories of her enforced visit to the South.

There she made many friends. Thus, with charming and bountiful Southern courtesy, Mrs. Whitfield said to her: " Come and be my guest until the war ends, if it ever does." An invitation thus given had an irresistible attraction for Mrs. McLure, and she visited " Gaineswood," the State residence of General and Mrs. Whitfield, where she long remained an honored thrice-welcomed guest until the war closed, when she returned to the North and from there to Philipsburg, Montana, where she joined her son, Charles D. McLure. At the venerable age of 87, Mrs. McLure still retains her noble attributes of mind and heart, nor have years robbed her of her many physical advantages. The form remains erect and her bright eyes retain their sparkle, and the firm lips and clear ringing voice proclaim the resolute soul which still rules from within the tabernacle of clay.

A visit to Mrs. McLure at her well appointed home is always a pleasure, and more a lesson and an inspiration to those who love brave souls, wherever and whatever age found. She is a Daughter of the Confederacy of St. Louis, and a lodge has been named in her perpetual honor. Her sympathies are still with the lost cause. And yet who shall say lost? Nothing is absolutely destroyed. Changed, may be, but not lost. The seed that quickens perishes, but its virtues abide in the sap of the tree. The South, glorious in the days of Washington and Jefferson — aye, and glorious in the days of Davis and Lee — is glorious to-day also; and promises even more glory in the future. With the South lost, the United States would be poor indeed, deprived as they would be of some of the best elements that go to build up a truly great nation. The security and glory of nations is not so much a question of extent of territory, as of quality of men.

The South has ever been rich in men, as is once more shown to the world in the late war with Spain. It was this quality of virile manhood that doubtless first attracted the heroic soul of Margaret A. E. McLure so irresistibly to espouse the cause of the Confederacy; if so, then it is safe to say that her last as well as her first instincts are right. Her fidelity to a cause is but fidelity to an ideal; and if woman be not faithful, what hope for man? In truth, it is such women as this venerable lady that make history heroic. It was Spartan mothers that made Sparta possible. Mrs. McLure is one of the most honored descendants of the Revolution.

McCULLOCH, Robert. Of patriotism, as of charity, it may be said: "they give twice who give promptly." If to strike for independence is ever noble, to be one of the first to rally to the call is to be eminently noble. It was because he was thus quick to respond, that we must regard as specially worthy of mention in this volume, the name of Andrew Lewis, Brigadier-General of the Continental Army, during the critical years of 1776–77. He served in the eastern parts of Virginia with headquarters at Williamsburg. This followed twenty years of constant service in Indian warfare. His statue forms one of the famous group around the Washington statue at Richmond, Va. Of this distinguished Revolutionary soldier, our esteemed fellow-citizen, Captain Robert McCulloch, is the great-great-grandson.

Captain McCulloch was born September 15, 1841, his paternal ancestry being from Amherst and Rockbridge counties, Va., and on the maternal side being from Augusta and Roanoke, Va. He lost both parents when quite young. Captain McCulloch was educated at the Virginia Military Institute at Lexington, Va., and was a cadet there in 1861, and in April of that year, as one of the corps of cadets, in obedience to orders of the Governor of Virginia, went to Richmond as an instructor in military tactics, being assigned to duty in drilling the volunteers assembling there for the terrible conflict between the two sections of the country. He continued in the Confederate service from April, 1861, to April, 1865; being first a drill-master with the corps of cadets, then a volunteer private in the Fourth Virginia Regiment, Stonewall Jackson's Brigade, at the first battle of Manassas, July 21, 1861; then an enlisted private in Company B, of the Eighteenth Virginia Infantry; then a Lieutenant of the same company; then Adjutant of the Eighteenth Virginia Infantry; and then Captain of Company B of the same regiment. This regiment was a part of Garnett's Brigade of Pickett's Division, Longstreet's Corps, Lee's Army of Northern Virginia. He was wounded five times, two of the wounds being received in Pickett's famous charge at Gettysburg on July 3, 1863, he being left lying on the field amongst the dead at the "high-water-mark" line of the Confederacy, and reported killed.

Soon after the close of the war he left Virginia, going to St. Louis and engaging in the street railway business, in which he still continues, occupying the position of Vice-President and General Manager of several different companies. His estimable wife, also a native of Rockbridge County, Va., accompanied him. She was Miss Emma Paxton, born of Revolutionary stock. They have three children: Richard, a graduate of Washington University and a civil and electrical engineer and now in charge of the street railways of Geneva, Switzerland; Roberta, a graduate of Vassar College; and Gracie, a student at Mary Institute.

WILLIAMS, Walter, of Columbia, Missouri, is the worthy descendant of one of that noble band of patriots who so valiantly fought for and assisted in achieving American Independence. His great-grandfather was John Carter Littlepage, a Captain of Virginia State troops.

Mr. Williams was born in Boonville, Missouri, July 2, 1864. He is the son of Marcus and Mary (Littlepage) Williams, both of whom were natives of Virginia. He graduated from the Boonville High School

at the age of fourteen years, learned the printer's trade in the Boonville *Topic* office, and at the age of twenty years, became editor and part owner of the Boonville *Advertiser*, the oldest Democratic newspaper in Central Missouri. In 1889 he sold his interest in the *Advertiser*, retired from its editorship, and accepted the position of bookkeeper in the Missouri State Penitentiary. Official life not being to his liking, he resigned within eight months, and accepted the editorship of the Columbia *Missouri Herald*. In 1895 he established *The Country Editor*, a monthly magazine published in the interest of newspaper men. In 1898 he became a stockholder in the Tribune Printing Company, of which Mr. Williams is Vice-President, and assumed also the editorship of the *Daily State Tribune*, published at Jefferson City by the Tribune Printing Company, which position he still holds, also that of editor of the Columbia *Missouri Herald*, and of *The Country Editor*.

Mr. Williams has contributed to various literary publications and was for two years editor of the *St. Louis Presbyterian*. He married, on June 30, 1892, Miss Hulda Harned, daughter of George Harned, of Vermont, Cooper County, Missouri. They have two children, Walter, Jr., and Helen. Mr. Williams has declined several invitations to become candidate for public office, the last being a petition signed by nearly 2,000 Democratic voters, a large majority of Boone County, to accept the office of representative. He was chosen president of the Missouri Press Association at the age of 23 years and of the National Editorial Association of the United States, before he was 28. He is a ruling elder in the Presbyterian Church, has served as moderator of the Missouri Presbytery, commissioner to the General Assembly and was chosen delegate to the Pan-Presbyterian Council of that church in Scotland by the General Assembly of the United States. He has held the presidency of the Boone County Sunday School Association and the Christian Endeavor Union. Mr. Williams is a Scottish Rite Mason. He is president of the Columbia Board of Education, president of the Missouri School Boards' Association, member of the Board of Curators of the University of Missouri, member of the Eugene Field Monument Association, chairman of the Century Club, member of the Board of Control of the Editors' Home established by the National Editorial Association of the United States. Mr. Williams was member of the building committee and chairman of the finance committee of the Columbia Presbyterian Church under the direction of which a $30,000 stone church edifice was builded in Columbia. During his presidency of the Columbia Board of Education two new school buildings have been erected at a cost of $80,000. He was chairman of the Citizens' Executive Committee which secured for Columbia the Missouri Midland Railroad upon the contribution of $20,000 bonus.

ROBERTSON, George, is the great-grandson of Joseph Robertson of Revolutionary distinction, and the son of James Register Robertson and Margaret (Barkley) Robertson, natives of Tennessee; grandson of George Robertson, a soldier of the War of 1812 and a resident of Greene County, Tenn. Joseph Robertson was born in Pennsylvania, was of Scotch-Irish descent. From Pennsylvania he, with other members of the family, settled in North Carolina, and was one of the Robertsons who took part in the battle of King's Mountain, one of the most noted fought in the South during the Revolutionary War.

James Robertson (of the same line) was one of the leaders of that courageous band who made their homes in the wilderness of Wautauga Valley, formed the Wautauga Republic (now part of Tennessee), which was the first to offer armed resistance to British oppression. (Ref. Life of Gen. James Robertson. Life of John Sevier, or the Commonwealth Builder: Ramsay's Annals of Tennessee.) Joseph Robertson, after leaving North Carolina, lived and died in Blount County, Tenn., and his son, George, was given a land warrant for his services, which he gave to James Register Robertson, his son.

The land under the warrant was located in Mahaska County, Iowa, and there George Robertson, our subject, was born, June 2, 1852. In 1867 his father located in Randolph County, Missouri, and went there with his family; here George completed his elementary education, and later attended Woods Academy at Moberly, and the State Normal, at Kirksville, Mo.

In 1872 he went to Audrain County, Mo., where he taught in the common schools for about four years, attending school at intervals. In March, 1876, he became a resident of Mexico, Mo., where he now resides, and began the study of law; and October of that year was admitted to the Bar, and opened an office in April, 1877 at which time he was elected City Attorney of Mexico, which office he held three terms.

(85)

In the fall of 1880 he was elected Public Administrator of Audrain County, and held the office one term. In January, 1885, was appointed Prosecuting Attorney of the county by Gov. John S. Marmaduke, and held that responsible office one year; making no effort to retain it as he had built up a fine practice which engaged his entire attention.

In 1886 he was appointed attorney for the Wabash Railroad; and in 1890 was appointed to same position for the Chicago & Alton, and still retains both positions.

Mr. Robertson has always been a staunch Democrat, but opposed the platform of his party as enunciated in Chicago in 1896, and was one of the delegates-at-large sent to the "Gold" Democratic Convention at Indianapolis of that year. In March, 1899, he was elected President of the Missouri Bar Association.

Mr. Robertson is a hard student, and has one of the finest private law and general libraries in Missouri. It is unnecessary to mention the professional and social standing of our subject; it is of the highest. He is an acknowledged leader of men, aggressive and courageous, and stands to-day upon the topmost rung of the ladder of success.

Mr. Robertson was married to Miss Laura Hiner, of Mexico, Mo., September, 1879. They have five children.

SHELLEY, George Madison, is entitled to representation in this work through the brave and heroic services of his great-grandfather, Beverly Stubblefield, who took part in many of the most noted and hard-fought battles of the Revolutionary War. He was commissioned Ensign in 1757; a 2nd Lieutenant, December 28, 1776; 1st Lieutenant, August 17, 1777; and Captain, June 17, 1781. He served in the Second and Sixth Virginia Regiments.

George Madison Shelley was born in Murray, Calloway County, Kentucky, May 2, 1848. He received his elementary education in the common and classical schools of Keokuk, Iowa, to which place his father's family had moved in 1849; subsequently graduating from a commercial college in Chicago, Ill., and Princeton College, New Jersey. At Princeton, he entered younger in years than any student admitted to that great institution of learning for a century. His early youth was spent in traveling in China, Australia, oriental countries, and South America, finally settling in California in the 60's, from whence he came to Missouri in 1868, locating in Kansas City, where he established himself in the dry goods business which he has continuously conducted ever since.

During his residence in Kansas City, he has served twice as its mayor, before reaching his twenty-ninth year, three times as police commissioner, and postmaster. He has been prominent in public affairs almost from the time of his arrival, repeatedly serving in the directories of railroads, banks, and various other important corporations.

Mr. Shelley is a self-made man, and has always been in the front ranks of those who have done so much toward the building up, prosperity, and progress of Kansas City.

He was married to Miss Scioto McAdow, of Chillocothe, Ohio, who is also a descendant of a Revolutionary hero of the same name. They have one child living, James M. Shelley.

GAGE, John Cutter, descends from pure English ancestry, and is of the sixth generation from John Gage, who was one of the Massachusetts company who came from England under the leadership of Governor John Winthrop, and landed in Salem on the 20th day of June, 1630. He was one of the signers of covenant of the First Church of Boston on August 27, 1630; was also one of the company of ten who, with John Winthrop, junior, were the original proprietors of Agawan, now Ipswich, Mass., from which place he went to Rowley in 1654, and from there to Bradford, Mass., where he died, March 24, 1672-3.

The line of descent from John to the subject of this sketch is as follows: Benjamin of Bradford, who married Prudence, daughter of Thomas Leavit of Rowley. He died Oct. 10, 1672. John, the son of Benjamin, born June 15, 1672, died in Bradford, Dec. 15, 1751. Married June 13, 1694, Sarah, daughter of David and Mary Hasletine. Thomas, son of John, was born Mar. 15, 1706; moved to Pelham, N. H., about 1621; was killed at Fort William Henry in the French and Indian War, Oct. 8, 1756. He married Phoebe, daughter of James and Johanna Frye, April 30, 1734. Jonathan, son of Thomas, was born at Pelham, N. H., July 5, 1735; he married Dorcas Swan of Methuen, Mass., Dec. 18, 1757. He was a soldier in the American Revolution and grandfather of our subject.

Frye Gage, son of Jonathan, was born in Pelham, N. H., in 1783; he married Keziah Cutter of the same town; to this union was born John Cutter Gage, in the town of Pelham, N. H., on the 20th day of April, 1835. His father was a New England farmer in comfortable circumstances. The childhood days of his son were spent at home, in the ordinary routine of the public schools, and the boys work on the farm. Such spare hours and days for play or recreation as he could indulge in from time to time, few and far between, were vividly improved by this boy of an active body and inquiring mind. At an early age he exhibited evidence of more than ordinary scholarship and ability, and was placed in Phillips Academy in Andover, where he prepared for college. In 1856 he graduated from Harvard College. Almost immediately upon graduation he wisely determined what his life business should be, and entered the law office of Abbott & Brown, in Lowell, Mass., who occupied a position in the front ranks of the foremost lawyers in Massachusetts. Here his assiduous industry and fidelity of purpose attracted the firm to such an extent that he was soon intrusted with some of the most important and difficult of the office work, which he always performed with care and accuracy, thereby acquiring the respect and confidence of not only his preceptors, but of their clients and others interested in the business of the office.

In 1858 he was admitted to the bar in Boston, Mass., Judge Morton presiding. Having some idea of the "Great West" and its boundless fields and innumerable opportunities he determined to take his chances and "grow up with the country." Leaving what seemed to him the crowded East, he soon found himself in St. Louis, where, within a very short time, he was admitted to the Missouri Bar. He remained there but a brief time, going to Kansas City, and planted himself and took deep root in the virgin soil of the then frontier town, at "the mouth of the Kaw." The town at that time was full of lawyers, of everybody and everything, and then had, perhaps, 5,000 people, white and black, more than it had at any time afterwards until 1866. He soon found himself in the midst of enmities and hostilities, engendered by the recent border war, hardly closed; the agitation of the slavery question at its greatest fury, and the presidential contest of 1860; soon followed by the waste, horrors and destruction of four years of civil war.

Conservative, true to his convictions, and to duty as he understood it, he was loyal to his government and held the confidence and respect of his fellow-townsmen, during all of these years of violence and discord.

He had just commenced the practice of law when the war began, yet continued it in the local courts when there were any, and before the Federal authorities civil and military, in matters where the services of a lawyer were required and allowed. In all matters, his patience, ability and integrity commanded the respect of the Federal officers, as well as the government of the State of Missouri.

The war was closely followed by an immense immigration to Kansas City from all parts of the country, litigation on a boundless scale ensued, and the services of the lawyer were in unusual demand, and there was no one in whom the people had, generally, more confidence, both as a lawyer and citizen, than in John Cutter Gage. He was retained upon one side of most of the cases, involving personal rights and life itself, as well as of business facts, cognizable by the State and Federal Courts, from the Justice of the Peace to the Supreme Court of the United States. In this great wilderness of litigation, this young attorney was among the foremost, developing unquestioned ability, brightly illumined by the best of motives and the highest integrity of purpose. This position as a lawyer and man, in the estimation of his fellow-citizens of Missouri, Mr. Gage has always held, and still holds.

As a citizen, during forty years of residence in Kansas City, he has always been true to the best interests of the city and State. No jobber, trickster, ringster, or corrupt contractor, has ever had, or claimed to have, a friend in John R. Gage; he has never been their attorney, either in the court room or in the privacy of his office. He is, and always has been, conservative, but liberal in advocating necessary public improvements to the full extent of the ability of the tax-payer.

In politics, Mr. Gage is, and always has been, a Democrat, but never an active intense partisan. He always holds the good of the public to be a greater good than mere partisan success. He has never been an office-seeker, but once consented to be a member of the General Assembly of Missouri, and was once a member of the Board of Public Works in Kansas City; in both positions he more than met the reasonable expectations of the public and his friends; further than this he never has consented to the use of his name as a candidate for any public office, although at times the blandishments of a seat in Congress with its attending honors, and the allurements and dignity of the mayoralty have insidiously been offered to him by the political siren, in art and style most seductive, yet he has always most steadily and sturdily declined the enticing temptation.

Mr. Gage was married to Miss Ida Bailey, of Monroe County, Mo., April 26, 1886. They have two children, John Bailey and Marion Mansur Gage.

With his estimable wife and children, he lives in his well appointed home in that quiet retirement so conducive to his and their happiness.

GROSS, George Peery, was born in Van Buren, Crawford County, Arkansas, November 21, 1847. He is the son of George and Lockey (Peery) Gross, his wife. George Gross was born in Alleghany City, Pennsylvania; he removed from there to Tennessee, thence to Caledonia, Mo. During this time he was engaged with his father in the manufacture of leather; later he went to Van Buren, Ark., where he became the proprietor of a hotel and stage line. He now lives with his son, the subject of this sketch.

Jacob Strauft Gross, paternal grandfather of our subject, married Mary Morrison, of Pittsburgh, Pennsylvania; he was a prominent leather manufacturer. He served in a Pennsylvania regiment in the War of 1812, and died in Van Buren, Ark., in 1854.

Col. George Peery Gross is entitled to representation in this work through the services of his great-grandfather, Capt. John Gross, of the Third Pennsylvania Regiment, commanded by Col. Woods, and served until the end of the Revolutionary War. He enlisted as First Lieutenant and was promoted Captain.

Col. George Peery Gross attended the common schools of his native county until he reached the age of fourteen and one-half years, when he entered the Confederate Army. He first served seven months in the Indian Territory under Confederate Gen. Steele. He then joined Gen. Parson's Missouri Brigade in the winter of '63, and was detailed to act as his orderly in the Red River campaign. His brigade fought Gen. Banks' Army Corps in Louisiana, then Gen. Steele's Division of the U. S. Army, at Jenkins Ferry, Ark. Col. Gross was then transferred to Col. Wm. Brooke's Regiment of Scouts, and served with portions of that regiment in Northwest Arkansas and Southwest Missouri. He remained with them until November, '64, when he returned South through the Indian Territory to Texas, thence back to Southern Arkansas, was transferred to Gen. James S. Fagan's Escort Company, there went into winter-quarters, where he remained until the close of the war, when his company surrendered at Little Rock, Ark.

Col. Gross then returned to Van Buren, entered the mercantile business, in which he continued until 1874, when he removed to Kansas City, Mo., where he accepted the position of traveling salesman for a wholesale hardware house, so continuing twelve years.

In 1886 he took charge of the sales department of another wholesale hardware firm, where he remained until 1888. For the next ten years thereafter, he represented several of the largest Eastern manufacturers. In February, 1898, he accepted the general agency of the Covenant Mutual Life Insurance Co. of St. Louis, with headquarters in Kansas City, actively representing that company until the beginning of the Spanish-American War.

May 14, 1898, he was commissioned Colonel of the Third Missouri U. S. Volunteers. His military service and rapid promotions are very interesting. On May 26, 1891, he was commissioned Captain and Quartermaster of the Third Regiment N. G. M. Resigned December 8, 1893. December 22, 1893, was commissioned First Lieutenant, Battery B., N. G. M. Recommissioned Captain and Quartermaster of Third Regiment, March 31, 1894. Was elected Lieutenant-Colonel of the Regiment, April 10, 1895, and elected Colonel of the Regiment October 4, 1895; and then his final commission in the U. S. volunteer service. He was ordered to Jefferson Barracks, Missouri, and with his regiment was, on May 14, 1898, mustered into the U. S. service.

May 29 he was ordered to Camp Alger, Va., remained there until August 6, when he was ordered with the Second Division of the Second Army Corps, to Thoroughfare Gap, Va. He was then ordered to report to Dunn Loring, Va., to act as president of the Board of Inquiry to investigate the case between Maj.-Gen. M. C. Butler and the Third Virginia Regiment. August 20 he was ordered back to Thoroughfare Gap to take charge of his regiment.

On August 24, the Second Division, Second Army Corps, was ordered to Camp Meade, Penn., remained there until September 7, when he was ordered with his regiment to Kansas City, and was there mustered out of service November 7, 1898.

Col. Gross is liberal and broad-minded in his views, and possesses a charming personality which makes him very popular with all classes. He has a host of friends who show their appreciation of his deeds by their loyalty to him.

BACKUS, Rev. Clarence Walworth, D. D., of Kansas City (eldest son of the Reverend Jonathan Trumbull Backus, D. D., LL.D., of Schenectady, New York, and Anne Eliza Walworth, daughter of Chancellor Reuben Hyde Walworth, LL.D., of New York State, who served as Colonel and Aide to Major-General Mooers in the War of 1812, and as Adjutant-General in the battles of Sept. 6th and 11th, 1814, at the invasion of Plattsburgh, New York, and whose father, Benjamin Walworth, was Quarter-master of Colonel Nicholl's New York regiment in the War of the Revolution. "Colonel Nicholl's New York regiment belonged to General George Clinton's brigade, which formed a part of Major-General Heath's division of Washington's army in Westchester, in the autumn of 1776. When New York City was evacuated by the Americans after the battle of Long Island, General Heath was in command at King's Bridge, Westchester County, and other posts in that neighborhood.

Upon General Howe's invasion of Westchester and the consequent retreat of our forces to White Plains, Nicholl's regiment was one of the four regiments left behind temporarily to guard the retreat and to forward the stores and provisions. In their turn they followed the rest of the army, taking the Albany road nearer to the river and stopping at Dobb's Ferry, where they received their baggage, etc., from the boats on which they had been forwarded.

The final position assigned to Heath's division at the battle of White Plains was on the main road of the village to the north of the courthouse. It occupied the heights on either side, forming the left wing of the American lines. When, on the 31st of October, the American Army swung back from its first position, taking Heath's division for a pivot, Heath occupied the same ground as before.

The final attack of the British on the 1st of November, was an effort to force Heath's position, and was a complete failure. Three days later Howe's entire encampment was broken up, leaving Heath's division in possession of the village.

Benjamin Walworth was the quartermaster of his regiment, but in the engagements at White Plains he acted as adjutant to Nicholl. In July, 1779, when Brant made his raid on Minisink, Benjamin Walworth was one of the volunteer party who went in pursuit of the savages." (See "The Walworths of America"—page 106.) Mrs. Ellen Hardin Walworth, a daughter of Colonel John J. Hardin of Jacksonville, Illinois, who was killed February 23d, 1847, at the battle of Buena Vista, in Mexico, married Mansfield Tracy Walworth, a son of Chancellor Walworth; is prominent in the society of the Daughters of the Revolution, and the "Woman's National War Relief Association" during the Spanish war, 1898, and her daughter, Miss Reubena Hyde Walworth, a graduate of Vassar College in 1896, distinguished herself as a nurse at "Camp Wikoff," "Montauk Hospital," where she laid down her life for the cause. She had said, "If I cannot fight, I can nurse," and she did not lose a patient.

On his father's side, the subject of this sketch is descended from William Backus, Sr., from Norwich, England, in 1637, one of the 35 original proprietors of Norwich, Connecticut, who established the town in 1660. He is a great-grandson of Major Ebenezer Backus of the 4th Connecticut Militia; and later, of the regiment of light horse at New York in 1776, from Lebanon, Connecticut (see "Connecticut Men in the Revolution," pp. 444 and 475). He is a great-grandson, through his father's mother, Elizabeth Chester, of Colonel John Chester of Wethersfield, Connecticut, distinguished in the War of the Revolution. He was Captain of the Wethersfield Company of Connecticut Militia at Lexington Alarm, April, 1775; Captain in 2nd Regiment, Connecticut Line, Colonel Joseph Spencer, from May 1st to December 17th, 1775; Major of Colonel Erastus Wolcott's regiment, Connecticut Militia, from December, 1775, to July, 1776; Colonel, 6th Battalion, Connecticut State troops, from June 20th to December 25th, 1776. At Lexington, Bunker Hill, and Long Island. He died November 4th, 1809. (See "Heitman's Historical Register of the Officers of the Continental Army," page 122, also Rosters of the Revolution Army and Navy, United States Army.)

"Colonel Chester especially distinguished himself at the Battle of Bunker Hill at the head of his company of volunteers. According to Frothingham's History General Warren's last words were addressed to the then Captain Chester. ' Chester, 'tis past. Haste! Lead our men from the unequal fight!' Trumbull's picture of the death of General Warren gives a good portrait of Captain Chester supporting the General." "Frothingham's Siege of Boston on page 111 and 112, says — General Humphrey speaks of Chester's company as the 'Elite Corps of the Army,' and ' as such was selected to escort General Putnam and Joseph Warren, the President of the Congress, to Charlestown, on the exchange of prisoners with the British."

"H. C. Hollister's History of Connecticut, Vol. II, on page 180, states: 'Connecticut, among others, was represented by the gallant Captain Chester from Wethersfield, graceful and chivalric with his independent company of high spirited men, who had not forgotten who their grandfathers were, nor what battles they had fought, and who were worthy, almost every one, to bear a colonel's commission, and lead a regiment in the face of any army that did not more than three times outnumber them."

"Sweet's History on page 7, states: 'Chester's Company was by far the most accomplished body of men in the whole American Army."

He was appointed Colonel in 1776, and was known as "*the friend*" of Washington. He was often a Representative, and for several years Speaker of the House, and in 1778 was State Counsellor; was Judge of Probate and County Court. In 1791 Washington appointed him Supervisor of Connecticut. He was the wealthy man of his region." (Genealogy of the Chester family.)

Dr. Backus is the ninth in descent from Governor William Bradford of the Mayflower, through his great-grandmother, Elizabeth Fitch Backus and her father, Colonel Eleazor Fitch, and her great-grandfather, Rev. Samuel Whiting, and her great-great-grandparents, Rev. William Adams and his wife, Alice Bradford, the granddaughter of Governor William Bradford, of the Mayflower.

He is the eighth in descent from Governor John Haynes, and the seventh in descent from Governor Thomas Welles.

His great-great-grandfather, Ebenezer Backus, Sr., married Abigail Trumbull, sister of the first Governor, Jonathan Trumbull, of Connecticut, and his great-grandfather's sister, Eunice Backus, married the second Governor Trumbull. It is from such relationship that his father and son get their name of Jonathan Trumbull.

In connection with this it might be interesting to state that his son, Jonathan Trumbull Backus, possesses a letter that comes down to him as an heirloom, written by General Washington to the first Governor Trumbull, dated July 20, 1788, just after Virginia had voted for the Constitution. It shows that the patriots of that day were disposed to guard against entangling alliances with foreign powers, and had their trials and oppositions at home. It also shows that Washington and his counsellors did not fail to recognize the hand of Providence in transpiring events. One hundred and four years after written, the letter becomes the property of one who, on his father's side, is related to Governor Trumbull, to whom the letter is written, and on his mother's side (a fourth cousin of General Washington), is related to the one who wrote the letter.

Governor Jonathan Trumbull was a wise patriot, and when General Washington needed counsel he was often wont to turn to the Governor, saying, "Let us consult Brother Jonathan." The following clipping from a New York paper is interesting in this regard:—

"The remains of this famous war Governor of Connecticut — this 'Brother Jonathan,' whom Washington nicknamed, and whose title has since been appended to Americans everywhere — lie in the old Trumbull tomb on Lebanon's beautiful and historic green in this county. A price was set upon the head of this brave old rebel Governor by the government of Great Britain. His was a remarkable family."
* * * "He was graduated from Harvard College in 1727." * * * "In 1739 was chosen Speaker of the House of Representatives, and was constantly in offices of trust and responsibility until 1783, when after having served as Governor of Connecticut through a period of fourteen more eventful and important years than any in the history of the country, he declined re-election." "In the earliest part of the controversy between Great Britain and the American Colonies, he was ever conspicuous for his zeal and patriotism in the cause of liberty. When the war broke out he was the only one of the governors of the thirteen colonies who stood staunch in the American cause. He was a great counsellor. Washington leaned heavily upon him during those dark days and it was to the fertile resources of ' Brother Jonathan ' that he ever turned for supplies and for the sinews of war. The phrase, ' We must consult Brother Jonathan,' used by Wash-

ington when he first took command of the Continental Army at Cambridge, was so often repeated by him that it became a byword with his staff and eventually, through the army, spread all over the Union and the world. 'Brother Jonathan' then became a national generic name for Americans, even as the title of 'John Bull' is recognized in England."

Dr. Backus was born at Schenectady, New York, April 20, 1846. Graduated at Union College, 1870, Princeton Theological Seminary 1873. Was previously educated in the public schools at Schenectady, and the Pennsylvania Military Academy, then located at Westchester, Pa., since removed to Chester.

From this Military Academy he went into the army as 1st Lieutenant, 97th New York State Volunteers. He served as Aid-de-Camp on the staff of Major-General Martin D. Hardin, and also on the staff of Major-General Wesley Merritt, in the valley south of Winchester, Va., in the fall of 1864, and from Five Forks to Appomattox in the spring of 1865. He was present at McLane's, and witnessed the meeting of General Phillip Sheridan with General John Gordon, and the historic parting of Generals Grant and Lee after the surrender. He was on General Merritt's staff on the Grand Review at Washington, D. C. While on General Hardin's staff, he was stationed at Washington, headquarters at the corner of Pennsylvania avenue and Nineteenth street, not far from the White House. Through General Hardin, a lifelong friend of President Lincoln, he was personally acquainted with the President, and frequently at the White House. During this time he was also well acquainted with prominent members of the Senate and Congress and the social life of that day, to which such acquaintances led. Together with General Hardin he was a guest at City Point in the family of General Grant early in 1865. And on April 1st, 1865, the evening before the evacuation of Richmond, he spent the night at General Grant's headquarters at Dabney's Mills taking supper with the General. July 18th, 1865, after the war, he was honorably discharged with his regiment, being mustered out. He rode on the staff of General Merritt at the dedication of General Grant's monument in 1897.

He has been a minister in the "Presbyterian Church in the United States of America," since April, 1873. Settled respectively at Northville and Northampton, N. Y., at Charlestown, Princeton, N. Y., at Victor, N. Y., and at Kansas City, where under the Presbytery of Topeka, he organized the Grand View Park, and the Western Highlands, churches of Kansas City; The First Presbyterian Church of Argentine, Kansas, all of which he served as their first pastor, and for a time he was in charge of the Walrond Avenue Mission, in Kansas City, Mo. He received the degree of D. D. from the University of Omaha.

April 30, 1873, he married Susan Maria Livingston Washington, daughter of James Augustine Washington, M. D., of New York City, and his wife Anna White Constable, the granddaughter of Gilbert Livingston of Red Hook Manor House, on the Hudson. Dr. Washington was the third cousin of General George Washington, through his great-grandfather, Lawrence Washington, the uncle of General Washington.

To Dr. Backus and his wife were born five children; only one son is living, Jonathan Trumbull Backus, who graduated from the University of Omaha, in 1899.

Dr. Backus is a member of the following Societies: Loyal Legion; Sons of the Revolution; Foreign Wars (in the State of Missouri); Royal Arch Mason (New York State). Description of the Backus Arms reproduced in this volume: *Arms* — Azure, a Chevron ermine between three doves argent. *Crest* — A dove argent: *Motto*, Confido in Deo.

GENTRY, Richard, was born in Boone County, Mo., Nov. 11th, 1846. He was raised on a farm and received his earlier education in the country log schoolhouse. In 1863 he entered the Kemper School for boys at Boonville, Mo., and progressed finely with his studies until the fall of 1864. When General Price made his raid into Missouri, his army passed through Boonville, and young Gentry, at the age of 17, enlisted as a Confederate soldier, and served until the close of the war in Gen. Shelby's Brigade. On his return home he entered the Missouri State University in 1865, and was graduated in 1868, having spent his vacations at work with the civil engineers in charge of the construction of the railroad and turnpikes of Boone Co. Adopting civil engineering as a profession, his education was shaped to qualify him for it. He at once obtained a position on the surveys of the Chillicothe & Omaha R. R., and subsequently was connected with the construction of the Chicago & Alton, the Iron Mountain, and other railroads.

On Nov. 11th, 1873, he married Susan E. Butler, daughter of Martin Butler, of Callaway County, Mo., and made Mexico, Mo., his home until 1880, and engaged in banking and farming. In 1879 and 1880 he became interested in silver mining in Colorado, and promoted successfully several large mining enterprises. In 1881 he moved to Kansas City, Mo., became interested in banking and cattle ranching in Colorado, and later in 1885 invested largely in Kansas City real estate, which he sold out at handsome profits, before the decline in values began. In 1889 he was one of the organizers of the Kansas City, Pittsburg & Gulf Railroad and one of its largest stockholders; and was its first General Manager and Chief Engineer. Under his management the first three hundred miles of the road were built and put in operation and the next two hundred miles located and partly constructed. In the fall of 1895 he resigned, and disposed of his interests in the railroad; his investments having proved very successful. He possessed good judgment in all business affairs. He is fond of large undertakings, and prefers to engage in enterprises that contribute to the growth and development of the country. His business methods are straightforward and honest. He has the courage to follow his own convictions in politics and religion as well as in business. He was raised an old school Presbyterian, but in later life inclined towards Unitarianism. In politics, he was a Democrat from his youth up, but in 1896 he was so opposed to the Free Silver platform of his party that he voted the Republican ticket.

Mr. Gentry is one of the charter members of Society of the "Sons of the Revolution" at Kansas City, Mo. He is of the seventh generation of Gentrys in the United States, and every one of his ancestors seems to have at some time been a soldier in defense of his country. His father — Richard Harrison[6] Gentry — was born Oct. 15, 1812, in Madison Co., Ky., and was wounded in the Florida war, while serving as Sergeant-Major of the Regiment of Mo. Vol. His grandfather, Major-General Richard[5] Gentry born in Kentucky, Aug. 21, 1788, served under General Harrison on the lakes in 1812, was Major-General of Missouri troops in the Black Hawk Indian War and at the request of Senator Benton accepted a commission as Colonel of Mo. Volunteers in the Florida Seminole War and was killed at the head of his regiment in the battle of Okeechobee, Florida, in 1837. His great-grandfather, Richard[4] Gentry, of Kentucky, born in Albemarle Co., Va., Sept. 26, 1763, was a Revolutionary soldier, having enlisted twice before he was 18 years old, and was present at the surrender of Cornwallis at Yorktown. His next ancestor down that line was David Gentry, born about 1725, and David's father, Nicholas Gentry, was born in New Kent Co., Va., in 1697, and both were engaged in the various Colonial Indian Wars; and the first of the name in this country — Nicholas Gentry — the emigrant, came as a British soldier in Jan., 1677, to assist in settling the Bacon rebellion, and in protecting the Virginia colonists from the Indians.

Mr. Gentry's mother, Mary Wyatt Gentry, was a daughter of John Wyatt, of Missouri — a Captain under General Jackson at New Orleans — and a granddaughter of Frank Wyatt, of Kentucky, who served seven years as a Revolutionary soldier. She was also a granddaughter of Major Benjamin Sharp, of Missouri, one of the heroes of the battle of "King's Mountain," during the Revolution. He was a contributor to the *American Pioneer* in 1843, and gives most interesting accounts of pioneer and Revolutionary times, and also a graphic description of the Battle of King's Mountain.

Mr. Gentry's great-grandfather, Nicholas Hawkins, of Kentucky, was also a soldier in the Virginia line during the Revolution. He was the father of Ann Hawkins Gentry, the wife of General Richard Gentry, of Missouri, who has the distinction of being the first woman ever appointed to a Federal office in the United States. At the instance of Senator Benton upon the death of her husband in 1837, President Van Buren appointed her to keep the Postoffice at Columbia, which position she held through successive administrations for thirty years, and resigned it in 1865.

Mr. Gentry's great-grandmother, Jane Harris Gentry, born Sept. 18, 1763, in Albemarle County, Va., emigrated to Kentucky with her husband, Robert Gentry, the Kentucky pioneer, in 1786. She was the granddaughter of Major Robert Harris, member of the House of Burgesses from Hanover County, Va., in 1740, whose mother, Temperance Overton Harris, was a granddaughter of Col. Robert Overton, who commanded the "Ironsides" at the battle of Dunbar under Cromwell, during the Commonwealth.

In August, 1899, at the second family reunion of the Gentrys at Meramec Highlands, Mo., Mr. Gentry was elected President and Historian of the Gentry Family Association of the United States. The descendants of Nicholas Gentry, the immigrant, now number many thousands in the United States.

Mr. Gentry lives at 2600 Troost avenue, Kansas City, Mo., at his very comfortable home, built by himself in 1883. He is the father of six promising children: Elizabeth, Richard Hardin, Ruth, Mary, Hellen. and Martin Butler.

CRUM, Rev. John Horace, S. T. D. This gentleman is a prominent descendant of Revolutionary stock, and is the chaplain of the Society of the Sons of the American Revolution of Kansas City, Mo. He is the great-grandson of Gaun Riddell, a private in Captain Oliver's Company, Colonel Doolittle's Regiment of Massachusetts Militia. Enlisted July 29th, 1775, discharged Dec. 23, 1775. Private in Captain Lawrence Kemp's Company, Colonel Leonard's Regiment of Massachusetts; enlisted February 3, 1777, discharged April 10, 1777; was also a private in Captain Hugh McCellan's Company, Colonel David Field's Regiment of New Hampshire; to march from Colrain to Bennington; re-enlisted September 22, 1777; discharged October 18, 1777.

Our subject was born in Preston, Chenango Co., N. Y., Dec. 23, 1831. His parents removed to Onondago County, a few miles from Syracuse, when he was two years of age, where his mother died in 1840, being the eldest daughter of John Riddell. The name is also spelled Riddle by some branches of the family. His father, Ruel Crum, was a farmer. After the death of his mother our subject made his home with an uncle with whom he remained until 1849. During this time his early education was obtained at the district schools. He afterwards attended select schools in Chenango County, and himself taught in different places until 1852, at which time he entered the preparatory department of Oberlin College and graduated from the college department in 1858. He then entered the theological department of the same institution with which he was connected two years.

In 1861 he married Eliza Tilden, a relation of Samuel J. Tilden, of N. Y. In 1862 he was ordained to the ministry, and founded the first Congregational Church at Traverse City, Michigan. After resigning his pastorate at Traverse City, he spent several years in teaching, about five years being employed as professor of Latin and Greek in the Pittsburg Central High School, Pittsburg, Penn. Dr. Crum then returned to the ministry, supplying the pulpit of Plymouth Congregational Church, Pittsburg, Penn., and Alleghany City. His other pastorates have been the Congregational Church, Antwerp, N. Y; 1st Presbyterian Church, Glovesville, N. Y; 1st Congregational Church, Winona, Minnesota, and 1st Congregational Church, at Terre Haute, Indiana; from which he accepted a call to his present pastorate, the Beacon Hill Congregational Church of Kansas City, Mo.

He received the degree of A. M. from his Alma-Mater in 1861; and in 1891 Olivet College, Michigan, conferred upon him the honorary degree of S. T. D.

Dr. Crum's ancestry on his father's side was, according to the best traditions, of Scotch origin, the name originally being spelled "Crombie," afterwards abbreviated to "Crumb," and, still later, to "Crum." Some of the older members of the family still continue the spelling of the name with a "b."

On his mother's side he is also of Scotch origin. His ancestors at an early day moved from Scotland to Londonderry, Ireland, whence four brothers emigrated about 1734 to New Hampshire, from which State their descendants have scattered over New England, and pretty much all over the United States.

HUTCHINGS, Charles Frederick, born in North Barton, Tioga county, New York, May 25th, 1846. He traces his genealogy on his father's side to Thomas Hutchings, a seaman in the British navy, who at the close of the war between Holland and England, about 1680, choosing to remain in America rather than return to England, swam ashore in the night from an English ship in the harbor of New York. Isaac Hutchings, the son of said Thomas, was also a sailor. He was captured by pirates, or what he deemed equivalent, forcibly impressed as a seaman into the naval service, but escaped from the piratical ship while at anchor in Long Island Sound, by jumping overboard, and after remaining in the water for a long time, and when nearly exhausted was discovered and rescued by a boatman and his daughter. He afterwards married the daughter, and in 1725 settled on Long Island. From this couple descended the numerous families of the name now residing in Ulster, Dutchess, and other counties along the Hudson river, and in central New York. The third in

(93)

the line was also named Thomas. The fourth in the line was Jonathan or John Hutchings, the great-grandfather and Revolutionary ancestor of the subject of this sketch. He served (rank not known) in Jacobus Swartwouts' regiment in the Revolutionary War. His name appears on the muster roll, dated August 20, 1776, " of men raised and passed muster in the county of Dutchess, N. Y., for Cornelius Van ———(roll torn).

After his Revolutionary service he settled in Luzerne county, Pennsylvania, and died there August 8th, 1826. His wife was Letitia Langdon. The next in the line, also John Hutchings, was born at Esopus, Ulster county, New York, October 1st, 1778, and died March 24th, 1853. His wife's name was Abigail Dean, who was born at Stamford, Connecticut, in 1780, and died June 27th, 1837.

Our subject is also the great-grandson of Percival Ashley, of Freetown, Mass., whose name appears among a list of Revolutionary officers of the Massachusetts Militia in the 14th Co., Captain Joseph Norton, of the 2nd Bristol Co., Regiment, Col. John Hathaway's. Commissioned August 10, 1779. Percival Ashley also appears with rank of Lieutenant on muster and pay-roll of Capt Joseph Norton's Co., Col. John Hathaway's Regiment, for service at Rhode Island. Enlisted Aug. 7, 1781; marched under order of Council, July 23, 1781.

He is also the great-grandson of Levi Rounsevill, who appears with rank of Captain on Lexington Alarm; roll of Captain Levi Rounsevill's Co., which marched on the alarm of April 19, 1775, from Freetown. He also appears with rank of Captain on muster roll of Captain Levi Rounsevill's Co., Col. David Brewer's Regiment, dated Aug. 1, 1775. Enlisted April 24, 1775. Time of service, 3 months, 15 days. He also appears with rank of Captain on Company Return, Col. David Brewer's regiment, dated Roxbury, Oct. 7, 1775. On "Coat Rolls" this service shows eight months.

The grandfather, John Hutchings, served in the American Navy under both Commodores Bainbridge and Decatur in the War of 1812 and the war with Tripoli. He settled at Dryden, Tompkins County, New York, at an early day and resided there when he died. He was an aggressive and outspoken abolitionist long before the general anti-slavery agitation began and his house was the place of resort of such men as Gerritt Smith with whom he co-operated in aiding runaway slaves to gain their freedom, his grist mill and farm buildings frequently furnishing them secure places of refuge and concealment from pursuers.

The next in line, the father of the subject of this sketch, was Samuel Dean Hutchings. He was born September 11th, 1808, at Dryden, New York, and died March 27th, 1878. He studied for the law but devoted most of his time to teaching and educational pursuits. He followed the profession of a teacher in the public schools of New York for more than thirty years, during which time he prepared a system of text-books for the common schools, adopting the orthography and orthorepy of Webster instead of Walker, which was then generally employed in school books. He was only prevented from becoming the pioneer in that reform by the unexpected appearance in print of the works of Charles W. Sanders, adopting the same methods, after his manuscripts had been completed and delivered to the printer. These books in manuscript form are still preserved in the family and are quite interesting relics of the early efforts in the reform of spelling and pronunciation.

On his mother's side the subject of this sketch traces his genealogy to James Ashley, who came to Boston from England between 1639 and 1650 and afterwards removed to Freetown, Bristol County, Massachusetts, which became the seat of numerous descendants, many of whom the war records of Massachusetts show served their country in the Revolutionary War. The first of the family concerning whom definite information had been obtained is the great-grandfather Percival Ashley, who was a Lieutenant in Colonel Hathaway's Regiment in the Revolutionary War. His wife was Gabriella De Miranville, the descendant of a Huguenot family. His sons, Colonel Simeon Ashley, at one time colonel of militia and Sheriff of Bristol County, and Dr. James Ashley, an eminent physician of New Bedford, at an early day settled in Tompkins County, New York. The latter was the grandfather of the subject of this sketch. He was born at Freetown, February 3rd, 1777, and died at Caroline, New York, December 9th, 1870. He married Betsey Rounseville, who was born at Freetown in 1784 and died December 3d, 1856. She was a daughter of Levi Rounseville, a Captain in the Revolutionary Service. The Grandfather, Dr. Ashley, like the grandfather,

(94)

John Hutchings, was an ardent anti-slavery advocate. He practiced medicine continuously for more than fifty years. The neighborhood in which he lived was principally settled by Virginians, who held slaves, New York then being a slave State. Against the prejudices of these people, his principal competitor in the profession, Dr. Joseph Speed, being a large slaveholder, he resolutely advocated the unconditional abolition of slavery. He also supported with great determination the Washingtonian Temperance movement which had in view the total suppression of the sale of intoxicating liquors in tippling shops. The daughter of Dr. Ashley, Betsey Rounseville Ashley, the mother of the subject of this sketch, was born at Caroline, Tompkins County, New York, August 15th, 1815. She was married to Samuel Dean Hutchings, November 29th, 1835, and still survives at the age of 84.

The following children were born of this marriage: John Hutchings, born December 31st, 1836, died April 2nd, 1892; James Ashley Hutchings, born September 29th, 1838; Samuel Dean Hutchings, born August 16th, 1840, died July 6th, 1842; Mary Ann Hutchings, born August 16th, 1842; Betsey Amanda Hutchings, born August 8th, 1844, died Nov. 18th, 1863; Charles Frederick Hutchings, born May 25th, 1846; Simeon Ashley Hutchings, born July 20th, 1848, died July 10th, 1864; Franklin Hutchings, born October 24th, 1859.

Two of the brothers of the subject of this sketch, James Ashley Hutchings and Simeon Ashley Hutchings, served as privates in the 10th and 5th New York Cavalry, respectively, in the late War of the Rebellion. The former participated in many of the most important engagements of the war and returned at its close unhurt. The latter, Simeon Ashley Hutchings, with many of his regiment, was taken prisoner in an engagement in Virginia soon after he entered the service. Nothing further was heard from him until after the war, when his grave was discovered as No. 3112 in the National Cemetery at Andersonville, Georgia, where were buried the victims of the terrible Andersonville Prison. He was only fifteen years old at the time of his enlistment. The surviving brothers, James Ashley Hutchings and Franklin D. Hutchings, reside at Kansas City, Kansas, the latter being a prominent lawyer and City Counsellor of that city.

The subject of this sketch was educated in the common schools, in Starkey Seminary in Yates County, and the Waverly Institute in Tioga County, New York. At the commencement of the Revolution he was taking a preparatory course for Harvard University but was compelled to abandon it by reason of the enlistment of his brothers in the army, his services being, for that reason, required at home. He afterwards commenced the study of law in the office of his elder brother, John Hutchings, a prominent lawyer at Waverly, New York. The latter removed to Lawrence where he soon took rank as one of the leading lawyers of the State of Kansas and at the time of his death, in 1892, represented as counsel some of the largest corporate interests in the country.

After the removal of his brother to Kansas, the subject of this sketch resumed his law studies there for a short time, but in 1865 went to New Orleans, Louisiana, and for some time was engaged in the Educational Department of the Freedman's Bureau, but in the spring of 1866 he removed to Charlotte, Easton County, Michigan, and completed his study of the law in the office of Hon. Henry A. Shaw and was admitted to practice. He returned to Kansas in 1867, locating in Neosho County, where he soon had a successful practice. In 1872 he was elected as a member of the Kansas House of Representatives, and, though one of the youngest, was one of its most prominent members, occupying the position of chairman of the judiciary committee investigating the celebrated Pomeroy-York bribery case. He was unanimously nominated by his party at the next election for State Senator but though certain of an election declined the nomination and has ever since devoted his entire attention to the practice of the law. He located in Kansas City, Kansas in 1885, and has since been connected as counsel with much of the important litigation of that city and State. On July 14th, 1869, he was married to Larooka Thornton Kinney at Jackson, Michigan, who was born January 14th, 1850. He has three children, Charlotte Frederica, born September 2nd, 1874, Samuel Dean, born December 23rd, 1877, and Paul Ashley, born Nov. 26th, 1886.

YOST, Charles Corey, is a prominent and popular descendant of one of the patriots of the War of Independence. He is the present capable and efficient Assessor of Kansas City, Mo. Mr. Yost was born in Rochester, Indiana, Dec. 29, 1860.

His great-grandfather, John H. Yost,

(95)

was a Hessian who served under General Washington in the war which brought to America her independence. After that war he took up his residence on a farm that is now the site of Fairmount Park in the western part of Philadelphia. On that site the grandfather (Yost) of our subject was born, and lived for several years. His great-grandfather on the maternal side came to America on the "Mayflower." In 1816 the family emigrated to the wilds of Indiana, locating on the Ohio river at Madison, Jefferson County, a small town where at the time were built all the ferry and merchant steamboats that plied on the Ohio river. When twenty-five years of age Mr. Yost married Miss Sarah Staton, a member of the noted Staton family of Kentucky. They had six children, three of whom died in infancy. Three sons grew to manhood, the eldest being J. H. T., the father of our subject.

In 1848 the grandfather Yost had a desire to try his fortune in California, attracted by the discovery of gold there, and in 1849 started for the Pacific slope, with his family, making the journey in a covered wagon drawn by an old ox team, and being six months on the journey. They passed within a few miles of Kansas City. They experienced many hardships and trials on the trip and were in constant danger of being attacked by the hostile Indian tribes infesting the plains. At length they arrived at Hangtown, now Placerville, and immediately began the search for wealth. For four years the father and sons worked hard, and at last fortune favored them at Drytown, where they found a good supply of gold. At length the father's health failed and he returned with his family to Madison, Indiana, purchasing a farm at Bryantsburg, about ten miles east of Madison, where he spent his remaining days.

John H. T. Yost, the father of our subject, was born at Madison, Jefferson County, Indiana, and accompanied his parents on their emigration to California. He was married in Bryantsburg, Indiana, in 1858, to Miss Roxana Selleck, daughter of John M. and Mary G. Selleck. They had three sons and two daughters, all of whom are yet living. For a year after their marriage they lived in Brandon, Mississippi, then returned to Madison, Indiana, and two years later removed to Rochester, same State, but within another year returned to Bryantsburg.

At the first call for troops Mr. Yost bade adieu to his family and entered the Sixth Indiana Regiment and served for three years. In July, 1865, Minnie, the eldest daughter, was born, and the parents removed immediately afterward to Indianapolis, where they resided for several years, the father becoming a prominent contractor there and laying the foundation for the great water-works plant, which is still in use. Afterwards he was called to construct similar works in other large cities, including De Moines, Iowa.

Being pleased with the west, he removed with his family to Fort Scott, Kansas, in 1871, and in December, 1872, took up his abode in Kansas City. He is ranked among the foremost contractors there. They had twelve children, but ten died in infancy, The two children living are Mrs. De Vasher and the subject of this sketch.

Charles C. Yost, whose name introduces this sketch, and who is the only surviving son in his father's family, was ten years of age when his parents came to Kansas City, and since that time he has been identified with its interests. He acquired good English education, graduating at the high school when only sixteen years of age. He then entered a grocery store, where he was employed as a clerk for two and one-half years, after which he entered into partnership with L. M. Berkley, carrying on a retail and wholesale grocery. For ten years they did a large and profitable business. During the real estate "boom" of 1885-6-7 the firm invested heavily in property, and being unable to realize on their investments, with scores of others they went down when the collapse came, necessitating an assignment. Subsequently Mr. Yost organized the Yost Grocery Company, and, as its manager, successfully conducted business for four years, when he sold out, in November, 1894. Immediately thereafter he established a novelty market, known as Yost's Market, conducted on a unique and ingenious plan of his own, which proved a great success. However, he sold his store, when in the spring of 1895 he was elected City Assessor. He was also one of the projectors and organizers of the Commercial Bank, which was subsequently merged into the Metropolitan Bank.

In 1883 was consummated the marriage of Mr. Yost and Miss Hattie M. Beedle, of Johnson County, Kansas, a representative of one of the early settlers.

Mr. Yost adheres to the party which his family has supported since its organization, and which his mature judgment sanctions as the one best calculated to advance the nation's interests. He is now chairman of the County Committee and the Assessment Committee of Jackson County; a member of the County Committee, Executive Committee, and Committee on Judges, Clerks, Speakers, and Finance; and was Treasurer of the Republican Committee from 1886 to 1892. Now Treasurer of City Committee and Chairman of the Executive Committee of the Missouri Republican Club, the largest Republican organization in the State of Missouri. He is a charter member of Republican Lincoln Club, the Masonic fraternity, the Knights of Pythias society, and the Junior Order of American Mechanics, the Modern Woodman, and the Modern Brotherhood.

Though he is young in years, the life of Mr. Yost has been fraught with many changes, some of which, to natures less sanguine and courageous than his, would have been exceedingly discouraging. His is a strong nature, not easily disturbed by adversity, which has often seemed to act as an impetus for renewed effort on his part, and thus using his difficulties as stepping-stones for something higher, he has climbed steadily upward. He has the regard of all who know him, and in the discharge of his official duties has displayed a marked fitness and fidelity to the trust reposed in him.

SWENTZEL, William Edward, is one of the most prominent descendants of the patriots of the Revolution, residing in Kansas City, Missouri. He is entitled to representation in this work through the services of his great-grandfather Frederick Swentzel, who was a private in the company of Captain Jasper Yates, Colonel Matthias Slough's Battalion, Lancaster County, Pennsylvania, Associators.

William Edward Swentzel was born in Lancaster, Pennsylvania, June 9, 1847, and educated in the public schools of his native town. He is the son of Henry and Mary Walker Swentzel. His father was a cabinet-maker in Lancaster, and lived eighty years, when he died; his wife also died there, and young William Edward was deprived of both parents at the tender age of six years.

Our subject began life on his own account in Lancaster at the age of nineteen as a clerk in an insurance office, where he remained one year. He then went to Chicago, Illinois, where he was connected with an insurance company for two years. He then engaged as clerk in the real estate and loan business until 1874.

His next move was the acceptance of a clerkship in the Bank of Creston, of Creston, Iowa, and continued as such until the business was absorbed by the Lombard Investment Co. in 1882, at which time he went to London, England, where he remained three years extending the business of the Lombard Investment Co. in England and Scotland; during this time he acted as director of an English Mortgage Company, for which he is now the American agent.

At the expiration of three years he returned to the United States, and was made manager of a branch office of the Lombard Investment Co. at Sioux City, Iowa. After remaining there about three years he was elected Vice-President of the Lombard Investment Co. and moved to Kansas City, Mo., and continued as such officer until April, 1893, when he resigned.

In the fall of 1893 he started in business for himself as a financial broker, representing a large number of English and American investors, who held Western investments; in addition to this he has been extensively engaged in making new loans and supplying his different clients with securities, which bring his career up to 1899.

Mr. Swentzel was married January 14, 1880, to Miss Carrie A. Kimball, of Grafton, New Hampshire, she being a great-granddaughter of Captain Peter Kimball of Revolutionary fame. Four children have been born to this union: Maud Kimball, Edward Reed, Marguerite Livonia and Lawrence Kimball Swentzel. Mr. Swentzel is a self-made man in every respect, genial, whole-souled, and very popular for his many noble and generous qualities. He is a member of the Sons of the Revolution, Kansas City, Mo., Chapter.

GRANT, Lee Wiley, a prominent lawyer and descendant of the patriots of the Revolution, was born in St. Louis, Mo., Jan. 17, 1863; was educated in the St. Louis High School and was graduated from the Washington University, St. Louis, in 1884.

He began the study of law in 1885, was admitted to the bar at St. Louis in 1886, and entered at once upon the practice of his profession, which he has continued ever since.

Mr. Grant's father was a prominent wholesale dealer in St. Louis for upwards of thirty years, coming to St. Louis in 1850. Our subject is a member of the Masonic and Knight Templar's fraternity, and of the Sons of the Revolution.

(97)

SPENCER, Hon. Selden Palmer. Great-grandson of Israel Selden Spencer, Private in the Company of Captain John Gates, Colonel John Ely, Connecticut State troops, 1777; also, Private in the Company of Captain Worthington; Private in the Company of Captain Hungerford.

Great-great-grandson of Israel Spencer, Captain in Colonel Charles Burrall's Regiment, Connecticut troops; served at Quebec and Ticonderoga, 1776.

Great-great-grandson of Colonel Samuel Selden, Colonel of the 4th Battalion, Wadsworth's Brigade, Connecticut State troops, 20th June, 1776; wounded and taken prisoner, 15th September, 1776, and died in prison in New York City, 11th October, 1776.

SWASEY, William Albert. Great-great-grandson of Ebenezer Swasey, Private in the Company of Captain Zebulon Gilman, Colonel Stephen Evans' Regiment, New Hampshire troops, which regiment joined the Continental army at Saratoga, September, 1777.

BAKER, George Arnold. Grandson of Amos Baker, Surgeon's Mate in Colonel Bradley's Regiment, Wadsworth's Brigade, Connecticut State troops, 1776.

Grandson of Isaac Gilbert, private in the Company of Captain Elihu Kent, in the Lexington Alarm, 1775; Private in the Company of Captain Oliver Hanchett, 2d Regiment, Connecticut troops.

PRINCE, Laurence Lempriere. Great-grandson of Lemuel Benton, Major of South Carolina Militia, 1781; Lieutenant-Colonel and Colonel of Militia attached to General Francis Marion's Brigade, 1782.

Great-great-grandson of Clement Lempriere, Captain of Sloop "Commerce;" captured August 7, 1775, off St. Augustine bar,

the brigantine "Betsy," Captain Lofthouse, of London, with 111 barrels and one-half barrel and thirty small kegs of gunpowder, and after spiking the two guns of the brigantine and transferring the powder to his own vessel, arrived safely at Charleston; Commander of the South Carolina ship of war "Prosper," 1775; member of the South Carolina Legislative Assembly, 1776.

DODDRIDGE, William Brown. Great-great-grandson of Gustavus Scott, member Association of Freemen, 1775; member of Maryland Convention, 1774; delegate to Maryland Congress, 1776; member of Committee on Observation and Safety.

Great-great-grandson of Samuel Love, member of Committee of Safety for Charles County, Maryland, also member of the Maryland Convention, 1775-1776; member of the Committee of Observation.

Great-great-great-grandson of Charles Jones, member Committee on Arms and Ammunition, Frederick County, Maryland, and Judge of Maryland Court, Frederick County, Maryland.

BLOCK, George Montgomery. — Great-great-great-grandson of Thomas Walker, Member of the Virginia House of Burgesses, 1775; was organizer of Plans of Defense and served on Second General Committee of Safety; Commissioner jointly with his son to treat with Pittsburg Indians on behalf of Colonies in 1777; President of Board of Commissioners to determine disputed line between Virginia and North Carolina, 1778; Member of Council of State for Virginia, 1777.

Great-great-grandson of Nicholas Lewis, Captain of Virginia Minute Men, and Colonel of Militia in the expedition of 1776 against the Cherokee Indians.

(98)

Vera Lawrence Siegrist,
Grand-daughter of Dr. J. J. Lawrence.

ROSTER

OF

ANCESTORS AND DESCENDANTS

OF SONS OF THE REVOLUTION AND
SONS OF THE AMERICAN REVOLUTION.

Ancestors in CAPITALS.

SONS OF THE REVOLUTION.

ADAIR, JOHN,
   Thayer, William Bridges.
   Thayer, Norton.
ADAMS, ISSACHER,
   Adams, Elmer Bragg.
ADAMS, ABEL,
   Adams, Frederick Cossette.
ADAMS, DANIEL JENIFER,
   Adams, Charles Breck.
ALBAN, GEORGE,
   Alban, Charles Willis.
ALLEN, EDWARD,
   Allen, Edward Archibald.
ALLEN, ETHAN,
   Hitchcock, Henry.
   Hitchcock, Ethan Allen.
   Hitchcock, George Collier.
ALLEN, WILLIAM,
   Rogers, Alfred Harrison.
ALLISON, ISAAC,
   Allison, James Williams.
ALVORD, DANIEL,
   Alvord, Daniel Smith.
ANKENY, PETER,
   Connelly, Alvin Henry.
ASHTON, JAMES,
   Ashton, Sidney Cornell.
ATWILL, NATHAN,
   Atwill, James William.
AVERY, EBENEZER,
   Randall, John Frederic.

AVERY, THOMAS,
   Miner, Edgar Samuel.
   Miner, William Avery.
AXTELL, HENRY,
   Cory, James Manderville.
BABER, WILLIAM,
   Crutcher, Edwin Ruthven.
BACKUS, EBENEZER,
   Backus, Clarence Walworth.
BAKER, REUBEN,
   Millard, Clifford Isaac.
BAKER, AMOS,
   Baker, George Arnold.
   Baker, Isaac Gilbert.
   Baker, William Street.
BALLARD, DANE,
   Ware, Charles Edwin.
BAMFORD, CHARLES,
   Coburn, James Mitchell.
BAMFORD, CHARLES, SR.,
   Coburn, James Mitchell.
BANKS, DAVID,
   Gould, David Banks.
BARNARD, BENJAMIN,
   Stuart, Lewis Batchelder.
   Stuart, James Lyall.
BARNES, JOSHUA,
   Brockett, Charles Andrew.
BARNETT, JAMES,
   Barnett, Julian.

ANCESTORS AND DESCENDANTS.

BARRET, WILLIAM,
   Barret, Richard Aylett.
   Barret, James Van Sweringen.
BARRET, CHISWELL,
   Barret, Richard Aylett.
   Barret, James Van Sweringen.
BARRETT, JAMES,
   Griffin, Frederick Ward.
BARSTOW, JACOB,
   Barstow, Charles Warren.
BARTLETT, JOSIAH,
   Orear, John Davis.
BARTLOFF, CRINEUS,
   Craft, Henry Gray.
BASCOMB, ELISHA,
   Bascomb, Joseph Dayton.
BATCHELDER, JOHN,
   Stuart, Lewis Batchelder.
   Stuart, James Lyall.
BATES, LEMUEL,
   Stiles, Edward Holcomb.
   Adams, Frederic Cossette.
BATES, ALPHEUS,
   Humphrey, Frank Waterman.
BAYLY, PIERCE,
   Asbury, Ai Edgar.
BEACH, GERSHOM,
   Beach, Jesse Waldo.
BEACH, ELIJAH,
   Middlebrook, Robert Brinsmade.
BEALL, ELISHA,
   Pettit, Henry McEwen.
BEBEE, JAMES,
   Brinsmade, Hobart.
   Middlebrook, Robert Brinsmade.
BEDINGER, DANIEL,
   Rust, George.
BELL, HENRY,
   Branch, Charles.
BENBURY, THOMAS,
   Creecy, Edmond Perkins.
BENTON, LEMUEL,
   Prince, Laurence Lempriere.
BERGEN, CHRISTOPHER,
   Galentine, William Axford.
BERRIEN, JOHN,
   William, James Seymour.
BERRY, THOMAS,
   Parry, Guerdon Groves.
BIGELOW, DAVID,
   Trask, Walter Bigelow.
BIGELOW, WILLIAM,
   Walker, Stoughton.
BIGELOW, CONVERSE,
   Bigelow, Edmund Sprague.

BIGELOW, JOSIAH,
   Bigelow, Edmund Sprague.
BINGHAM, STEPHEN,
   Clarke, William Bingham.
BISHOP, JOHN,
   Duckworth, William King.
BLACKBURN, THOMAS,
   Harding, Eugene Fauntleroy Cordell.
BLACKWELL, THOMAS,
   Skinker, Thomas Keith.
   Skinker, Charles Rives.
BLAISDELL, ABNER,
   Shapleigh, Alfred Lee.
   Shapleigh, John Blasdel.
   Shapleigh, Richard Waldron.
   Shapleigh, Frank.
BLISS, CALVIN, SR.,
   Bliss, George Francis Fuller.
BLOSS, ZADOC,
   Bloss, Orlando Powers.
   Bloss, Fred Leonard.
BLOSS, WALTER,
   Bloss, Orlando Powers.
   Bloss, Fred Leonard.
BOOTH, JAMES, SR.,
   Middlebrook, Robert Brinsmade.
BOOTH, JOSIAH,
   Orear, John Davis.
BOWEN, CONSIDER,
   Case, George Bowen.
BOTELER, HENRY,
   Boteler, William Clarence.
BOWMAN, SAMUEL,
   Rollins, Hamilton Bowman.
BOYD, JOHN,
   Boyd, William Goddin.
BRACKETT, WILLIAM,
   Newcomb, George Amos.
   Newcomb, Norton,
BRADLEY, TIMOTHY,
   Bradley, Timothy Cookson,
BRIDGES, JOHN,
   Thayer, William Bridges.
   Thayer, Norton.
BRIGGS, SAMUEL,
   Carr, Robert Elisha.
BRINKERHOFF, JACOB,
   Brinkerhoff, Jacob Oscar.
   Brinkerhoff, James Hunt.
BRINSMADE, ABRAM,
   Brinsmade, Hobart.
   Middlebrook, Robert Brinsmade.
BRITTAIN, JOSEPH,
   Brittain, John Sherrard.

BRITTAIN, JOSEPH,
   Brittain, John Sherrard, Jr.
BROWN, JOHN,
   Brown, Willis.
BROWN, WILLIAM,
   Douglas, Archer Wall.
BRYANT, JOHN,
   Bryant, John Allen.
BUCK, AMOS,
   Lahee, Eugene Horace.
BUCKNER, AYLETT,
   Barret, Richard Aylett.
BURNHAM, WESLEY,
   Burnham, Michael.
BURRILL, JOHN, JR.,
   Atwill, James William.
BURRILL, JOHN, SR.,
   Atwill, James William.
BURRIS, THOMAS,
   Ragland, Samuel Hobbs.
BURTON, JUDSON,
   Middlebrook, Robert Brinsmade.
BUSHNELL, GIDEON,
   Bushnell, Albert.
BUSSEY DE, COUNT, J. B. C., L.D.
   Dyer, Ezra Hunt.
BUTLER, WILLIAM,
   Butler, William David.
   Butler, William Morton.
CALVERT, CORNELIUS,
   Dunn, James.
CAMPFIELD, JABEZ,
   Campfield, Charles Henry.
CAREY, ARCHIBALD,
   Hutchinson, William Christy.
CARGILL, DAVID,
   Ford, Harry Kane.
CARPENTER, AMASA,
   Walker, Stoughton.
CASE, OLIVER,
   Case, Theodore Spencer.
CASEY, JOSEPH,
   Casey, Alexander Marshall.
CHAMBERS, BENJAMIN,
   Shultz, Llewellyn Brown.
CHAPEL, JOHN,
   Chapel, William Wallace.
CHENEY, WILLIAM,
   Perry, Albert.
CHESTER, JOHN,
   Backus, Clarence Walworth.
CLARK, ROBERT,
   Groves, John Garner.

CLARK, ZELOTUS,
   Clark, Charles.
CLAYPOOLE, ABRAHAM GEO.,
   James, Thomas.
   James, William.
CLEMENT DE VILLENEUVE, AUGUSTINE,
   Lawrence, Joseph Joshua.
CLEMENT, MOSES,
   Gilbert, Matthew James.
COBURN, SIMON,
   Coburn, James Mitchell.
COIT, SAMUEL,
   Day, Robert Coit.
COLEMAN, THOMAS,
   Tootle, Milton, Jr.
   Tootle, John James.
   Weakley, Laurence O'Neill.
   Weakley, Armstrong Beattie.
   Logan, John Sublett.
CORDER, JOHN,
   Corder, John Elias.
CORY, ELNATHAN,
   Cross, Charles Sumner,
CRESAP, JOSEPH,
   McCarty, Richard Justin.
CROCKETT, ANTHONY,
   Wood, John McKee.
CROSS, ZACHARIAH,
   Funkhouser, Robert Monroe.
CROWELL, JOSEPH,
   Edgar Charles Bloomfield.
CUSHMAN, NATHANIEL,
   Cushman, George Henry.
CUTHBERT, ANTHONY,
   Cuthbert, Charles McIntosh.
CUTTER, SAMUEL,
   Wyman, Henry Purkitt.
   Wyman, Edward.
   Wyman, Leigh.
   Wyman, Charles Hadley.
   Wyman, Frank.
   Morton, Isaac Wyman.
DANA, WILLIAM,
   Snedaker, John Harvey.
DANE, BALLARD,
   Ware, James Bissell.
DAVIDSON, WILLIAM,
   Sloan, Ewing McGready.
   Sloan, Charles William.
   Sloan, Robert Tarlton.
   Ewing, Henry Watkins.
DEAN, SETH,
   Dean, William Brewer.
DEGRAFF, ISAAC,
   Toll, Philip Riley.

ANCESTORS AND DESCENDANTS.

DEWESS, WILLIAM,
  Gadsden, Paul Trapier.
DEWOLF, JOSEPH, SR.,
  Close, Frederick DeWolf.
DEWOLF, ELISHA,
  DeWolf, Edwin Allis.
DEWOLF, MARK ANTHONY,
  Howe, Alfred Leighton.
DOLPH, MOSES,
  Dolph, Moses.
  Dolph, Clifford Myron.
DRINKWATER, DANIEL,
  Healey, Edwin Sprague.
DUFFIELD, WILLIAM,
  Motter, Louis.
  Motter, Isaac.
DUTTON, THOMAS,
  Comstock, Freeman Jonathan.
EASTMAN, JOSEPH,
  Walker, Stoughton.
EASTMAN, MOSES,
  Walker, Stoughton.
EATON, WILLIAM,
  Root, George Eaton.
  Root, Ralph Sellew.
EATON, EBENEZER,
  Gilbert, James Spofford.
EBENEZER, RICHARDSON,
  Mill, Charles David.
EDGAR, WILLIAM,
  Edgar, Charles Bloomfield.
EDMUNDS, THOMAS,
  Edmunds, Henry Littleton.
EDWARDS, JOHN,
  Gadsden, Paul Trapier.
ELKINS, HENRY,
  Perkins, John Walter.
ELLERBE, THOMAS,
  Ellerbe, Christopher Pegues.
ELY, JOHN,
  Gregory, Alfred.
EMERSON, THOMAS,
  Carpenter, George Oliver.
EVANS, ROBERT,
  Mitchell, Arthur Sanford.
FAIRBANK, JOSIAH, 2d.,
  Fairbank, Lemuel Gulliver.
FASSETT, JONATHAN,
  Fassett, Daniel Dobbins.
FAY, SHEREBIAH,
  Fay, William Henry.
FIELD, JEREMIAH,
  Field, John Telfair.
  Field, William Boyd.

FISHER, HENRY,
  Smith, William Medill.
FITZRANDOLPH, NATHANIEL,
  Edgar, Charles Bloomfield.
FLEET, JOHN,
  Fleet, Alex. Fred'k.
FLEMING, WILLIAM,
  Sullivan, Andrew McClure.
FLOYD, BENJAMIN,
  Newcomb, Norton.
  Floyd, William Harris, Jr.
FLOYD, DANIEL,
  Floyd, Russell Greene, M. D.
FLOYD, NOAH,
  Newcomb, Norton.
  Floyd, William Harris, Jr.
FOSTER, JOSEPH,
  Foster, William Davis.
FRAZIER, JOHN,
  Frazier, James William.
FULLER, MATTHEW,
  Fuller, Andrew Jackson.
FULLER, WILLIAM,
  Fuller, George Washington.
FULLER, WILLIAM,
  Fuller, William Harvey.
GADSDEN, CHRISTOPHER,
  Gadsden, Paul Trapier.
GAGE, BENJAMIN,
  Raeder, Francis Henry.
GARDNER, JOHN,
  Grover, George Sheets.
GARRARD, JAMES,
  Bierbower, James Culver.
GATES, SILAS,
  Gates, Edward Payson.
GAY, EBENEZER,
  Butler, James Gay.
GAYLORD, LEVI,
  Gaylord, Hal.
GEORGE, JOSEPH,
  George, Henry Lewis.
GENTRY, RICHARD,
  Gentry, Richard,
  Shelton, Richard Theodore.
GENTZELL, ADAM,
  Wilder, George Webb.
GILBERT, ISAAC,
  Baker, George Arnold.
  Baker, Isaac Gilbert.
  Baker, William Street.
GILBERT, WILLIAM,
  Rivers, Tyree Rodes.
GIST, NATHANIEL,
  Blair, James Lawrence.

GOODRICH, JOHN H.,
　　Close, Frederick DeWolf.
GORDON, PETER,
　　Clark, William Voorhies.
GOULD, JOSEPH,
　　Gould, David Banks.
GOULD, ABRAHAM,
　　Northrop, Sandford.
GRIFFITH, HENRY,
　　Welsh, Milton.
GRISWOLD, PHINEAS,
　　Adams, Frederick Cossette.
GREEN, JOHN,
　　Green, John.
　　Green, John, Jr.
GREEN, TIMOTHY,
　　Rogers, Alfred Harrison.
GREENE, JAMES,
　　Stewart, Seymour.
GREENE, JAMES,
　　Greene, Henry Alexander.
GREENWOOD, MOSES,
　　Greenwood, Moses, Jr.
GREGG, SAMUEL,
　　Gregg, William Henry.
　　Gregg, William Henry, Jr.
　　Gregg, Norris Bradford.
GREGORY, JOHN,
　　Moore, Walton Norwood.
GREGORY, WALTER,
　　Gregory, Charles Rush.
GULLIVER, LEMUEL,
　　Fairbank, Lemuel Gulliver.
GULLIVER, JOHN,
　　Fairbank, Lemuel Gulliver.
GUSTINE, LEMUEL,
　　Witherspoon, Thomas Casey.
HADLEY, MOSES,
　　Wyman, Henry Purkitt.
　　Wyman, Edward.
　　Wyman, Leigh.
　　Wyman, Charles Hadley.
　　Wyman, Frank.
HAHN, JOHN,
　　Harman, Jacob Frank.
HALLET, JOSEPH,
　　Delafield, Wallace.
HARDING, ABIEL,
　　Harding, James.
　　Harding, Eugene Fauntleroy Cordell.
　　Harding, Chester.
HARDIN, JOHN,
　　McHenry, Estill.
　　Harwood, John Tevis.

HARRINGTON, HENRY WILLIAM,
　　Powe, William Robbins.
HARRIS, JOHN,
　　Woodson, Archelaus Marins.
HARRIS, JOHN,
　　Woodson, Benjamin Jordan.
　　Harris, John.
　　Woodson, Charles Ransom, M. D.
HARRIS, SAMUEL,
　　Harris, Charles Leonard.
HARRISON, BENJAMIN,
　　Harrison, John Scott.
　　Harrison, Archibald Irwin.
HARRISON, BENJAMIN,
　　Drummond, Charles Randle.
HARRISON, BENJAMIN,
　　Drummond, Harrison Irwin.
　　Drummond, John N.
HARRISON, RICHARD,
　　Chidsey, Conley.
HARTWELL, SAMUEL,
　　Brown, Frank Arthur.
HARVEY, WILLIAM,
　　Husted, Edward Chapin.
HASKELL, JONATHAN,
　　Lawton, William Arthur.
HAVERSTICK, WILLIAM,
　　Mellier, Walter Gallatin.
HAYWARD, LEMUEL,
　　Hayward, Francis Morse.
HEALD, EPHRAIM,
　　Sargent, Clarence Spalding.
HEALEY, ELIPHAZ,
　　Healey, Edwin Sprague.
HELM, THOMAS,
　　Ragland, Samuel Hobbs.
HEMPSTEAD, STEPHEN,
　　Kennett, William Potts.
HENDERSON, BENJAMIN,
　　Newcomb, Norton.
HEPP, JOHN,
　　Gaiennie, Frank.
HICKS, GEORGE,
　　Powe, William Robbins.
HODGES, EZEKIEL,
　　Hodges, William Romaine.
HOKE, HENRY,
　　Hoke, Charles Henry.
HOLCOMB, HEZEKIAH,
　　Stiles, Edward Holcomb.
HOLLAND, JAMES,
　　Rivers, Tyree Rodes.
HOLLAND, GEORGE,
　　Holland, Robert Afton.

HOPKINS, STEPHEN,
    Martin, George Edward.
HOPKINS, SAMUEL,
    Hopkins, Innis.
HOPKINS, MARK,
    Hopkins, Henry.
HOPKINS, STEPHEN,
    Martin, George Edward.
    Preston, Thomas Jefferson.
HOWARD, EBENEZER,
    Elliott, Howard.
HOWARD, SAMUEL,
    Elliott, Howard.
HOWE, PERLEY,
    Howe, Alfred Leighton.
HOVEY, PHINEAS,
    Trask, Isaac Rogers.
    Trask, Walter Bigelow.
HUBBARD, JONATHAN,
    Hubbard, Robert Morris.
    Hubbard, Henry Fitch.
HUGHES, JOSEPH,
    Barton, William.
    Barton, Kimber Lewis.
    Barton, James Southworth.
HUGHES, WILLIAM,
    Barton, William.
    Barton, Kimber Lewis.
    Barton, James Southworth.
HUGHES, WILLIAM,
    Barton, George Allen.
HUMRICHOUSE, PETER,
    Hanenkamp, Richard Pindell, Jr.
HUNTOON, JOSIAH,
    Harmon, Horatio Loomis.
HUMPHREY, JAMES,
    Humphrey, Frank Waterman.
HURD, ABRAHAM,
    Bushnell, Albert.
HURD, CRIPPEN, SR.,
    Mosher, George Clark.
HUTCHINS, HEZEKIAH,
    Dana, Leslie.
IVES, SAMUEL,
    Ives, Halsey Cooley.
IVES, TITUS HOEL,
    Ives, Halsey Cooley.
JACKSON, EDMUND,
    Jackson, Charles Christopher.
JACKSON, EPHRAIM,
    Jackson, George Edward.
    Jackson, Ephraim.
    Jackson, Edward Fisher.

JENKINS, EBENEZER,
    Jenkins, Hermon Dutilh.
JENNINGS, JACOB,
    Alexander, St. Clair.
JENNINGS, JACOB,
    Alexander, St. Clair.
JOHNSON, EZRA,
    Cadle, Henry.
JONES, CHARLES,
    Doddridge, William Brown.
JORDAN, JOHN,
    Jordan, John Manning.
JULIAN, JOHN,
    Wood, John McKee.
KELLOGG, AARON,
    White, Henry Kirke.
KEMPTON, RUFUS,
    Parker, Charles David.
KENDRICK, SAMUEL,
    Kendrick, Justin Smith.
KERCHEVAL, JOHN, 2D,
    Parry, Guerdon Groves.
KEY, JOHN,
    Shannon, Thomas.
KIMBALL, SAMUEL,
    Kimball, Thomas Dudley.
KIMBALL, DANIEL,
    Raeder, Francis Henry.
KIRKLAND, SAMUEL,
    Lathrop, Gardiner.
KLINE, JACOB,
    Field, John Telfair.
    Field, William Boyd.
KNIGHT, JONATHAN,
    Bacon, Walter Clark.
KNIGHT, SAMUEL,
    Adams, William Knight.
LAMPREY, DANIEL,
    Cadle, Henry.
LAMAR, MARION,
    Welty, Edwin Arthur.
LAMPREY, JOHN,
    Cadle, Henry.
LANE, SIMON,
    Cadle, Henry.
LANE, NATHAN,
    Coburn, James Mitchell.
LANGSTAFF, JOHN,
    Hockaday, Augustus.
LAWRENCE, LEVI,
    McCarty, Evans.
LAYN, JOHN,
    Coburn, James Mitchell.

LEE, RICHARD HENRY,
  Lee, Arthur.
  Lee, John Fitzgerald.
  Lee, William Hill.
  Rust, George.
LEMPRIERE, CLEMENT,
  Prince, Laurence Lempriere.
LEONARD, ABIEL,
  Smith, Abiel Leonard.
LEWIS, ISAAC,
  Hyde, Ira Barnes.
LEWIS, NICHOLAS,
  Block, George Montgomery.
LEWIS, ANDREW,
  McCulloch, Robert.
  McCulloch, Richard.
LINCOLN, LEVI,
  Humphrey, Frank Waterman.
LITTLEPAGE, JOHN CARTER,
  Williams, Walter.
LONGSTRETH, BARTHOLOMEW,
  Longstreth, Charles Howard.
LOVE, SAMUEL,
  Doddridge, William Brown.
LOW, JOHN,
  Trask, Isaac Rogers.
  Trask, Walter Bigelow.
LYMAN, JOSEPH,
  Dana, Leslie.
MANSON, NEHEMIAH,
  Faxon, Frank Allen.
  Faxon, Henry Darlington.
MANSUR, WILLIAM,
  Sanders, Joseph Warren.
MARSHALL, ICHABOD,
  Kendrick, Justin Smith.
MARSHALL, THOMAS,
  Casey, Alexander Marshall.
MARSHALL, THOMAS, JR.,
  Casey, Alexander Marshall.
MAYO, JOSEPH,
  Crutcher, Edwin Ruthven.
MCCALLA, DANIEL,
  Witherspoon, Thomas Casey.
MCCLARY, ANDREW,
  McClary, Harvey Clark.
MCDOWELL, SAMUEL,
  Casey, Alexander Marshall.
MCELWEE, JAMES,
  McElwee, Lucien Claude.
MCFERREN, WILLIAM,
  Clendening, Edwin McKaig.
MCGRATH, JOHN,
  Reid, William Magraw.

MCINTOSH, LACHLAN, JR.,
  Cuthbert, Charles McIntosh.
MCINTOSH, WILLIAM,
  Cuthbert, Charles McIntosh.
MCKEE, JAMES,
  Watson, Claude Leslie.
MCKEEN, HUGH,
  McKeen, Charles Stone.
MCLAUGHLIN, JOHN,
  Brown, James Newton.
MEADE, RICHARD KIDDER,
  Funsten, Robert Emmett.
MIDDLEBROOK, STEPHEN, SR.,
  Middlebrook, Robert Brinsmade.
MITCHELL, EDWARD,
  Glasgow, Edward James, Jr.
  Glasgow, William Jefferson.
MONTAGUE, JOHN,
  Wilder, Edward Bliss.
MOORE, JOSEPH,
  Moore, Samuel Wallace.
MOORE, ROGER,
  Pope, William Spencer, Jr.
MOORE, JAMES,
  Duckworth, William King.
MORELAND, WILLIAM,
  Carter, Charles Moreland.
MORGAN, JONAS,
  Morgan, George Hagar.
MORRILL, LABAN,
  Bradley, Timothy Cookson.
MORRIS, JONATHAN FORD,
  Hays, Charles Melville.
  Hays, David Hunt.
MORRIS, JOSEPH,
  Hays, Charles Melville.
  Hays, David Hunt.
MORRIS, LEWIS,
  Marshall, Wm. St. John Elliot.
MORTON, WILLIAM,
  Edmunds, Henry Littleton.
MOTHERSHEAD, NATHANIEL,
  Fife, Charles Boss.
MOTT, SAMUEL,
  Burnett, Willard Elmer.
MOULTON, DAVID,
  Moulton, John Henry.
MUNGER, ELIAS,
  Munger, Lyman Paige.
MUSSER, GEORGE,
  Mellier, Walton Gallatin.
NELSON, THOMAS,
  Meredith, Jonathan Cushing.

ANCESTORS AND DESCENDANTS.

NEWCOMB, THOMAS,
   Newcomb, George Amos.
   Newcomb, Norton.
NEWHALL, EZRA,
   Ravold, Henry Jacques, M. D.
NUNELY, HENRY,
   Rainwater, Charles Cicero.
OBER, JOSEPH, JR.,
   Obear, Frank.
OLIVER, DOUGLAS,
   Campbell, James Alexander.
OREAR, JOHN DAVIS,
   Orear, John Davis.
OSBORNE, BENNETT,
   Scruggs, Milus Dickey.
PALMER, ELIAS SANFORD,
   Palmer, Clarence Steuben.
PARKER, ABRAHAM,
   Parker, George Washington.
   Parker, Clarence Farleigh.
   Parker, Charles Morton.
   Wiley, Charles Samuel.
   Wiley, Clifford.
PARKER, NATHANIEL,
   Parker, James Henry, Jr.
PARSONS, ELDAD,
   McCarty, Evans.
PATEE, EDMUND,
   Clayton, Alvah Patee.
PAYNE, JOSEPH,
   Karnes, Joseph Van Clief.
PAYNE, WILLIAM,
   Scott, Henry Clarkson.
   Scott, William Samuel.
PEALE, CHARLES WILSON.
   Lockwood, James Yeatman.
PEARLE, SIMEON,
   Riggs, Manfred Moses.
PEGUES, CLAUDIUS, JR.,
   Ellerbe, Christopher Pegues.
PERKINS, JAMES,
   Perkins, John Walter.
PERLEE, EDMUND,
   Pugsley, Charles Azariah.
PERRY, CHRIS. RAYMOND,
   Rodgers, Robert Slidell.
PETTIBONE, GILES,
   Dyer, Ezra Hunt.
PETTIBONE, JONATHAN,
   Dyer, Ezra Hunt.
PETTINGILL, ANDREW,
   Ewing, Arthur Eugene.
PHELPS, ROGERS,
   Phelps, Herbert Wilson.

PLATT, BENJAMIN,
   Wood, Horatio Dan.
POMEROY, SETH,
   Lathrop, Joseph.
   Lathrop, William Addison Howe.
POSEY, THOMAS,
   Baker, William Street.
POST, ROSWELL, 2d,
   Post, Truman Augustus.
   Post, Martin Hayward.
POWE, THOMAS,
   Powe, William Robbins.
POWE, THOMAS,
   Powe, Thomas Erasmus.
POWELL, LEVIN,
   Atkinson, Robert Chilton.
PRATT, JOHN,
   Pratt, Charles Alexander.
PRATT, BENJAMIN,
   Humphrey, Frank Waterman.
PRESTON, STEPHEN,
   Preston, Thomas Jefferson,
PRESTON, WILLIAM,
   Douglas, Walter Bond.
PRICE, WILLIAM,
   Barton, William.
   Barton, Kimber Lewis.
   Barton, James Southworth.
PRIMM, JOHN,
   Primm, Alexander Timon, Jr.
PURCELL, GEORGE,
   Hill, Charles Chase,
   Hill, Will Winfield.
   Hill, Frank Miller.
PUTNAM, ISRAEL,
   Dana, Israel Putnam.
QUARLES, ROBERT,
   Scott, Walter Scott.
QUISENBERRY, JAMES,
   Ragland, Samuel Hobbs.
RAGLAND, JAMES, SR.,
   Ragland, Samuel Hobbs.
RAYMOND, HEZEKIAH,
   Raymond, Francis, Jr.
RICH, JOSHUA,
   Rich, Irving Hale.
RICHARDSON, NATHAN,
   Walker, Stoughton.
RINGGOLD, WILLIAM,
   Holland, Frank Edwin.
ROBARDS, GEORGE,
   Barret, Richard Aylett.
ROBERTSON, JOSEPH,
   Robertson, George.

ROBINSON, JONATHAN,
  Grant, Lee Wiley.
ROGERS, ANDREW,
  Rogers, Alfred Harrison.
ROGERS, WILLIAM,
  Trask, Isaac Rogers.
  Trask, Walter Bigelow.
ROLLINS, HENRY,
  Rollins, Curtis Burnam.
  Rollins, George Bingham.
  Rollins, Edward Tutt.
  Rollins, Hamilton Bowman.
  Hockaday, Rollins Mills.
ROLLINS, ICHABOD.
  Moses, Frank Demming.
ROLL, JOHN,
  Cross, Charles Sumner.
ROWELL, DANIEL,
  Rowell, Clinton.
RUSSELL, PHILIP,
  Campbell, James Alexander.
RUTHERFORD, ROBERT,
  Rust, George.
SALMON, GEORGE,
  Salmon, Harvey Wallis.
SANDS, JOHN,
  Sands, James Thomas.
SANDS, SAMUEL,
  Sands, James Thomas.
SCHUREMAN, JAMES,
  Peppard, Joseph Greer, Sr.
SCOTT, GUSTAVUS,
  Doddridge, William Brown.
SEWALL, DUMMER,
  Sewall, Frederic Norris.
SEGAR, SAMUEL,
  Segur, Frederick Wilkinson.
SELDEN, SAMUEL,
  Spencer, Selden Palmer.
  Delafield Wallace.
SEVIER, JOHN,
  King, Edword Austin.
SCRUGGS, WILLIAM,
  Scruggs, Milus Dickey.
SHAPLEIGH, ELISHA,
  Shapleigh, Alfred Lee.
  Shapleigh, John Blasdel.
  Shapleigh, Richard Waldron.
  Shapleigh, Frank.
SHERWOOD, ADIEL,
  Sherwood, Thomas Adiel.
  Sherwood, Adiel.
SHEWELL, ROBERT,
  Lloyd, Henry Albert.

SHOCKEY, CHRISTIAN.
  Shultz, Chauncey Forward.
  Shultz, John Andrew Jackson.
  Shultz, Llewellyn Brown.
SHUBRICK, THOMAS, SR.,
  Gadsden, Paul Trapier.
SHUBRICK, THOMAS,
  Gadsden, Paul Trapier.
SHURTLEFF, ICHABOD, 2,
  Parker, Charles David.
SINCLAIR, BENJAMIN,
  Dana, Israel Putnam.
SINKLER, THOMAS,
  Dana, Israel Putnam.
SINKLER, PETER,
  Mitchell, Charles Dwight.
SKINNER, WILLIAM,
  Creecy, Edmund Perkins.
SMITH, FRANCIS,
  Smith, George Edward.
SMITH, COMFORT,
  Leach, Francis Augustus.
SMITH, JAMES,
  West, Parker Whitney.
SMITH, OLIVER,
  Alvord, Daniel Smith.
SMITH, DANIEL,
  Smith, Edward Calhoun.
  Smith, Lewis Motter.
  Holland, Frank Edwin.
  Holland, Charles Littleton.
SMITH, STEPHEN,
  Howe, Alfred Leighton.
SNOW, ABIJAH,
  Preston, Thomas Jefferson.
SNOW, DAVID,
  Lombard, James Lewis.
SPALDING, EBENEZER,
  Spalding, Elliott.
SPALDING, SAMUEL,
  Sargent, Clarence Spalding.
SPALDING, SAMUEL,
  Sargent, Clarence Spalding.
SPAULDING, SAMUEL,
  Harvey, George Irving.
SPENCER, ISRAEL,
  Spencer, Horatio Nelson.
  Spencer, Selden Palmer.
SPENCER, ISRAEL SELDEN,
  Spencer, Horatio Nelson.
  Spencer, Selden Palmer.
SPENCER, JOSEPH,
  Delafield, Wallace.

ANCESTORS AND DESCENDANTS.

SPOTSWOOD, JOHN,
   Lemoine, Edwin Spotswood.
   Matthews, Edmund Orville.
   Matthews, William Nisbet.
   Nisbet, William Wood.
STANLEY, JOHN,
   Brown, Willis.
STEARNS, EDWARD,
   Wyman, Henry Purkitt.
   Wyman, Edward.
   Wyman, Leigh.
   Wyman, Charles Hadley.
   Wyman, Frank.
   Morton, Isaac Wyman.
STEARNS, REUBEN,
   Walker, Stoughton.
STEELE, PEREZ,
   Tuttle, George Marvine.
   Tuttle, Herbert Edward.
STEELE, DAVID,
   McCord, William Hallack.
   McCord, James Hamilton.
   McCord, Samuel Steele.
   McCord, Francis.
   McCord, George Lawrence.
   McCord, Robert Hamden.
STICKNEY, ELIPHALET,
   Miller, George Dana Boardman.
STILES, GIDEON,
   Stiles, Edward Holcomb.
STOUGHTON, SAMUEL,
   Walker, Stoughton.
STOUT, ABRAHAM,
   Hill, Ewing.
   Hill, Josiah Charles.
   McBee, Augustine Ewing.
STRYKER, ABRAHAM,
   Voorhees, William Perrine.
SUFFERN, JOHN,
   Craft, Henry Gray.
SWAN, ROBERT,
   Mosman, Chesley Augustus.
SWASEY, EBENEZER,
   Swasey, William Albert.
SWENTZEL, FREDERICK,
   Swentzel, William Edward.
SYMMES, JOHN CLEVES,
   Harrison, John Scott.
   Harrison, Archibald Irwin.
TARBOX, SOLOMON,
   Bacon, Frederick Hampden.
TAYLOR, IGNATIUS,
   Branch, Thomas Innis.
TAYLOR, RICHARD,
   Casey, Samuel Lewis.
   Taylor, John Rodgers Meigs.

TAYLOR, REUBEN,
   Campbell, Walter Taylor.
TEN EYCK, JACOB,
   Field, John Telfair.
   Field, William Boyd.
TERRY, SAMUEL,
   Terry, John Henry.
   Terry, Robert James.
THAYER, ICHABOD,
   Thayer, Amos Madden.
THAYER, ICHABOD, JR.,
   Thayer, Amos Madden.
THAYER, ISAAC,
   Thayer, William Bridges.
   Thayer, Norton.
THORNTON, ANTHONY,
   Barret, Richard Aylett.
THOMPSON, PETER,
   Wright, Herbert Perry.
TRACY, JOHN,
   James, John Faraday.
TRAPIER, PAUL, JR.,
   Gadsden, Paul Trapier.
TRAPIER, PAUL, SR.,
   Gadsden, Paul Trapier.
TRASK, EBENEZER, JR.,
   Trask, Isaac Rogers.
   Trask, Walter Bigelow.
TRASK, EBENEZER, SR.,
   Trask, Isaac Rogers.
   Trask, Walter Bikelow.
TRIGG, JOHN,
   Groves, John Garner.
   Garner, Edward Samuel.
TRIPLETT, SIMON,
   Triplett, John Richards.
TODD, LEVI,
   Carr, Robert Elisha.
TUTTLE, CHARLES,
   Tuttle, Daniel Sylvester.
   Tuttle, George Marvine.
   Tuttle, Herbert Edward.
VAN DOREN, JACOB,
   Harbeson, Frank O'Ferrell.
VARNUM, JOSEPH BRADLEY,
   Coburn, James Mitchell.
VENOY, ANDREW,
   Lucas, John Baptiste Charles.
VOORHEES, JOHN,
   Voorhees, William Perrine.
VOORHIES, DANIEL,
   Clark, William Voorhies.
VOSE, JOSHUA,
   Fairbank, Lemuel Gulliver.

ANCESTORS AND DESCENDANTS.

WAGGENER, ANDREW,
 Casey, Nicholas Waggener.
 Casey, Samuel Lewis.
WAGNER, PETER,
 Wagner, Arthur Lockwood.
WALKER, PHINEAS,
 Walker, Stoughton.
WALKER, THOMAS,
 Block, George Montgomery.
WATERMAN, ASA,
 Waterman, Sherman Jewett.
WEEKS, JONATHAN,
 Weeks, Edwin Ruthven.
WHALEY, JAMES,
 Jackson, Charles Christopher.
WHEELER, SAMUEL,
 Case, George Bowen.
 Ross, John Alexander.
WHITE, JOHN,
 White, Henry Kirke.
WHITE, JONAS,
 Elliott, Howard.
WHITE, LUKE,
 White, John Barber.
WHITE, VASSALL,
 White, Henry Kirke.
WILDER, JOHN,
 Wilder, Edward Bliss.
WILDER, ABEL,
 Wilder, George Webb.
WILLIAMS, JOHN,
 Groves, Frank Simpson.
 Simpson, Frank.
WILLIAMS, JOSEPH,
 Hayward, Harry Erwin.

WILSON, THOMAS,
 Wilson, George Neal.
WILSON, WILLIAM,
 MacMurray, Junius Wilson.
WINSTON, WILLIAM,
 Barret, Richard Aylett.
 Barret, James Van Sweringen.
WITT, ABNER,
 Witt, Thomas Dudley.
WOOD, DAVID,
 Wood, Horatio Dan.
 Nisbet, William Wood.
WOOD, GEORGE,
 Wood, Horace Walter.
 Woodard, Dudley Graves.
WOODHULL, JOHN,
 McCune, Harry Long.
WOODWARD, NATHANIEL,
 Woodward, Calvin Milton.
WOOL, ISAIAH,
 Field, John Telfair.
WORK, JAMES,
 Bacheller, Roscoe Morrow.
WRIGHT, JOB,
 Sands, James Thomas.
WYETH, EBENEZER,
 Wyeth, Huston,
 Wyeth, Parker Campbell.
WYMAN, NEHEMIAH,
 Wyman, Henry Purkitt.
 Wyman, Edward.
 Wyman, Leigh.
 Wyman, Charles Hadley.
 Wyman, Frank.
 Morton, Isaac Wyman.
YOUNG, CALVIN,
 Young, Thomas Crane.

Total Membership July 1, 1898, 378.

Number of ancestors represented, 438.

SONS OF THE AMERICAN REVOLUTION.

NOAH ADAMS,
    Duston Adams.
    Robert Adams, Jr.
LEMUEL GATES,
    Edward Lawrence Adreon.
JOHN TOLMAN,
    John Tolman Alden.
JOHN DURKEE,
    Henry Edward Bartling.
ELISHA BASCOME,
    Joseph Dayton Bascome.
WILLIAM RADFORD,
    Western Radford Bascome.
ABRAHAM CLARK,
    Jonas Clark.
    Lee Clark.
    Edgar Wright Clark.
    William Jones Clark.
    Albert Bonesteel Bates.
    W. Scott Bates.
JAMES WALSWORTH,
    Harmon Bell.
THOMAS WALKER,
    Henry Frey Berkley.
AARON MERSHON,
    Charles Edward Blackmar.
JOHN DAVIS,
    Harmon Joseph Bliss.
NICHOLAS LEWIS,
    Charles Allen Bonfils.
RICHARD PITKIN,
    William Willard Boyd.
BENJAMIN LODGE,
    Robert Emmett Brier.
SILAS MORTON.
    Charles Edward Briggs.
NICHOLAS CABELL,
    Edward Carrington Cabell.
    Ashley Cabell.
    Joseph Carrington Brown.
THOMAS BRAGG,
    John Logan Bruce.
ABRAHAM DE FOREST,
    Lawrence James Buckman.
    William John Brewster.
WILLIAM TUCKER,
    Gordon Wood Bull.
    Charles Richard Bull.
JOHN HALL,
    Eugene La Forest Burrell.

JOSHUA BROOKS,
    Charles Newell Brooks.
DANIEL BOWKER,
    Seth Dean Bowker.
JABEZ CAMPFIELD,
    Charles Henry Campfield.
ELIAS BREEVORT,
    James Spencer Cannon.
ISRAEL SHREEVE,
    Israel Shreeve Carter.
FIELDING LEWIS,
    William Farley Carter.
CARTER HENRY HARRISON,
    George Alfred Castleman.
    Lewis Castleman.
    David Castleman Webb.
JEROME CLARK,
    Hinman Holden Clark.
JOHN CLARK,
    Jefferson Kearney Clark.
CHARLES HAYES,
    George Dillard Clayton.
JOHN CLELAND,
    William Henderson Cleland.
NATHAN COLE,
    Amedee Berthold Cole.
    Nathan Cole.
SAMUEL COMSTOCK,
    Thomas Griswold Comstock.
JOHN JACKSON,
    Benjamin Franklin Coombs.
    Harry Ledden Coombs.
WILLIAM CRAIG,
    Charles Lacy Craig.
SAMUEL T. CRAM,
    George Taylor Cram.
NATHAN CRANE,
    Charles Samuel Crane.
BENJAMIN LINCOLN,
    William Shattuck Lincoln.
    Benjamin Lincoln Crosby.
GAUN RIDDLE,
    John Horace Crum.
JAMES HUNTER,
    Robert Hunter Dalton.
CHRISTIAN DANNAKER,
    Christian A. Dannaker.
NICHOLAS DAVIS,
    Alexander Davis.

MATTHIEU DEREVAUX,
    Armand Derevaux.
DAVID DIFFENDERFER,
    William Irving Diffenderfer.
    David Michael Diffenderfer.
ELEAZOR DODD,
    Samuel Morris Dodd.
SOLOMON DALEY,
    Charles Henry Duffer.
JOSEPH CROWELL,
    Timothy Bloomfield Edgar.
DAVID BURT,
    Guy Dunsmore Edwards.
DENNIS FIELDER,
    Boyd Ward Fielder.
AMOS BARNES,
    William Carl Feld.
STEPHEN FOGG,
    Josiah Fogg.
    James Eads Fogg.
JOHN FREEMAN,
    William Lightfoot Freeman.
    Mortimer Leslie Freeman.
THOMAS FOX,
    Horace Fox.
JOHN RIPPEY,
    John M. Fulton.
JONATHAN GAGE,
    John Cutter Gage.
HENRY HARTER,
    Herbert Harter Getman.
GEORGE RUTLEDGE,
    Victor Rutledge Gibson.
JOSEPH GOULD,
    David Banks Gould.
JOEL DICKINSON,
    Joseph Lancaster Griswold.
JOHN GROSS,
    George Perry Gross.
JOHN IMPEY DAWSON,
    Walter Scott Haddaway.
DAVID BEACH,
    Herbert Spencer Hadley.
JOSEPH HARRIMAN,
    David Samuel Harriman.
    Joseph Lee Harriman.
JAMES HARRISON,
    Edwin Harrison.
ELISHA NILES,
    Charles Folsom Hatfield.
JOHN THRELKELD,
    Elijah Hawkins.
ALEXANDER HENDERSON,
    James Alexander Henderson.
    Frank Littleberry Henderson.

SAMUEL HILL,
    Henry Edward Hill.
HENRY ROGERS,
    John Beriah Holman.
JOSEPH HOAR,
    William Bradford Homar.
JOSEPH HOSMER,
    James Kendall Hosmer.
TITUS WATSON,
    James Clark Horton.
SAMUEL HOYT,
    True Worthy Hoit.
RICHARD HUGHES,
    Charles Hamilton Hughes.
    Clarence Hamilton Hughes.
    Henry Lawther Hughes.
THOMAS COLBY,
    William Lee Huse.
PERCIVAL ASHLEY,
    Charles Frederick Hutchings.
WILLIAM WILLIAMS,
    Moses Jackman Harrington.
ROBERT HARDAWAY,
    William Augustus Hardaway.
RICHARD IRWIN,
    James Harvey Irwin.
SAMUEL BUTLER,
    Anthony Francis Ittner.
THOMAS JEWETT,
    Irwin Scovell Jewett.
JOSEPH BATES,
    James Lucas Johnson.
EBENEZER BREWSTER GOULD,
    James Mills Jones.
    Gould Ely Jones.
    George Lafayette Jones.
    Lawrence Monroe Jones.
MOSES JONES,
    John Logan Jones.
SAMUEL JORDAN CABELL,
    Meredith Dabney Jones.
CHARLES JONES,
    George Robinson Jones.
ABRAHAM GOSS,
    Horace Kephart.
ISAAC WILSON,
    Thomas Jefferson Sanders.
RUFUS LANDON,
    Lucius Hoyt Landon.
RICHARD STOCKTON,
    Clarence McKean Lattimore.
WILLIAM LEIGHTON,
    George Eliot Leighton.
SAMUEL LEWIS,
    Edward Simmons Lewis.

SAMUEL LINDSLEY,
  Malcolm Augustus Lindsley.
ANDREW VANOY,
  John B. Charles Lucas.
GARVIN McCOY,
  Thomas Lewis.
ALEXANDER LOW,
  James Wright McClees.
JOHN McCREERY,
  Wayman Crow McCreery.
JOHN McLARAN,
  Charles McLaran.
RICHARD McLURE,
  Charles Derrickson McLure.
JOSHUA HOMANS,
  Robert Emmett McMath.
JOHN STEPHENSON,
  Isaac Morgan Mason.
STEPHEN MAYFIELD,
  George Washington Mayfield.
  William Henderson Mayfield.
JAMES BEAN,
  Edward James Mellen.
REUBEN BAKER,
  Clifford Isaac Millard.
NATHANIEL HUNT,
  George William Moore.
MOSES REEVES,
  Melvin Reeves Moore.
  Illion Everett Moore.
HENRY MORRILL,
  Henry Leighton Morrill.
ELIAS MUNGER,
  Lyman Page Munger.
JOSEPH WILLIAMS,
  Charles McClung Napton.
JOHN JACK,
  Samuel J. Niccolls.
WILLIAM NOEL,
  Henry Martin Noel.
JAMES O'FALLON,
  James Joseph O'Fallon.
  Harris Taylor O'Fallon.
TIMOTHY OLMSTEAD,
  George Petrie Olmstead.
GAIUS PADDOCK,
  Gaius Paddock.
  Gaius Foster Paddock.
OLIVER BARRETT,
  Galen W. Pearson.
PATRICK HENRY,
  Allan Bowie Pendleton.
HUGHES, WOODSON,
  Thomas Mosley Pendleton.

ELIJAH HUNGERFORD,
  Elijah Hungerford Phelps.
DANIEL RUSSELL,
  William Magruder Phillips.
ENOCH POND,
  John Clark Pond.
JONATHAN PERKINS,
  Frederick Wellington Perkins.
ZEBULON PEASE,
  Albion Parsons Pease.
WILLIAM LAWSON,
  Benjamin Franklin Qualtrough.
JOHN ALEXANDER BROWN,
  William Henry Reed.
WILLIAM CHURCHILL,
  Edgar Edrington Reel.
  Charles Gordon Reel.
  Frank Saugrain Reel.
  William Cochrane Reel.
BENJAMIN ROBINSON,
  Emmett Montgomery Reily.
JONATHAN WHEELER,
  Orran Scott Richards.
GEORGE ROBARDS,
  John Lewis RoBards.
  Archy Crump RoBards.
ABNER ROBBINS,
  Alexander Robbins.
  Nelson Chapman Robbins.
JAMES RUSSELL,
  Daniel Renouard Russell.
JACOB SAMPSON,
  Clark Hamilton Sampson.
CALEB HOWELL,
  George Howell Shields.
  George Howell Shields, Jr.
JAMES SIMONDS,
  Nathaniel Putnam Simonds.
JOHN SINGLETON,
  Benjamin Reynolds Singleton.
NATHANIEL GREENE,
  Peyton Horatio Skipwith, Jr.
ISAIAH SLAVENS,
  Luther Clay Slavens.
  Luther Clay Slavens, Jr.
  Hiram Collier Slavens.
  James Leander Slavens.
WILLIAM DAVIDSON,
  Ewing McGready Sloan.
CHARLES MILLS,
  Greenfield Sluder.
LEVI SMITH,
  Sheridan Sol Smith.
ALEXANDER McDOUGALL,
  Ellsworth Stryker Smith.

(112)

SAMUEL SOUTHER,
  Eustace Everett Souther.
  Latham Timothy Souther.
OLIVER SPAULDING,
  James Franklin Spaulding.
  Frank Carr Spaulding.
JOHN STAMPS,
  William Samuel Stamps.
  William Charles Stamps.
WILLIAM STANARD,
  Edwin O. Stanard.
PHILEMON BARNES,
  Melvin Hall Stearns.
PETER STICHTER,
  Franklin Goodhart Stichter.
ABRAHAM STICKNEY,
  William Albert Stickney.
ZEBINA DAY,
  William Crandall Streator.
BEVERLY B. STUBBLEFIELD,
  George Madison Shelly.
ANDREW MCADOW,
  James Madison Shelly.
EAIVES TAINTER,
  William Henry Harrison Tainter.
JOSEPH THOMPSON,
  Hugh Miller Thompson.
WILLIAM ROGERS,
  Isaac Rogers Trask.
JOHN TREAT,
  Samuel Treat.
ICHABOD TUTTLE,
  Thomas Benton Tuttle.
AMOS SINGLETON,
  Stephen Prince Twiss.
JABEZ WRIGHT,
  Charles Edward Thompson.
JOHN YOST,
  Charles Cory Yost.

WILLIS RIDDICK,
  Richard Webb Upshaw.
  Thomas Edmund Upshaw, Jr.
THOMAS DENTON,
  Edward Vail,
  Robert Weygant Vail.
JACOB VAN DOREN,
  Henry Allen Van Doren.
ADAM VINCIL,
  John Davis Vincil.
  James Edwin Vincil.
ASA WALBRIDGE,
  Cyrus Packard Walbridge.
JAMES WALKER,
  Jacob Lupton Walker.
JOHN F. BRADT,
  John Bradt Wands.
  John Clark Wands.
SIMEON WELLS,
  Harvey Jesse Wells.
JOHN WHITMAN,
  Charles Edward Whitman.
JOHN WALLS,
  Thomas D. Windiate.
MOSES CHASE,
  James Edgar Withrow.
THOMAS YALE,
  Charles Yale.
THOMAS WILSON,
  Michael Wilson Yeakle.
JAMES D. COLT,
  Calvin Cogswell Colt.
JOHN STROPE,
  George Wilson Strope.
JOHN HALL,
  Frederick Albert Smith.
JONATHAN VEAZEY,
  Charles Mackey Veazey.
ABNER ROBBINS,
  Alexander Henry Robbins.